Alternative Assessment

Evaluating Student Performance in Elementary Mathematics

Ann Arbor Public Schools

DALE SEYMOUR PUBLICATIONS

Managing Editor: Michael Kane
Project Editor: Mali Apple
Production: Barbara Atmore
Design: Side by Side Studios
Cover Illustration: D. J. Simison

This book is published by Dale Seymour Publications, an imprint of the
Alternative Publishing Group of Addison-Wesley.

Order number DS33200
ISBN 0-86651-691-3

4 5 6 7 8 9 10-MA-96

DALE
SEYMOUR
PUBLICATIONS
P.O. BOX 10888
PALO ALTO, CA 94303

Made from
Recycled Paper

Contents

Acknowledgments

The project staff wish to thank and acknowledge the efforts of people who contributed ideas and reviewed portions of this book. Their input and comments were especially helpful. Appreciation and a special thanks also go to many other teachers, curriculum specialists, and administrators who contributed ideas and suggestions.

Charles Allan	Michigan Department of Education
Betty Burton	Ann Arbor Public Schools
Randall Charles	San Jose State University
Terrence Coburn	Oakland Schools
Arthur Coxford	University of Michigan
LeAnn Corkins	Ann Arbor Public Schools
Dianne Davis	Ann Arbor Public Schools
Louise Hickey	Ann Arbor Public Schools
Linda Kolnowski	Detroit Public Schools
Jean Kelsey	Ann Arbor Public Schools
Matthew Krigbaum	Ann Arbor Public Schools
Steven Leinwand	Connecticut Department of Education
Ronald Ludwig	Ann Arbor Public Schools
Alexander Norrie	Peel Board of Education
Joseph Payne	University of Michigan
Linda Peters	Ann Arbor Public Schools
Nancy Shiffler	Ann Arbor Public Schools
Albert Shulte	Oakland Schools
Adele Sobania	Livonia Public Schools
Doris Sperling	Ann Arbor Public Schools
Anne Towsley	University of Michigan, Flint
Nancy Vogt	Ann Arbor Public Schools
Linda Warrington	Ann Arbor Public Schools
June Williams	Ann Arbor Public Schools
Persis Wirth	Ann Arbor Public Schools

About the Authors

This project was funded in part under a grant awarded by the Michigan State Board of Education under the Dwight D. Eisenhower Mathematics and Science Program. These materials were developed by teachers from the Ann Arbor Public Schools under the direction of Ann Beyer, Mathematics Coordinator.

Authors

Susan Bates
Ann Beyer
Connie Corwin
Patricia Fischer
Sally Freeman
Jeffrey Gaynor
Corrine Grace
Karen Henderson
Patricia Johnston
Martha Keefe
Trudy Lewis
Frances Marroquin

Marilyn Mckelvey
Beth Molnar
Laura Roth
Alease Roy
Patricia Rutz
Robin Rutz
Michele Snyder
Ruth Spangler
Jan Starr
Patricia Tracey
Marilyn Treutler

Project Coordinator/Editor: Ann Beyer
Associate Editors: Connie Corwin, Sally Freeman
Artist/Illustrator: Paul Beyer
Typist/Illustrator: Lynda Clewell

Ann Arbor Public Schools

Office of Curriculum and Instruction • 2555 South State Street • P.O. Box 1188
Ann Arbor, Michigan 48106 • (313) 994-2230

Board of Education

Administration

Ann Arbor Public Schools — Administration

William Wade, Interim Superintendent of Schools
Hayward Richardson, Deputy Superintendent for Instructional Services
Doreen Poupard, Assistant Superintendent for Curriculum and Instruction
Ron Williamson, Executive Director for Curriculum and Instruction
Clifford Weber, Executive Director for Research and Instruction
Ann Beyer, Mathematics Coordinator

List of Activities by Content Area

Content Area	Title	Grade	Page	Interviews	Observations	Portfolios	Student Self-Assessment	Performance Tasks	Student Writing	Manipulative	Representational	Abstract
All	Cooperative Task	3–6	100		•			•				
	Performance Review	3–5	47	•				•				
	Pluses and Wishes	3–5	44									
	Student Self-Assessment	4–5	46									
	Student Problem-Solving Journals	2–5	33									
	Weekly Math Work Portfolio	3–5	35									
Addition and Subtraction	Addition and Subtraction with Regrouping	3–4	67						•			•
	Facts Through Ten	2	131									
	Modeling Addition and Subtraction	2–4	182		•			•		•	•	•
	Number Families	1–2	206		•			•			•	
Algebraic Ideas	Checking out Order of Operations	6	85		•			•			•	•
	Constructing Tables and Graphs to Solve Equations	4–6	97					•			•	
	Explaining Patterns in the Environment	K–2	129	•						•		
	Missing Addends	2–6	180	•				•		•		•
	Patterns	K–2	210	•	•			•		•		
	Patterns and Sequences	3–5	219					•	•		•	
	Story to Fit Equation	1–6	277					•	•			•
	Understanding Patterns	K–2	297		•			•		•		
	Working with Patterns	K–1	311	•	•			•		•	•	
Arithmetic and Numeration	Number Theory Clues	5–6	208	•	•				•			•
Calculators	Checking out Order of Operations	6	85		•			•			•	•
	Check It Out	4–6	88		•			•		•	•	
	Reading with Numbers	2–5	257		•			•		•	•	
	Using Calculators Correctly	2–6	302		•			•		•		•
	0 to 100%: How Well Did You Score?	4–5	318			•	•	•	•		•	•
Estimation and Mental Computation	Checking out Order of Operations	6	85		•			•			•	•
	Division Facts	3–5	116				•	•				•
	Estimation and Mental Computation in Addition	3–5	121					•	•			•
	Estimation in Multiplication	5–6	125	•	•							•
	Estimation of Quantity	K–2	127	•				•		•		
	Measuring and Estimating Length	2–3	176					•		•		
	Multiplication/Division Facts	3–5	196	•				•				•
	Nonstandard Measurement: Guess and Check	2–4	203		•			•		•		
	Place Value and Estimation	1–3	223		•			•		•		•
	What's in a Shape?	6	304		•			•	•		•	•

Content Area	Title	Grade	Page	Interviews	Observations	Portfolios	Student Self-Assessment	Performance Tasks	Student Writing	Manipulative	Representational	Abstract
Fractions, Decimals, Ratio, and Percent	Body Ratios	6	73		•			•	•	•		•
	Decimal and Whole Number Place Value	4–5	104	•				•			•	
	Decimals	4–6	108		•			•		•		
	Fraction Models	3–5	136		•			•		•		
	Multiplying Fractions	6	201			•	•	•	•		•	•
	Ratio	5	255	•						•		•
	Understanding Fractions	5–6	291						•		•	•
	Writing About Fractions	4–6	313						•		•	•
Geometry and Spatial Sense	Building Geometric Shapes on the Geoboard	1–2	75	•				•		•		
	Circles	4–6	91					•		•	•	
	Defining Lines, Rays, Segments, and Angles	5–6	110						•			•
	Hands-on Geometry and Measurement Test	5–6	139					•		•	•	•
	Identifying Geometric Shapes and Solids	1–2	156		•			•		•	•	
	Identifying Shapes in the Environment	1–2	158		•			•		•	•	
	Is It or Isn't It?	3–6	160						•			•
	Lines, Rays, Angles, Line Segments	5–6	170		•			•		•		
	Positional Relationships	K–1	232	•	•			•		•		
	Solid Geometry	3–6	262					•	•	•	•	•
	Sorting Geometric Solids	2–4	275		•			•		•		
	Triangles	3–6	287					•			•	
Mathematical Thinking	Analyzing Word Problems	2–6	71	•		•		•		•	•	•
	Estimation and Mental Computation in Addition	3–5	121					•	•			•
	Math in Everyday Life	3–6	174						•			•
	Story to Fit Equation	1–6	277					•	•			•
Measurement	Body Ratios	6	73		•			•	•	•		•
	Calendar	K–2	77	•				•			•	
	Hands-on Geometry and Measurement Test	5–6	139					•		•	•	•
	High Five: Telling Time	2–3	144	•				•		•	•	
	How Does It Feel?	4–6	147	•				•		•		
	How Long Does It Take?	K–2	149	•				•			•	
	Linear Measurement	2–4	164		•			•		•		
	Measuring and Estimating Length	2–3	176					•		•		
	Money Counts!	1–3	186					•			•	
	Money Values	2–4	189	•				•		•		

Content Area	Title	Grade	Page	Interviews	Observations	Portfolios	Student Self-Assessment	Performance Tasks	Student Writing	Manipulative	Representational	Abstract
	Nonstandard Measurement: Guess and Check	2–4	203		•			•		•		
	Perimeter and Area on the Geoboard	3–6	217	•	•	•				•		
	Perusing Perimeter	3–6	221	•				•			•	
	Quarter Time	2–3	252	•				•		•	•	
	Time and Sequence	K–1	279	•	•			•			•	
	Time to Tell Time	1–3	284	•				•			•	
	Understanding Time	3	299						•		•	•
	Working with Kragels	3–5	308	•	•			•		•	•	
Multiplication and Division	Checking Division	4–6	82						•			•
	Division Chart	4–6	113	•				•				•
	Division Facts	3–5	116				•	•				•
	Division Pictures	4–5	118					•			•	•
	Modeling Division	3–5	184	•						•		
	Multi-digit Multiplication	4–5	192					•	•		•	•
	Multiplication/Division Facts	3–5	196	•			•					•
	Understanding Multiplication Facts	3–4	294	•					•		•	•
Place Value	Place Value and Estimation	1–3	223		•			•		•		•
	Place Value: Building Numbers	2–3	226		•			•		•	•	•
	Place Value: Explaining Numbers	2–3	228		•			•		•	•	•
	Reading with Numbers	2–5	257		•			•		•	•	
	Regrouping Using Base 10 Blocks	2–4	260		•			•		•		
Problem Solving and Logic	Analyzing Word Problems	2–6	71	•			•	•		•	•	•
	Body Ratios	6	73		•			•	•	•		•
	Explaining Patterns in the Environment	K–2	129	•						•		
	How Does It Feel?	4–6	147	•				•		•		
	How's It Going?	2–6	153				•				•	•
	Number Theory Clues	5–6	208	•	•				•			•
	Patterns	K–2	210	•	•			•		•		
	Patterns and Sequences	3–5	214					•	•		•	
	Primary Problem Solving	K–1	236	•						•		
	Problem Solving Strategies	2–6	241	•							•	•
	Problem Solving: Strategies and Process	4–6	243			•	•	•	•		•	•
	Sorting by Attributes	K–2	269					•		•		
	Story to Fit Equation	1–6	277					•	•			•
	Understanding Patterns	K–2	297		•			•		•		
	Working with Patterns	K–1	311	•	•			•		•		

Content Area	Title	Grade	Page	Interviews	Observations	Portfolios	Student Self-Assessment	Performance Tasks	Student Writing	Manipulative	Representational	Abstract
Statistics and Probability	Catch Your Breath	5–6	80		•	•	•	•	•		•	•
	Constructing and Interpreting Graphs	3–6	94			•		•	•		•	•
	Creating and Interpreting Graphs	K–2	102	•				•		•		
	Line Plots	3–6	167			•		•	•		•	•
	Probability Using Objects	3	238	•				•		•		
	Sorting and Graphing	K–2	267		•			•		•		
	Understanding a Bar Graph	3–6	288					•			•	
	Yesterday's News	4–6	316		•	•		•	•		•	•
	0 to 100%: How Well Did You Score?	4–5	318			•	•	•	•		•	•

List of Activities by Title

Title	Grade	Content Areas	Page	Interviews	Observations	Portfolios	Student Self-Assessment	Performance Tasks	Student Writing	Manipulative	Representational	Abstract
Hands-on Geometry and Measurement Test	5–6	Geometry and Spatial Sense Measurement	139					•		•	•	•
High Five: Telling Time	2–3	Measurement	144	•				•		•	•	
How Does It Feel?	4–6	Measurement Problem Solving and Logic	147	•				•	•			
How Long Does It Take?	K–2	Measurement	149	•				•			•	
How's It Going?	2–6	Problem Solving and Logic	153				•			•		•
Identifying Geometric Shapes and Solids	1–2	Geometry and Spatial Sense	156		•			•		•	•	
Identifying Shapes in the Environment	1–2	Geometry and Spatial Sense	158		•			•		•	•	
Is It or Isn't It?	3–6	Geometry and Spatial Sense	160						•			•
Linear Measurement	2–4	Measurement	164		•			•	•			
Line Plots	3–6	Statistics and Probability	167				•	•	•		•	•
Lines, Rays, Angles, and Line Segments	5–6	Geometry and Spatial Sense	170		•			•	•			
Math in Everyday Life	3–6	Mathematical Thinking	174						•			•
Measuring and Estimating Length	2–3	Measurement Estimation and Mental Computation	176					•	•			
Missing Addends	2–6	Algebraic Ideas	180	•				•	•			
Modeling Addition and Subtraction	2–4	Addition and Subtraction	182		•			•		•	•	•
Modeling Division	3–5	Multiplication and Division	184	•				•	•			
Money Counts!	1–3	Measurement	186					•			•	
Money Values	2–4	Measurement	189	•				•	•			
Multi-digit Multiplication	4–5	Multiplication and Division	192					•	•		•	•
Multiplication/Division Facts	3–5	Multiplication and Division Estimation and Mental Computation	196	•			•					•
Multiplying Fractions	6	Fractions, Decimals, Ratio, and Percent	201			•	•	•	•		•	•
Nonstandard Measurement: Guess and Check	2–4	Measurement Estimation and Mental Computation	203		•			•		•		
Number Families	1–2	Addition and Subtraction	206		•			•			•	
Number Theory Clues	5–6	Arithmetic and Numeration Problem Solving and Logic	208						•			•
Patterns	K–2	Algebraic Ideas Problem Solving and Logic	210	•	•			•		•		
Patterns and Sequences	3–5	Algebraic Ideas Problem Solving and Logic	214					•	•		•	
Performance Review	3–5	All	47	•			•					
Perimeter and Area on the Geoboard	3–6	Measurement	217	•	•	•				•		
Perusing Perimeter	3–6	Measurement	221	•				•			•	

Title	Grade	Content Areas	Page	Interviews	Observations	Portfolios	Student Self-Assessment	Performance Tasks	Student Writing	Manipulative	Representational	Abstract
Place Value and Estimation	1–3	Place Value / Estimation and Mental Computation	223		•			•		•		•
Place Value: Building Numbers	2–3	Place Value	226		•			•		•	•	•
Place Value: Explaining Numbers	2–3	Place Value	228		•			•		•	•	•
Pluses and Wishes	3–5	All	44									
Positional Relationships	K–1	Geometry and Spatial Sense	232	•	•			•		•		
Primary Problem Solving	K–1	Problem Solving and Logic	236	•						•		
Probability Using Objects	3	Statistics and Probability	238	•				•		•		
Problem-solving Strategies	2–6	Problem Solving and Logic	241	•							•	•
Problem Solving: Strategies and Process	4–6	Problem Solving and Logic	243			•	•	•	•		•	•
Quarter Time	2–3	Measurement	252	•				•		•	•	
Ratio	5	Fractions, Decimals, Ratio, and Percent	255	•						•		•
Reading with Numbers	2–5	Calculators / Place Value	257		•			•		•	•	
Regrouping Using Base 10 Blocks	2–4	Place Value	260					•		•		
Solid Geometry	3–6	Geometry and Spatial Sense	262					•	•	•		•
Sorting and Graphing	K–2	Statistics and Probability	267		•			•		•		
Sorting by Attributes	K–2	Problem Solving and Logic	269					•		•		
Sorting Geometric Solids	2–4	Geometry and Spatial Sense	275		•			•		•		
Story to Fit Equation	1–6	Mathematical Thinking / Problem Solving and Logic / Algebraic Ideas	277					•	•			•
Student Problem-Solving Journals	2–5	All	33									
Student Self-Assessment	4–5	All	46									
Time and Sequence	K–1	Measurement	279	•	•			•			•	
Time to Tell Time	1–3	Measurement	284	•				•			•	
Triangles	3–6	Geometry and Spatial Sense	287					•			•	
Understanding a Bar Graph	3–6	Statistics and Probability	288					•			•	
Understanding Fractions	5–6	Fractions, Decimals, Ratio, and Percent	291						•		•	•
Understanding Multiplication Facts	3–4	Multiplication and Division	294	•					•		•	•
Understanding Patterns	K–2	Problem Solving and Logic / Algebraic Ideas	297		•			•		•		
Understanding Time	3	Measurement	299						•		•	•
Using Calculators Correctly	2–6	Calculators	302		•			•		•		
Weekly Math Work Portfolio	3–5	All	35			•		•		•	•	
What's in a Shape?	6	Estimation and Mental Computation	304		•			•	•		•	•
Working with Kragels	3–5	Measurement	308	•	•			•		•	•	
Working with Patterns	K–1	Problem Solving and Logic / Algebraic Ideas	311	•	•			•		•		

Title	Grade	Content Areas	Page	Interviews	Observations	Portfolios	Student Self-Assessment	Performance Tasks	Student Writing	Manipulative	Representational	Abstract
Writing About Fractions	4–6	Fractions, Decimals, Ratio, and Percent	313						•		•	•
Yesterday's News	4–6	Statistics and Probability	316		•	•		•	•		•	•
0 to 100%: How Well Did You Score?	4–5	Statistics and Probability Calculators	318			•	•	•	•		•	•

Introduction

National, state, and local attention is being given to restructuring mathematics education to address

- what mathematics should be taught,
- how mathematics should be taught, and
- how to assess the mathematical achievements of students.

Two purposes of assessment are to improve instructional decision making and to improve student learning. Educators are always looking for ways to improve the alignment of curriculum, instruction, and assessment. Areas of focus include expanding how students can demonstrate their mathematical achievements and how educators can gain better information about students. Consequently teachers are being encouraged to explore and implement a wide range of assessment strategies and techniques.

In 1991 the Ann Arbor Public Schools received a grant to work on alternative classroom-based assessment in elementary mathematics. The focus of the project was on helping teachers expand their use of alternative assessment techniques and on developing assessment activities and lessons that modeled various strategies. This book, which is the product of the project, was partially funded by the 1991 Dwight D. Eisenhower Discretionary and Exemplary Program Grant for Elementary and Secondary Mathematics.

The first part of the book includes generic sections on performance indicators (including holistic and analytic scoring), assessment strategies, and record-keeping formats. These sections may be used at any grade level and in any subject area as general information about alternative assessment.

Following the general background sections is a collection of field-tested assessment activities. While the assessment activities and examples illustrate many different techniques, they are specific to mathematics. The intent in this book is to model alternative assessment as a natural extension of classroom activities and lessons.

ASSESSMENT MODEL

The following assessment model was used in creating the lessons and activities in this book.

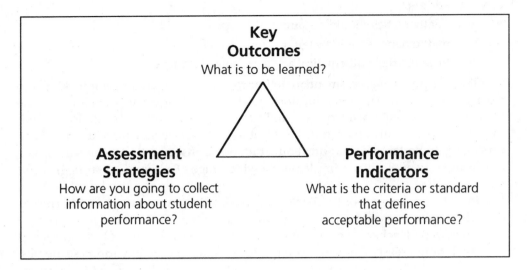

OUTCOMES

Outcomes such as those described in *Curriculum and Evaluation Standards for School Mathematics* (NCTM, 1989), as well as state and local standards and objectives, define important mathematical concepts and processes; that is, *What is to be learned?*

ASSESSMENT STRATEGIES

The NCTM standards cite the need to change the processes and methods by which student information is collected. Much has been said about the need to use alternative assessment techniques (e.g., observations, student writing, portfolios, student self-evaluation, interviews, performance tasks). These techniques address the question, *How are you going to collect information about student performance?* (See pages 11–57)

PERFORMANCE INDICATORS

Performance indicators answer two basic types of questions: What does the outcome look like at various developmental levels? What is the criterion or standard that defines acceptable performance? Performance indicators help you determine students' levels of performance and attainment. They establish benchmarks against which student performance can be compared. This comparison helps you determine student and class strengths and weaknesses, and subsequently, plan for improved instruction. (See pages 3–10)

Performance Indicators

One aspect of improving teacher observation and reflection about student performance is to have a clear picture of what student performance tells you about
students' levels of understanding. Richard Stiggins, from Northwest Regional Edu-
cational Laboratory, says to think of it as target practice.

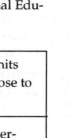

Who frequently misses the target?	Who consistently hits the outer rings?	Who consistently hits the bull's eye or close to it?
Students who do not understand the concept or process (the outcome)	Students who are developing the outcome	Students who understand and can apply the outcome

As educators, we want all students to be able to hit the bull's eye consistently
(understand an outcome). Some students do this consistently. Others have pretty
good aim, consistently hitting the target, but not the bull's eye (are developing the
outcome). An Ashley Brilliant quote—"I may not be perfect, but parts of me are excel-
lent"—does a good job of describing this group of students. The third group of
students routinely misses the target, the arrows falling short of the mark (do not
understand the outcome).

FOR YOUR REFLECTION

The following figure provides a format for generating and using your own performance indicators.

	Students who are not understanding the concept or process (the outcome)	Students who are developing the outcome	Students who understand and are applying the outcome
What are the performance indicators for the outcome at the various developmental levels?			
At what level are my students performing? Which students are at each level?			
What do I need to do instructionally?			

Think of an important outcome you recently taught. Reflect on your students' performance. Think of students falling into one of three categories:
- students who did not understand the outcome
- students who were developing the outcome (but not quite there yet)
- students who attained the outcome and could apply it and communicate it

In each column make a quick draft of behaviors or indicators that would describe those types of students. Think of this as a first draft. It does not need to be perfect; it does not need to be complete; it does not need to be in parallel form; but it does need to identify the distinguishing attributes for each performance level.

Now think about individual students and write their names in the appropriate categories. Once you have completed the task, answer the following questions:

- Were you able to record all the students in a given class?
- If not, what could you do to assess the remaining students' level of proficiency?
- What insights do the data provide that will help you plan your next steps?
- In light of this information about student performance, what do you need or want to do instructionally?
- What can you do to provide extended opportunities for students who are at the beginning stages?
- What can be done to more flexibly extend and enrich the experience for students who are demonstrating the desired level of proficiency?

USING PERFORMANCE INDICATORS AND OBSERVATION TO IMPROVE INSTRUCTION

You were just introduced to one simple strategy for both generating and using performance indicators as a self-help tool for improving instruction. By clustering student performance into three general categories, you can begin to reflect in a more meaningful way about your students' performance and behaviors and subsequently use this information in your instructional planning. This actually becomes a three-step process of reflection and observation:

- generating (through reflection and observation) performance indicators for key outcomes
- observing and recording student behavior and performance
- reflecting on student performance data to monitor students' performance and to improve instructional decisions

Project teachers indicated that this process truly caused them to look more closely at student performance and the relationships between curriculum, instruction, and assessment. Teachers self-reported that this reflective process helped them view classroom practice with new eyes. Thinking through the performance indicators helped them to be more observant of and analytical about student behavior, which in turn caused them to rethink how to do things instructionally.

AN EXAMPLE

One project teacher assumed she would need one to two weeks to work on time concepts. Using this model, she developed a mini interview, which, along with the performance indicators, is described in this book. The interviews took about one minute per student and were given during free moments such as recess, reading time, and student work time. She found that only five students needed any extended work on the concepts for which she was intending whole class instruction. Consequently she was able to plan some short review lessons for the whole class, insert enrichment activities, reallocate time for other mathematical concepts, and redesign the instructional activities for the students who needed additional work on the time concepts.

Teachers found the following things to be particularly helpful:

1. Reflecting on the level of performance they wanted provided a clarity of focus that helped them be more analytical and reflective in their daily observations of student performance. Performance indicators were helpful in a variety of ways as well (e.g., to increase comfort level in using observation as a valid assessment technique, to create better ways for evaluating work analytically or holistically, to reflect on student progress over the course of a year, to serve as sample comments to use in writing narrative reports, to code observations).

2. It was easiest to work with generating indicators at just three levels. Teachers usually described the two extremes first (those who did not understand and those who had attained the concept) and then the middle (those who are developing the concept).

3. Four strategies typically were used to generate performance indicators:
   - reflecting on previous students' performance and products
   - brainstorming what it might look like and then testing it (e.g., a guess-and-check strategy)
   - assuming that what it looks like is unknown and observing students' behavior as they complete a related task
   - collecting and analyzing student products, which have been divided into three piles representing the three performance levels

4. Performance indicators do not need to be generated for all outcomes or lessons. Pick some key areas for focused instruction. Then use these standards to help monitor student performance and growth over time. Performance indicators may be used to generate a scoring rubric for holistic and analytic scoring of student products.

5. The following table shows generic samples of performance indicators for some mathematical concepts. They are intended to trigger your own thinking. Because of the age of your students or the level of development of the concept in your grade, some of the samples may not be applicable or may be in the wrong column. Move them, change them, and provide other, more specific indicators that are appropriate for your students.

Notes

- Sample performance indicators, written by the contributing teachers, are provided in the assessment activities. You may wish to modify them in light of your observations of students at your grade level.

- The Record Keeping Formats section, page 58, describes one method for using performance indicators and recording student performance.

Sample Performance Indicators

Not Understanding	Developing	Understanding/Applying
CONCEPT UNDERSTANDING (e.g., MULTIPLICATION, SYMMETRY)		
• does not routinely model concept correctly • cannot explain concept • does not attempt problems • does not make connections	• demonstrates partial or satisfactory understanding • can demonstrate and explain using a variety of modes (e.g., oral, written, objects, models, drawings, diagrams) • is starting to make how and why connections • relates concept to prior knowledge and experiences • can create related problems • accomplishes tasks, though minor flaws	• correctly applies rules or algorithm on how to manipulate symbols • connects both how and why • can apply concept in new or problem situations • can see and explain connections • accomplishes tasks and goes beyond
UNDERSTANDING THE PROBLEM OR SITUATION		
• does not attempt the problem • misunderstands the problem • routinely requires explanation of problem	• copies the problem • identifies key words • may misinterpret or misunderstand part of the problem • may have a sense of answer	• can restate or explain the problem coherently • understands key conditions • eliminates unnecessary information • identifies needed information • has a sense of answer
APPLIES STRATEGIES, CONCEPTS, PROCEDURES LOGICALLY		
• makes no attempt • relies on others to select and apply strategies • provides work that is not understandable • cannot explain work or strategy adequately • selects inappropriate strategies • is not logical or orderly in implementation	• uses strategy if told • recognizes strategy • can explain strategy • uses a limited number of strategies • can select a strategy, but may need assistance in its implementation • can present work in an acceptable manner	• generates new procedures • extends or modifies strategies • knows or uses many strategies • uses strategies flexibly • knows when a strategy is applicable • presents work logically and coherently
VERIFIES RESULTS		
• does not review calculations, procedures • does not recognize if answer is/isn't reasonable	• reviews calculations, procedures • can ascertain reasonableness if questioned	• checks reasonableness of results • recognizes unreasonableness
EXTENDS THE PROBLEM, MAKES CONNECTIONS		
• does not attempt to make extensions • does not make connections • cannot extend ideas to new applications • does minimum expected	• can recognize similar problems or applications • makes connections • can apply ideas to new applications	• proposes and explores extensions • can create parallel problems by varying conditions of original problem
MATHEMATICAL COMMUNICATION		
• has difficulty communicating ideas • withdraws from discussions • cannot bring thinking to conscious level • does not use/misuses terms • offers unrelated information	• expresses ideas in rudimentary form • can support explanations with models, drawings, etc. • may need some assistance or prompts in refining skills • uses terms appropriately	• communicates clearly and effectively • explains thinking process well • can communicate ideas in several forms (orally, in writing, drawings, graphs)

Not Understanding	Developing	Understanding/Applying
USE OF MATERIALS		
• needs more exploration with materials • cannot use materials without assistance • watches to see how others are doing it, before trying it on own • does not attempt to use materials	• generally uses materials effectively • may require occasional assistance	• uses materials effectively and efficiently
ESTIMATION		
• makes unrealistic guesses • does not use strategies to refine estimates • cannot model or explain the specified strategy • cannot apply strategy even with prompts	• refines guesses or estimates by partitioning/comparing, etc. • can model, explain, and apply a strategy when asked • has some strategies, others are not yet in place • uses estimation when appropriate	• makes realistic guesses or estimates • refines estimates to suggest a more exact estimate • uses estimation when appropriate • recognizes and readily uses a variety of strategies
COLLECTS, ORGANIZES, AND DISPLAYS DATA		
• makes no attempt • cannot proceed without direction and assistance • makes major mistakes in collecting or displaying data	• can collect and display data, given a method to record • has minor flaws in collecting and or displaying data • can correct errors when pointed out	• can collect and display data in an organized manner • accurately and appropriately labels diagrams, graphs, etc.
SUMMARIZES, INTERPRETS RESULTS		
• makes no attempt to summarize or describe data • can answer simple questions related to data • needs prompts	• summarizes and describes data appropriately • can generate and answer questions related to data • can communicate results in rudimentary form	• draws valid conclusions and interpretations • makes generalizations • communicates results clearly and logically
MEASUREMENT (LENGTH, MASS, CAPACITY)		
• makes direct comparisons between objects • can order objects according to measure • can distinguish differences in measurements	• can compare and order using non-standard units • can estimate and measure using non-standard units • can estimate and measure using standard units • can solve related problems	• can estimate and measure using standard units • can select appropriate measurement units for task • can use fractional increments to measure • can solve related problems
PROVIDES ROTE RESPONSES TO ___ FACTS THROUGH ___		
• cannot readily or correctly cite facts • can model facts with objects and drawings	• knows some facts readily • pauses, needs to stop and figure out unknown facts • uses strategies or objects to ascertain unknown facts	• can accurately provide answers to ___ facts in ___ minutes • knows facts without having to use strategies or objects
MATHEMATICAL DISPOSITION (VALUES, LIKES MATHEMATICS)		
• demonstrates anxiety or dislike of mathematics • withdraws or is passive during math time • gives up easily, is easily frustrated during math • needs frequent support, attention, feedback	• applies self to task • is actively involved in learning activities • is willing to try new methods • does what is asked, but may not take initiative	• demonstrates confidence in work • is persistent, will try several approaches; does not give up • is curious; demonstrates flexibility • asks many questions

Holistic and Analytic Scoring

Performance indicators can be used to develop holistic and analytic scoring rubrics.

Comparison of Scoring Methods

Holistic scoring awards one score, which focuses on the total performance.	**Analytic scoring** awards points for each of several major components, phases, or objectives.

HOLISTIC SCORING OF STUDENT WORK

Holistic scoring awards one score, which represents an evaluation of the total performance. Rating criteria should reflect specific and important elements of a solution to a problem. Drafting performance indicators will be useful in developing the rating system (e.g., 0 points for no attempt, 1 point for inadequate product or solution, 2 points for acceptable product or solution, 3 points for superior product or solution).

The following chart demonstrates general criteria and indicators to consider in determining your rating scale.

	Inadequate Product or Solution	Acceptable Product or Solution	Superior Product or Solution
	Not Understanding the Concept	**Developing the Concept**	**Understanding/Applying the Concept**
Understanding Why and How	▲ Demonstrates no or little evidence of understanding ▲ Does not accomplish tasks ▲ Makes critical or many mistakes	▲ Demonstrates partial or satisfactory understanding ▲ Understands major aspects, though parts may be missing ▲ Accomplishes tasks, though minor flaws	▲ Clearly understands outcome ▲ Can demonstrate in-depth, extended understanding ▲ Accomplishes tasks and goes beyond ▲ Shows special insights
Communication	• Has difficulty communicating ideas and explanations • May answer simple questions • Does not use/misuses terms • Offers unrelated information	• Can communicate successfully on some aspects but not others • Expresses ideas in rudimentary form • May need some assistance or prompts	• Communicates clearly and effectively • Explains thinking process well • Can communicate ideas in several forms (orally, in writing, drawings, graphs)
Use of Materials	• Needs more exploration with materials • Cannot use materials without assistance • Watches to see how others are doing it before trying it on own • Does not attempt to use materials	• Generally uses materials effectively • May require occasional assistance	• Uses materials effectively and efficiently

ANALYTIC SCORING OF STUDENT WORK

Analytic scoring awards points for each major component, phase, or objective of the task being performed. To use analytic scoring, do the following:

1. Break down the task into major components, subtasks, concepts, processes, or objectives.

2. Identify which of these you want to assess.

3. Articulate what each component to be assessed looks like developmentally.

   a. What behaviors indicate that the student does not understand the concept or is just at the introductory level?

   b. What behaviors indicate progress toward understanding the concept?

   c. What behaviors indicate attainment of and ability to apply the concept?

4. Assign point values.

SAMPLE PERFORMANCE TASK WITH RATING CRITERIA

Performance Task

Suggested Grades

3-6

Content Areas

Statistics and Probability

Strategies

Interviews

Observation

Portfolios

Student Self-Assessment

➤ Performance Task

➤ Student Writing

Outcome

■ To use graphs to record, interpret, and show trends in data.

Materials

■ Graph paper

Assessment Activity

Have students collect and record data (e.g., homework scores, temperatures, minutes watching TV, spelling scores) for a certain period (minimum of eight scores), and then have them make a graph by following these instructions:

1. Use your data to make a line graph.

2. Make sure you divide and label the axes correctly.

3. Make sure you graph all the data correctly.

4. Write a brief report describing and interpreting your graph.

Notes

■ This activity is adapted from "Opening Doors to Alternatives: A Different Look at Assessment" by S. Stevens.

■ Both a holistic and an analytic scoring method are provided so you can compare the two techniques.

Rating and Criteria for Holistic Scoring

3 points—Understanding and Applying the Concept

▲ The student can independently construct a correct graph.

▲ Axes are correctly divided.

▲ Increments on axes are proportional.

▲ Increments reflect the total range of the data.

▲ All points are graphed without error.

▲ The graph and axes are labeled correctly.

▲ The student can describe and interpret the graph.

2 Points—Developing the Concept

▲ The student needs prompts to complete the graph.

▲ Errors can be corrected once they are pointed out.

▲ The graph contains minor errors.

▲ With prompting, the student can identify and explain the trends in the data.

1 Point—Not Understanding the Concept (any one of the following is unacceptable)

▲ Even after the teacher shows how to divide the axes and to determine the increments, the student cannot complete the task.

▲ The student creates the graph without help, but with major errors (e.g., increments and divisions are not accurate).

▲ The student cannot graph the points to match the data without help from someone else or cannot correct errors once they are pointed out.

▲ The student cannot describe and interpret the graph.

Rating and Criteria for Analytic Scoring

Independence

2: The student constructs a graph without being told what to do or how to do it.

1: The student needs assistance in construction or interpretation.

0: The student cannot complete the task.

Construction of Graph

2: Axes are correctly divided; increments are proportional and reflect range of data; graph is correctly labeled; points are graphed without error.

1: The graph contains only one or two minor errors; errors are corrected when pointed out.

0: The graph contains more than two errors; the graph is inaccurate or incomplete; the student cannot correct errors.

Interpretation and Presentation of Trends

2: The student is able to describe and interpret data; information is clearly and coherently communicated.

1: The student needs some assistance in describing or interpreting data or in communicating results.

0: The student cannot describe or interpret data, even with prompts; the student does not attempt to interpret data or communicate results.

The Assessment Strategies

Following are explanations of and some examples for six assessment techniques you may want to try in your classroom.

ASSESSMENT STRATEGIES

INTERVIEWS
OBSERVATIONS
PORTFOLIOS
STUDENT SELF-ASSESSMENT
PERFORMANCE TASKS
STUDENT WRITING

Background information is provided for each of the six assessment strategies. Included are a brief description, a list of evaluation purposes, general notes, and practical ideas for how to get started, as well as how to refine techniques (e.g., beginning users, intermediate users, advanced users). Sometimes student samples and sample activities are provided.

WE ENCOURAGE YOU TO EXPLORE DIFFERENT ASSESSMENT OPTIONS, WITH A REMINDER: MAKE IT WORK FOR YOU, NOT OVERWORK YOU.

DESCRIPTION

Interviews involve observing and questioning students to get a better idea of the student's thinking processes, level of understanding, ability to make connections, ability to apply concepts, and so on. Interviews may be formal or informal, individual or small group. Formal or structured interviews generally involve a selected sequence of tasks or problems and specific categories of questions. The assessor observes the student(s) performing the assigned task. Based on what was observed, questions are asked about what the student(s) did, how the student(s) perceived the situation, and so on. Notes are recorded during or soon after the interview. A parallel could be drawn to doing individual reading conferences or small group discussions to assess reading comprehension.

EVALUATION PURPOSES

- To gain insight into the student's thinking, performance, or attitude
- To diagnose problems students are having
- To determine the level of understanding
- To encourage students to reflect on their thinking

NOTES

1. Interviews allow careful observation of performance and provide the following:
   a. an opportunity to get detailed information about what the student is thinking and doing
   b. time for the assessor to probe more deeply into the student's thinking
   c. as much structure or flexibility as the assessor needs or wants
2. Therefore you may want to try informal interviews and to limit formal interviews for the following:
   a. assessing important behaviors that cannot be assessed more easily by using other techniques
   b. diagnosing the developmental level of individual students
3. Not all students need to be interviewed on a given set of tasks. Select a predetermined number or set of students whom you desire to assess more intensely.
4. Establish a friendly, relaxed atmosphere.
5. For an at-risk student, do the task and have the student tell what she or he thinks you are doing and why.
6. Decide whether and how you will score students, as well as whether to record data on students' actions and thoughts.
7. Observe and listen as the student completes the task. Allow plenty of wait time so that the student can give thoughtful responses. Do not interrupt a student when he or she is thinking. Ask probing questions to clarify what the student is thinking or doing. Refrain from teaching or asking leading questions. (You may want to wait to ask questions until after the task has been completed.)

BEGINNING USERS

1. Try some informal interviews. Develop one or two interview questions related to the current unit. Explain to the class that you will be taking a few students from class to interview them. As students work on assignments, take one or two students from class and interview them. Pick students at various performance levels so that you get a sense of the range of responses to expect. The first time you try this, you may want to develop and use a script, keeping all questions the same. Decide whether you want to ask clarification or extension questions; it may be helpful to think carefully about the subject of the interview so that good follow-up questions can be raised.

2. As students complete a problem-solving activity, ask them to explain how they solved the problem. Practice asking follow-up questions.

3. Design a mini interview (e.g., three mental computation problems) that you can give to all students. Design a way to keep a record of student responses.

4. Think about one interview question that would help you determine whether a student truly understands a concept or process. Try the question on two students—one you feel really does understand the concept or process, and one you feel does not. Compare the responses with what you anticipated.

INTERMEDIATE USERS

1. Modify the interviews, record-keeping devices, and so on to meet your own needs. Modify individual interviews by asking extension or clarification questions as needed. Look for ways and times to incorporate more informal interviews into your schedule.

2. Work on using structured or formal interviews. Think about outcomes you want to assess by means of interviews, and begin to develop interview activities and record-keeping formats. Develop a list of possible extension and clarification questions. Pilot your sample interviews. Continue refining your skills.

ADVANCED USERS

An advanced user demonstrates one or more of the following characteristics:

- ability to interpret both verbal and nonverbal behaviors
- a management system that allows her or him to effectively and efficiently use interviews as means of assessment
- a set of interview questions and techniques for assessing curricular and instructional goals
- comfort in altering assessment interviews based on individual student responses

SAMPLE INTERVIEW QUESTIONS

The following set of questions could form the basis of an interview. It was modified from a sample interview described by E. Labinowicz in *Learning from Children: New Beginnings for Teaching Numerical Thinking*. Questions and statements to the student are in bold type. It is assumed questions to probe or clarify will be asked if necessary.

1. Establish rapport with the student.

2. Provide a pool of blocks or tiles. Introduce the task as one relating to multiplication.

   Use the blocks (tiles) to show me 3 times 4. Explain what you are doing.

3. Provide graph paper and a pencil. Ask the student to shade the small squares to show "5 times 6" (spoken) or 5×6 (written).

Shade the small squares to show me 5 times 6.

4. **Suppose you forgot what 7 times 8 was; show me a way to figure out the answer.**

5. **Yvonne has 4 boxes with 7 apples in each box. How many apples does Yvonne have?** After the answer is provided, **How did you get that answer?**

6. **Write or tell me a story problem for this problem.**
   (Give notation "8 × 3".)

7. Show a multiplication problem; e.g.,   13
                                        × 12

Estimation	• **Guess how big the answer to 13 × 12 will be.**
	• **How did you decide?**
Computation	• **Let's see how you work out 13 × 12.**
Explanation	• **How would you explain what you did to a second grader?**
	• **When you multiplied (point to the two ones), what were you really multiplying?**
Demonstration	Provide base 10 blocks.
	• **How would you show the multiplication problem 13 × 12 with these blocks?**
Connection	• **When you multiplied (point to 1 × 1, 2 × 1, etc.) what were you really multiplying?**
	• **Make up a problem that would fit these numbers using multiplication.**

PRIMARY ASSESSMENT INTERVIEWS

The Ann Arbor Public Schools staff have been exploring alternative ways to assess the mathematics achievement of our primary grade students. A Primary Mathematics Assessment Committee, comprised of kindergarten, grade 1, and grade 2 teachers, designed fifteen- to thirty-minute interviews that included evaluation strategies and record-keeping forms. The interviews reflected a few outcomes of the hands-on primary mathematics curriculum.

Students were provided a variety of hands-on materials (beans, cubes, crayons, etc.) to use as they demonstrated their understanding of mathematical ideas.

The interviews are included here as a model of how you could put together a grade-appropriate kit that would be ready to use whenever you wished to assess a student. The interview tasks, materials lists, and record-keeping forms follow.

In the interview scripts, what the interviewer says is in bold type. The grade 2 script activities 2, 3, and 4 are also appropriate for grade 3.

Because many teachers use the *Mathematics Their Way*™ program, some of the assessment tasks were adapted from the *Mathematics Their Way*™ *Summary Newsletter*.

Kindergarden Scripts

1. One-to-one Correspondence

Materials

beans

Script

Place five beans on the table in front of the student.

Count these beans out loud for me.

If the student counts correctly, go to script 2.

If the student makes an error, have him or her try a second time.

Show me how you counted the beans.

Record Keeping

	No	Yes
▲ No response	▲ Does not touch each bean once and only once	▲ Touches each bean once and only once

2. Conservation of Number (6)

Materials

beans

Script

I am going to make two rows of beans.

Make one horizontal row of six beans, and then make another.

Beans in each row should be placed in one-to-one correspondence.

Does each row have the same number of beans?

If the student says yes, spread out the beans in one row to make it look longer.

Does each row have the same number of beans?

Have the student explain his or her answer.

0	1	3	5
▲ No response	▲ Does not conserve at 6	▲ Conserves at 6 ▲ Insufficient or no explanation	▲ Conserves at 6 ▲ Provides valid-explanation

3. Number to Five

Materials

beans

Script

Push the beans on the table into a pile.

Place five beans in my hand. (Pause for the student to do this.)

Now how many beans do I have?

I am going to hide some. Tell me how many I am hiding.

Hide beans in the following order.

I have two beans. How many am I hiding?

I have five beans. How many am I hiding?

I have one bean. How many am I hiding?

I have three beans. How many am I hiding?

I have zero beans. How many am I hiding?

I have four beans. How many am I hiding?

Try a smaller number if the student is hesitant or consistently responds incorrectly.
Whether the answer is right or wrong, do not show the student the beans you have in your closed fist.

Record Keeping

0	1	3	5
▲ No response	▲ 3 Family ▲ Instantanoeus, correct responses	▲ 4 Family ▲ Instantanoeus, correct responses	▲ 5 Family ▲ Instantanoeus, correct responses

4. **Instant Number Recognition (2–5)**

Materials
beans

Script
Have a pile of beans on the table.
> **Close your eyes. I'll tell you what I am doing, but keep your eyes closed. I am putting the beans in groups. When I am ready, I will have you open your eyes. Then I will say a number. I want you to point to the group of beans that matches that number.**
> **Do not count the beans. Just point.**

While you are talking, make random piles of two, three, four, and five beans.
> **Open your eyes. Point to five beans.**
> **Point to three beans.**
> **Point to two beans.**
> **Point to four beans.**

Record Keeping

	No	Yes
▲ No response	▲ Verbally or physically counts the beans ▲ Points to incorrect group	▲ Instant recognition ▲ All correct

5. **Identify Shapes**

Materials
circle, triangle, rectangle, square

Script
Place a circle, triangle, square, and rectangle in your hand so they are hidden from the student.
Starting with the circle, place one at a time on the table.
> **What is this shape?** (circle)
> **What is this shape?** (triangle, placed on a base)
> **What is this shape?** (square)
> **What is this shape?** (rectangle, placed on a long base)

Record Keeping

	No	Yes
▲ No response	▲ Did not know all 4 shapes	▲ Knew all 4 shapes

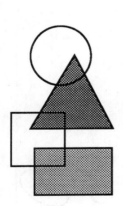

6. Number Order Cards (0–10)

Materials
index cards with numerals written on them

Script
Have a set of number cards in your hand.

These cards are out of order. Put them in order, starting with zero.

Hand the student the set of cards.

Record Keeping

	No		Yes
▲ No response	▲ Some cards in order ▲ Seems confused about some numbers		▲ Puts all cards in order

7. Sort and Classify

Materials
variety of old crayons

Script
Now you will do some sorting for me.

Place a pile of old crayons in front of the student.

Sort these into groups by color.

The crayons with paper and without paper.

The crayons that are whole and broken.

The crayons that are fat and skinny.

After each sort, push the crayons back into a pile.

Record Keeping

	No		Yes
	▲ No response	▲ Does not sort correctly	▲ Sorts correctly
Color			
Paper/No Paper			
Whole/Broken			
Fat/Skinny			

8. Numeral Recognition (1–20)

Materials
number strip and Unifix® cubes

1	2	3	4	5	6	7	8	9	10
11	12	13	14	15	16	17	18	19	20

Script
Put a number strip and Unifix® cubes on the table.

Here is a number strip and some Unifix® cubes. I am going to say a number. Cover it with a Unifix® cube.

Place a Unifix® cube on the number 8.

on the number 16.

on the number 5.

on the number 12.

on the number 15.

on the number 9.

on the number 11.
(Only the phrase is necessary after the initial direction.)

Record Keeping

0	1	3	5
▲ No response	▲ Does not recognize any numerals	▲ Recognizes all 1-digit numerals ▲ Misses some 2-digit numerals	▲ Recognizes all numerals ▲ Can quickly cover with a Unifix® cube

9. Graphing

Materials

1-in. graph paper, Unifix® cubes (7 orange, 3 red, 5 green, 2 brown)

Script

Place a pile of Unifix® cubes (7 orange, 5 green, 3 red, 2 brown) and 1-in. graph paper on the table.

Here are a sheet of graph paper and some Unifix cubes. Make a color graph by placing all these Unifix® cubes on the paper.

If the student completes the graph correctly, continue.

You may provide a prompt.

If the student has not completed the graph correctly, score it, clear the graph, make it correct, and then continue.

Tell me two things about your graph.

Prompt and, if necessary, say:

Tell me something else about your graph.

Record Keeping

MODELING

0	1	3	5
▲ No response	▲ Places cubes randomly ▲ Does not complete task	▲ Needs prompts to complete the graph	▲ Completes the graph without any help

EXPLANATION

0	1	3	5
▲ No response	▲ Makes inappropriate interpretive statements	▲ Makes one appropriate interpretive statement	▲ Makes two appropriate interpretive statements

Grade 1 Script

1. Estimation

Materials

   beans, index card

Script

   Place 24 beans on the table in front of the student.

   Guess how many beans are in this pile.

   If the student does not make a guess within 5 seconds, lay your card over the pile and prompt the student to make a guess.

Record Keeping

0	1	3	5
▲ No response	▲ < 15 or > 34	▲ 15 – 19 or 30 – 34	▲ 20 – 29

2. One-to-one Correspondence

Materials

   beans (from script 1)

Script

   Count the beans out loud for me.

   If the student counts correctly, go on to script 3.

   If the student makes an error, give him or her a second chance.

   Count these again. Point to the beans as you count out loud.

   If the student counts correctly, continue.

   If the student still does not count correctly, make a pile of 12 beans and have the student count it.

   Count this pile for me. Point to the beans as you count out loud.

Record Keeping

0	1	3	5
▲ No response	▲ 12 with one try	▲ 24 on second try	▲ 24 with one try

3. Counting Backward from 24

Materials

   beans

Script

   Have you ever counted backward, like from five: five, four, three, two, one? Would you count backward from 24 for me?

   If the student starts with 23 and performs correctly, accept it. Go on to script 4.

   If the student cannot count backward by rote, use the beans.

   **Here are 24 beans. I am going to take one away. How many are left?...
   And if I take away another one?**

Do this until the student has finished counting backward.
If a student is not successful on his or her second try, have him or her repeat this entire process using 19.
If she or he is not successful with 19, repeat the process using 10.

Record Keeping

0	1	3	5
▲ No response	▲ Can count backwards from 10 or 19 (circle one)	▲ Correctly counts backwards from 24 using bean prompt	▲ Correctly counts backwards from 24 rotely without bean prompt

4. Conservation of Number (10)

Materials
    beans

Script
    I am going to make two rows of beans.
    Using the same pile of beans, make one horizontal row of 10 beans, and then make another row.
    Beans should be placed in one-to-one correspondence.
        Does each row have the same number of beans?
    If the student says yes, spread out the beans in one row to make it look longer.
        Does each row have the same number of beans?
    Have the student explain her or his answer.

Record Keeping

0	1	3	5
▲ No response	▲ Does not conserve at 10	▲ Conserves at 10 ▲ Insufficient or no explanation	▲ Conserves at 10 ▲ Provides valid explanation

5. Number to Six

Materials
    beans

Script
    Use the same pile of beans.
        Place four beans in my hand. (Pause)
        Now how many beans do I have?
        I am going to hide some. Tell me how many I am hiding.
    Hide in the following order.
        I have three beans. How many am I hiding?
        I have zero beans. How many am I hiding?
        I have two beans. How many am I hiding?
        I have one bean. How many am I hiding?
        I have four beans. How many am I hiding?
    If the student responds quickly and accurately, try a larger number.

0	1	3	5
▲ No response	▲ 4 Family ▲ Instantaneous, correct responses	▲ 5 Family ▲ Instantaneous, correct responses	▲ 6 Family ▲ Instantaneous, correct responses

6. Sort and Classify (two categories that overlap)

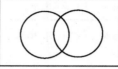

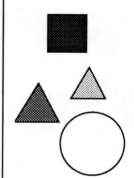

Materials

   attribute materials (e.g., attribute blocks), sorting mat

Script

   Place a sorting mat and attribute blocks in front of the student. Withhold the *small red square*, the *small blue triangle*, the *large red triangle*, and the *large yellow circle*.

   You are going to do some sorting. This circle is for the red pieces, and this circle is for triangles. Here are some colored shapes. Choose any three pieces, and place them on your sorting mat.

   Probe if the student places any incorrectly.

   Now I am going to give you some pieces to place. Decide where each piece goes. Put it there. Then tell me why it goes there.

   Hand the student one piece at a time in this order: *small red square*, the *small blue triangle*, the *large red triangle*, *large yellow circle*.

   Probe or prompt when necessary.

   Ask the student to rethink if an error is made.

   Use additional pieces if you feel you need to reassess something.

Record Keeping

0	1	3	5
▲ No response	▲ Unable to sort correctly	▲ Sorts main attributes ▲ Makes errors with intersection ▲ Makes errors with what is outside	▲ Can sort correctly ▲ Can provide a rationale

7. Oral/Written Story (for an equation symbolically given and stated)

Materials

   cards with the equations $4 + 3 = 7$ and $5 - 2 = 3$ on them

Script

   Show the student the equation card $4 + 3 = 7$. Do not state the sentence.

   Tell me a story to go with this number sentence.

   Prompt the student if he or she is hesitant or confused.

   Tell me a story about horses/cats/puppies to go with this number sentence.

   Even if the student had trouble with the first card, show the student the equation card $5 - 2 = 3$. Do not state the sentence.

   Prompt if necessary.

Record Keeping

ADDITION

	No	Yes
▲ No response	▲ Story or statement was inappropriate or incorrect	▲ Story was appropriate

SUBTRACTION

	No	Yes
▲ No response	▲ Story or statement was inappropriate or incorrect	▲ Story was appropriate

8. Problem-Solving Story

Materials

beans, paper and a pencil, picture, story card

Script

Now I am going to tell you a story. You may use beans, paper and pencil, or do it in your head.
Provide beans, paper, and pencil.
Show the student the marbles picture.
This is a picture of bags of marbles.

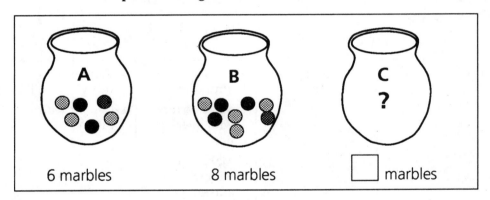

A 6 marbles

B 8 marbles

C ? ☐ marbles

Sara has 18 marbles. She has 6 marbles in bag A and 8 marbles in bag B.
How many marbles does she have in the last bag?
Have the student explain his or her answer.
How did you get your answer?
Sara has 18 marbles.

Record Keeping

SOLUTION

0	1	3	5
▲ No response	▲ Incorrect answer	▲ Minor error in execution	▲ Correct answer

0	1	3	5
▲ No response	▲ Inappropriate strategy	▲ Partially correct ▲ Errors in implementation	▲ Appropriate strategy ▲ Able to explain strategy

Grade 2 Script

1. Conservation of Number (10)

Materials
> beans

Script
> **I am going to make two rows of beans.**
> Have a pile of beans on the table. Make one horizontal row of 10 beans, and then make another row. Beans should be placed in one-to-one correspondence.
> **Does each row have the same number of beans?**
> If the student says yes, spread out the beans in one row to make it look longer.
> **Does each row have the same number of beans?**
> Have the student explain her or his answer: **Can you tell me why?**

Record Keeping

0	1	3	5
▲ No response	▲ Does not conserve at 10	▲ Conserves at 10 ▲ Insufficient or no explanation	▲ Conserves at 10 ▲ Can provide a valid explanation

2. Build a Number

Materials
> place value boards, squared or base 10 materials (or beans, bean sticks, portion cups, Unifix® cubes), paper, pencil

Script
> Show the numeral card 16.
> **What is this number?**
> Correct the student if he or she gives an incorrect answer.
> **Use these materials to show me this number.**
> *Point* to the six. Do not say, "Six."
> **What does *this part* mean? Could you show me with your beans?**
> Accept his or her answer without probing.
> *Point* to the one. Do not say, "One."
> **What does *this part* mean? Show me with your beans.**

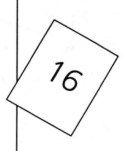

If the student performs correctly, go to script 3. If the student performs incorrectly, probe. For example:

> **You showed me all these** (point to 16 objects) **for this number** (point to card with 16 on it)
> **and these** (point to 6 objects) **for this part** (point to 6)
> **and this** (point to object) **for this part** (point to 1 on card).
> **What about the rest of the pieces** (point to the extras that the student did not use)?
> **Why are pieces left over?**
> **Can you tell me any more?**

Record Keeping

0	1	3	5
▲ No response	▲ Cannot create place value model for a number ▲ Cannot explain relationship of digits and numerical value	▲ Can create place value model ▲ Has difficulty explaining the model ▲ Has difficulty explaining the relationship of the digits and numerical value	▲ Can build and explain the model ▲ Can explain the relationship of the digits and numerical value

3. Regrouping with Addition

Materials

place value boards, squared or base 10 materials (or beans, bean sticks, portion cups, Unifix® cubes), paper, pencil, addition card

Script

Place all of the base 10 materials on the table.

Have the student clear his or her board.

Show the card with 16 + 17 written on it.

> **Add these numbers. You may do it in your head or on paper.**

Have the student explain how he or she got his or her answer: **Tell me how you got that answer.**

> **Show me with these materials a way you can solve the problem.**
> **Explain what you are doing/did?**

Have the student explain, using the pieces, the procedure he or she had just described.

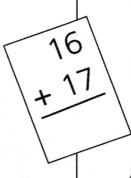

Record Keeping

0	1	3	5
▲ No response	▲ Incorrect answer	▲ Minor error in execution	▲ Correct answer

0	1	3	5
▲ No response	▲ Cannot model regrouping ▲ Cannot create place value model	▲ Can model regrouping with a prompt or probe ▲ Can create place value model ▲ Has difficulty building model	▲ Can model regrouping ▲ Can create place value model ▲ Can correctly build both numbers

MODEL

0	1	3	5
▲ No response	▲ Cannot explain how to regroup ▲ Cannot explain model ▲ Cannot explain relationship of digits and numerical value	▲ Has difficulty or makes errors when demonstrating regrouping ▲ Has difficulty explaining the model ▲ Has difficulty explaining relationship of digits and numerical value	▲ Can explain how to regroup ▲ Can explain the model ▲ Can explain relationship of digits and numerical value

EXPLANATION

4. Regrouping with Subtraction

Materials

place value boards, squared or base 10 materials (or beans, bean sticks, portion cups, Unifix® cubes), paper, pencil, subtraction card

Script

Have on the table the materials the student preferred . Show to the student the card with 34 – 17 written on it .

Subtract these numbers. You may do it in your head or on paper.

Have the student explain his or her answer: **Tell me how you got your answer.**

Show me 34 with your materials.

Show me, as you explain, how you subtracted 17.

Record Keeping

SOLUTION

0	1	3	5
▲ No response	▲ Incorrect answer	▲ Minor error in execution	▲ Correct answer

0	1	3	5
▲ No response	▲ Cannot model regrouping ▲ Cannot create place value model	▲ Can model regrouping with a prompt or probe ▲ Can create place value model ▲ Has difficulty building model	▲ Can model regrouping ▲ Can create place value model ▲ Can correctly build both numbers

EXPLANATION

0	1	3	5
▲ No response	▲ Cannot explain how to regroup ▲ Cannot explain model ▲ Cannot explain relationship of digits and numerical value	▲ Has difficulty or makes errors when demonstrating regrouping ▲ Has difficulty explaining the model ▲ Has difficulty explaining relationship of digits and numerical value	▲ Can explain how to regroup ▲ Can explain the model ▲ Can explain relationship of digits and numerical value

5. Story Card: Problem Solving Without a Picture

Materials
card with story printed on it, sorting mat, blank cards

Script

I am going to tell you a story. You may use your paper and pencil, if you wish.
Place the story card in front of the student so she or he can see it as you read aloud.

Two trees are in a yard. One tree has 5 baby birds in it. The other tree has 3 baby birds in it. How many feet are there all together?
Give the student time to work.

Explain how you solved the problem.

Record Keeping
SOLUTION

0	1	3	5
▲ No response	▲ Incorrect answer	▲ Minor error in execution	▲ Correct answer

0	1	3	5
▲ No response	▲ Inappropriate strategy	▲ Partially correct ▲ Errors in implementation	▲ Appropriate strategy ▲ Able to explain strategy

6. Sort and Classify: Two categories that overlap

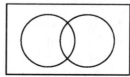

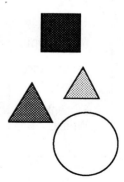

Materials

> attribute materials (e.g., attribute blocks), sorting mat

Script

> Place attribute blocks and a sorting mat in front of the student.
> Withhold the *small blue square,* the *small yellow circle,* the *large yellow square,* and the *small red triangle.*

> *Part A*
>> **You are going to do some sorting. This circle is for the yellow pieces. This circle is for squares. Here are some colored shapes. Choose any three pieces, and place them on your sorting mat.**
>
> Probe if the student places any incorrectly.
>> **Now I am going to give you some pieces to place. Decide where each piece goes. Put it there. Then tell me why it goes there.**
>
> Hand the student one piece at a time in this order: *small blue square,* the *small yellow circle,* the *large yellow square,* and the *small red triangle.*
> Probe or prompt when necessary.
> Ask the student to rethink if he or she makes an error.
> Use additional pieces if you feel you need to reassess something.

> *Part B*
>> **This time you get to sort any way you would like.**
>
> When the student has decided the labels, make out cards for the student and place them above the circles over previously used labels.
>> **Place five pieces.**
>
> Have the student give you reasons why he or she placed pieces where he or she did.
> Select two or three pieces, and have the student place them for you and explain why they go there.

Record Keeping

GIVEN THE CATEGORIES

0	1	3	5
▲ No response	▲ Unable to sort correctly	▲ Sorts main attributes ▲ Makes errors with intersection ▲ Makes errors with what is outside	▲ Can sort correctly ▲ Can provide a rationale

OBSERVATIONS

DESCRIPTION

You observe an individual, small group, or class during an activity to assess some aspect of student behavior or attitude. While observing students, you record observations and may ask evaluative or probing questions.

EVALUATION PURPOSES

- To observe the processes students use to solve problems and to complete tasks or products
- To collect data on behaviors that are difficult to assess by other methods
- To monitor overall classroom performance to ascertain whether students are attaining the intended objectives (e.g., Do I need to re-teach? Are students ready to move on? Are groups on task?)

NOTES

1. Limit observations to what cannot be more readily evaluated by other techniques (e.g., attitude toward problem solving, selection and implementation of a specific strategy, modeling a concept with a manipulative, ability to work effectively in a group, persistence, concentration).

2. Ask students questions that will help you better understand their behavior and understanding (e.g., What did you do first? Why? Can you describe your solution? Will you explain what you are doing? What should you do next? Can you describe any patterns you see?)

3. Record and date your observations briefly and objectively during or soon after the observation. Develop a shorthand system.

4. Frequently recorded observations will point out students whom you have not observed for a while. For example, just tallying on a seating chart those students who have responded to questions will make you more aware of interesting patterns.

5. Experiment with different recording formats until you find ones that are useful and user friendly. Sample forms, along with helpful hints, are provided in this book.

6. Observe students in a natural classroom setting so you can see how they respond under normal conditions. It is easier to observe students' behavior if they are working in small groups rather than alone.

7. Have an observation plan, but be flexible enough to note other significant behavior. You may find it helpful to limit the number of students or the number of things for which you are observing.

BEGINNING USERS

1. Initially, limit the number of behaviors or students being observed. For example, pick one specific aspect of your students' behavior that you would like to evaluate. Write the behavior at the top of a sheet of paper so you can collect data about the class in an anecdotal form.

> **BEHAVIOR: Sticks to the task until a solution is reached**   10-10-91
>
> Sally – tried but then asked for help
> Sam – tried 3 things, then got one to work
> R.J. – tried adding all the numbers; it didn't look
>   right so gave up

2. Select one of the record-keeping formats described in the book. Try it out, and analyze how well it worked. Make modifications to make it work better for you. If it just did not work, try a different one.

INTERMEDIATE USERS

1. Experiment with different record-keeping formats, and refine them to fit your needs.
2. Select a limited number of behaviors to observe. Consider performance indicators or rating scales that you could use. Select two or three students to observe each class period when they are directly involved in a related activity. Record your observations.
3. Observe students, and develop performance indicators for the three levels (not understanding, developing, applying). Keep the performance indicators on file.

ADVANCED USERS

1. Create your own checklists (with or without rating scales), and consistently use them to evaluate certain aspects of students' performance or attitude. Keep an ongoing record of observations.
2. Continue developing performance indicators that can be used to help you be consistent in your assessment of students.

Strategies
Interviews
Observations
➤ Portfolios
Student Self-Assessment
Performance Tasks
Student Writing

PORTFOLIOS

DESCRIPTION

A portfolio is a collection of student-produced work and support documentation that shows evidence of a student's learning. A portfolio reflects a student's development and progress over time on a variety of concepts, processes, skills, and attitudes.

You may collect samples from all students on a common assignment or task and may include the best pieces in a student's portfolio.

EVALUATION PURPOSES

- To provide a multidimensional perspective by including different indicators of the breadth and depth of a student's learning
- To provide a chronology of the student's progress and development on important concepts, processes, skills, and attitudes
- To provide a clear and comprehensive profile
- To focus on what the student has attained
- To encourage teacher-student reflection and interaction about the student's performance

NOTES

1. Portfolios may include the following types of items:

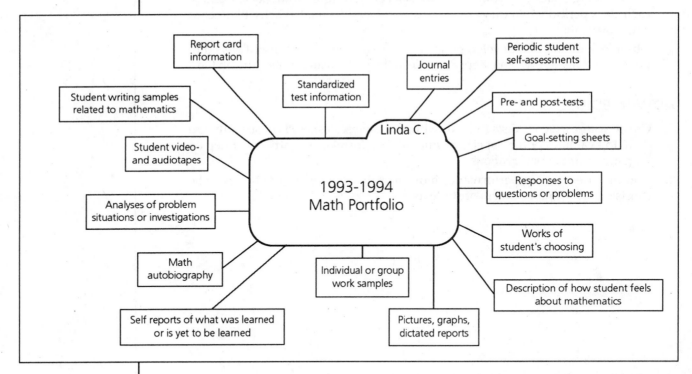

2. Students should be actively involved in assessing and selecting their work. Planned opportunities should be provided for them to present and explain their own portfolios to outside observers (e.g., to parents during a conference).

3. Because portfolios show what one knows rather than what one does not know, they provide opportunities to improve student self-image.

4. Items in a portfolio should be dated.

5. Portfolio pieces may be assessed by analytic or holistic scoring.

BEGINNING USERS

1. Begin collecting pieces to have a profile on each student or to make comparisons. Your collection may be somewhat random (e.g., without feeling a need to collect on a variety of math strands or on major outcomes).

2. Collect a certain number of pieces each quarter to get a sense of growth over time. In this case it may be helpful to pick some samples from the same strand.

3. Try a *Portfolio on the Wall*. Establish a bulletin board for displaying student work. Each week students select and post their best work, along with a brief paragraph about why they selected that particular piece. As new pieces are posted, the previous "best piece" goes into the student's portfolio. The portfolio may be shared with the parents at conference time or at the end of a grading period.

4. Think about six things you would put into a portfolio during the next month. Include these activities in the next month, and get some portfolios started. Continue this throughout the school year. If students want to add other things as well, let them.

5. You might not have any specific criteria for evaluating pieces initially. As you collect and compare samples, however, you may see some patterns or get ideas for setting criteria.

INTERMEDIATE USERS

1. Develop and implement a portfolio plan. Consider your curricular priorities in designing your plan.

My Portfolio Plan

1. Use two small group problem-solving experiences each week to get portfolio pieces.
   - Have students individually write descriptions of how they solved the problem.
   - At the end of the week, have each student select one of the two to include in the portfolio.

2. Put pretests, posttests, quizzes, and one work sample for each unit into the portfolio.

3. Have each student write a math autobiography.

4. Let each student pick five pieces each quarter, including a written explanation of why each was chosen, to be put into his or her portfolio.

---

2. Begin identifying and trying various criteria for evaluating pieces (e.g., understands the problem and conditions, can correctly compute 50 facts in 5 minutes). You might consider finding another interested colleague and work together on developing and trying different criteria and on improving your management system.

3. Consider having students help select, describe, or evaluate their work. Explore providing planned times or opportunities for students to share and discuss their portfolios with other people. Consider having students write why they selected certain pieces for their portfolio.

ADVANCED USERS

1. Systematically review your curricular and instructional priorities. Determine where assessment is adequate and where more is needed. Decide what actual evidence, as well as what support evidence, should be included in student portfolios. Be sure the portfolios reflect student achievement or progress on major outcomes.

2. Implement and refine criteria for evaluating pieces. Evaluation also might include student self-evaluation.

3. Staff of the entire school could pursue use of the portfolio in an organized manner across multiple grade levels.

4. Identify pieces that best exemplify change over time, best work, and typical work.

Student Problem-Solving Journals

Outcomes

- To gain confidence in problem-solving ability.
- To keep a journal to provide a record over time of one's increased ability to think and reason mathematically.

Materials

- Word/story problems (from, for example, TOPS Problem Solving Card Decks from Dale Seymour Publications) written on the board three mornings a week
- Journal for each student (journals can be made from blank paper with construction paper covers folded together and stapled in the middle)

Assessment Activity

1. Direct students to begin three days each week with their problem-solving journal, using two problems of different levels of difficulty.
2. Let students choose which problem they wish to solve after problems are read to class.
3. Show students how to record their work on a four-part page.
   a. Write the question asked.
   b. Record the important information given (e.g., a picture).
   c. Write the equation or number sentence.
   d. Write the solution and how you feel about today's work.

a
b
c
d

(For a quick assessment, you might use the method described in *How to Evaluate Progress in Problem Solving* by R. Charles et al.)

4. After 15 minutes, collect the journals.
5. Without journals, have students discuss as a group how they solved the problem.

Notes

- Work recorded in a journal allows you to see how the student's confidence grew each time.
- At the start of the year, use just one problem for the whole class to solve and discuss.
- Model and record on the board how students will later fill in their journals.
- Not all students may be able to do all parts at start. Explain that they get credit for each part finished.
- Use a holistic scoring for the student's work, focusing on the total work, not just the answer.
- As needed, note in the students' journals any questions and ideas you have.

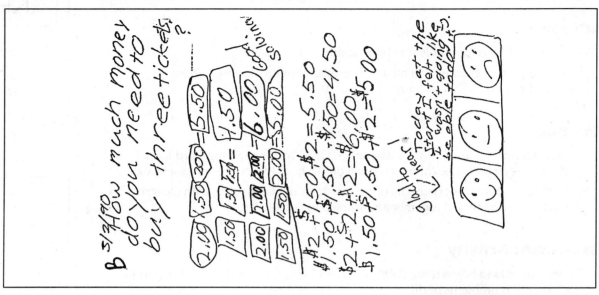

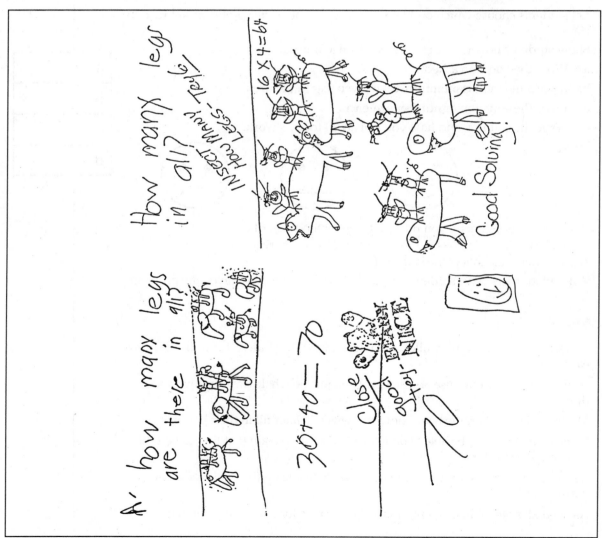

Weekly Math Work Portfolio

Materials

■ A five-day math journal with a cover sheet and an answer sheet (see following pages for a sample journal)

■ Pencil

Assessment Activity

1. Have students complete one day's assignment in the math journal each day. Each day should be devoted to a different topic, such as:

   Day 1   Graphs and tables

   Day 2   Computational review problems

   Day 3   Story problems

   Day 4   Problems related to the current unit of study

   Day 5   Problems related to past units of study

2. Grade the work each night, and return it to students the next day. On day two, students have the responsibility of correcting day one's mistakes and of completing day two's assignment. This process continues throughout the week.

3. Record scores or grades, and place them in students' portfolios.

Notes

■ To save time, attach an answer sheet to each journal. Put the answer sheet on backward to avoid having to flip through the pages to grade them. This makes it possible to grade all of the journals in a few minutes.

■ One way to motivate students to carefully complete the daily assignments is to reward them. Make a class chart and a wizard hat for each student like the ones below. Place each student's hat outside the chart. Move a student's hat to level one after he or she receives an "A" or a "B" on the weekly math journal. Each subsequent week that the student earns an "A" or a "B," move the student's hat up one level. When a student's hat is moved to level 4, the student earns a "free week" coupon, which entitles him or her to skip a week of math journal work. Students may use their "free weeks" whenever they choose.

■ The next five pages are a model of a math work portfolio with a cover and activities.

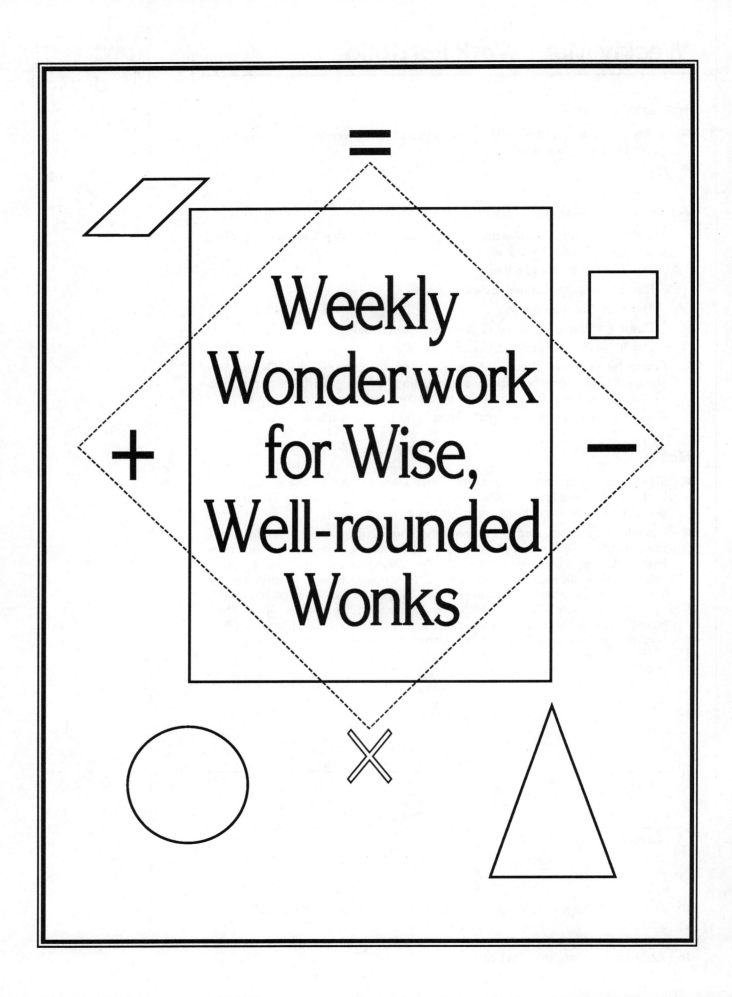

TAKING TIME

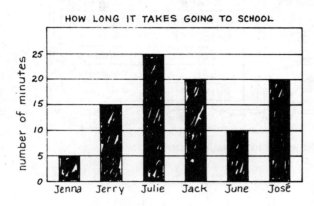

HOW LONG IT TAKES GOING TO SCHOOL

You can't tell everything from a graph.
Use the graph to answer the questions.
Draw a line through the questions that *cannot* be
answered from the graph.

Who takes 20 minutes going to school? _____

How many minutes does June take going to school? _____

Who takes longer going to school, Julie or Jack? _____

Who has the farthest to go? _____

How many minutes does Jim take going to school? _____

Is Julie late to school if she starts at 8:00 AM? _____

Does José get to school before Jerry? _____

When does Jenna get to school if she starts at 8:25? _____

Does June walk faster than Jenna? _____

How many more minutes does it take Jack than Jerry? _____

Who takes the longest going to school? _____

If Jenna, Jerry, Julie, Jack, June, and José start at the same time,

who gets to school first? _____

Reproduced from *Developing Skills with Tables and Graphs*, Book A by Elaine C. Murphy, © 1981 by Dale Seymour Publications

You can add more open-ended questions to any worksheet. For example:

1. Explain why you could not answer each question you drew a line through.

_____

_____

2. Write two statements about the information in the graph.

_____

_____

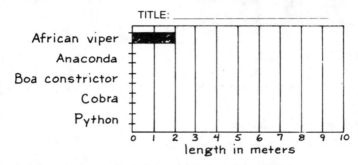

SNAKES ALIVE!

Mary read that some snakes are very long.

She saw this chart.

Snake	Length
African viper	2 meters
Anaconda	8 meters
Boa constrictor	3 meters
Cobra	2 meters
Python	9 meters

Complete the bar graph to show the information about snakes.

TITLE: _____

African viper
Anaconda
Boa constrictor
Cobra
Python

0 1 2 3 4 5 6 7 8 9 10
length in meters

Answer the questions about your graph.

What is the title of your graph? _____

How many bars are on the graph? _____

How long is the anaconda? _____

How long is the cobra? _____

Which bar is longest? _____

Which bar is shortest? _____

Which bar shows 3 meters long? _____

Which bar shows 10 meters long? _____

Which bar shows 5 meters long? _____

Reproduced from *Developing Skills with Tables and Graphs*, Book A by Elaine C. Murphy, © 1981 by Dale Seymour Publications

Open-ended questions you could add to this worksheet:

3. How much longer is the python than the African viper? _____
   How do you know?

_____

4. Give an example of a question about these snakes that cannot be answered with the information in the graph.

_____

5. Write two statements about the information in the graph.

_____

_____

Day 2

6.   409
   × 7

7. 58 × 13 =

8. 9$\overline{)34}$

9. 2,982 + 763 + 52 =

10.   84
   × 6

11. 24$\overline{)843}$

12. 447 − 399 =

13.   5,940
  + 9,552

Day 3

Jesse paints beautiful pictures of people. Every time he paints 5 pictures, he puts them into a box and sends them to a gallery. Last year he filled 8 boxes. This year he wants to fill 12 boxes. This year he has already created 50 paintings. This year Jesse is going to show his work at an art exhibition. He will bring 24 of his best paintings to the show. The art gallery has 4 walls. Jesse wants to hang the same number of paintings on each wall.

14. How can you find how many pictures Jesse painted last year?

15. How many pictures did he paint last year?

16. How many pictures does he want to paint this year?

17. How many paintings should be hung on each wall of the gallery?

18. How many more paintings must Jesse create to reach his goal for the year?

Day 4

Estimate each sum to the nearest *whole number*. (For example, you would estimate 4.2 + 8.7 as 4 + 9 to get an estimate of 13.)

19.　18.7　20.　345.8　21.　100.9　22.　45.89　23. 12.111
　　+ 5.1　　　+　0.7　　　+ 23.5　　　+　1.6　　　+ 5.812

Estimate each sum to the nearest tenth. (For example, you would estimate 4.235 + 5.18 as to 4.2 + 5.2 to get an estimate of 9.4.)

24.　34.5　25. 13.764　26. 43.278　27.　50.90　28.　25.79
　　+ 1.56　　+ 4.011　　+20.819　　+ 9.2　　　+ 8

Day 5

Use the number 2,473,986.150 to answer questions 29 to 33.

29.　What number is in the *ten thousands* place?

30.　What number is in the *tens* place?

31.　What number is in the *hundred thousands* place?

32.　What number is in the *ones* place?

33.　What number is in the *hundredths* place?

34.　Frank has $10.00. He spends $4.96 on a book. How much money does he have left?

35.　Is 321.903 an even or an odd number?

36.　Find the perimeter of the following figure.

32.7 cm

25.13 cm

37.　Find the perimeter of the following figure.

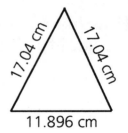

17.04 cm　17.04 cm

11.896 cm

STUDENT SELF-ASSESSMENT

DESCRIPTION

Students are asked to reflect on, make a judgement about, and then report on their own behavior and performance. Usually the reports are made in response to specific questions or statements designed to elicit feedback on selected aspects of their experience, behavior, feelings, and so on. The responses may be used to evaluate both performance and attitude.

EVALUATION PURPOSES

- To gain information on how students view their own performance
- To collect data on student attitudes, feelings, opinions, views, and so on
- To provide student-supplied information that cannot be obtained elsewhere

NOTES

1. The usefulness of self-assessment data depends on how honestly students report their feelings, beliefs, intentions, thinking processes, and so on. To provide information that helps them improve themselves and that helps you provide more appropriate experiences, establish a climate that encourages honest, thorough responses.

2. Students need models. Model evaluating your own performance, or provide examples. Another strategy is to introduce constructive feedback. Models help students develop their sense of standards for their own performance.

3. Self-assessment activities used for grading purposes may influence the frankness of students' responses.

4. Some sample self-assessment strategies are provided.

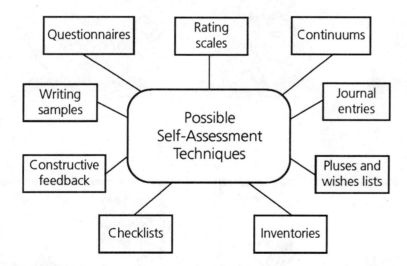

5. Let students do a private self-assessment that no one else sees. This allows for an honest sense of their own level of understanding and performance.

Strategies

Interviews

Observations

Portfolios

➤ Student Self-Assessment

Performance Tasks

Student Writing

1. Have students evaluate or comment on what happened in class, how their group worked, and so on. Or have them comment on each other's work or your presentation. In these cases students are not evaluating themselves; that dimension will be added later as they gain experience assessing performance.

2. Have students respond to simple statements or questions about their own performance.
   - Describe what contributions you made to the group.
   - What could you have done to make your group work better?
   - How could you have improved your performance?
   - How do you feel about what you learned or achieved today? Why do you feel that way?
   - My plan for what I will accomplish tomorrow is _____ .
   - What questions do you still have?

3. Provide happy faces. Have students circle one of the faces and write why they circled that face.

Two variations on this idea are clowns and a roller coaster. Enlarge or reduce them to fit on the bottom of the worksheet you are using.

1.

2.

3.

4. Have the students complete a Pluses and Wishes Chart.

1. Involve students in providing written or tape-recorded retrospective reports about their performance.

STUDENT REFLECTION: FOCUS QUESTIONS ON PROBLEM SOLVING

Use the following questions to help you look back and describe your thinking as you worked the problem.

1. How did you get started? What were your first thoughts?

2. Did you use any problem-solving strategies discussed in class? Which ones? How did they work out? How did you find your solution?

3. Did you try anything that did not work? How did you feel about it?

4. Did you find a solution? Did you check your answer in any way? Were you sure you were correct? Why or why not?

Adapted from *How to Evaluate Progress in Problem Solving* by R. Charles et al.

2. Pilot the use of inventories, continuums, or rating scales for collecting self-assessment data on selected aspects of the program. Involve students in drafting forms, criteria, and so on.

3. Have cooperative working groups debrief on their behavior and performance. Have them write what went well, what was difficult or problematic, and an improvement goal.

ADVANCED USERS

1. Integrate student self-assessment into the total program. Help students identify their strengths and weaknesses, and plan accordingly. Provide opportunities for reflection and self-evaluation.

2. Work on constructive feedback between students. Do a lot of modeling first, and then move to your making one positive statement and one area for improvement. The student then will pick another classmate to make a positive and an improvement comment as well.

3. Identify and implement several self-assessment techniques for focus throughout the school year. Work continuously with students on upgrading their skills at self-assessment.

4. Consider working on goal setting based on the interaction and comparison between the teacher's and the student's assessment of performance.

Pluses and Wishes

Outcome

■ To evaluate the learning experience, including one's own and others' productivity.

Materials

■ Lined paper
■ Pencil

Assessment Activity

1. The Pluses and Wishes Chart is a good closure activity that causes student reflection and self-evaluation.

2. The purpose of a Pluses and Wishes Chart is two-fold:

   a. To get students to be specific about things that were helpful or that went well, as well as things that were problematic

   b. To get students to self-evaluate

3. After completing an activity, have students make an evaluation T, labeling one column "Pluses" and the other "Wishes."

4. Students must write three specific things that went well or were helpful in the "Pluses" column. In the "Wishes" column they must write three specific things that were problematic, they didn't understand, could be improved, and so on.

Pluses	Wishes

   Initially none of the items need be self-evaluation. Eventually students should have at least one thing in each column that is self-evaluation.

5. (Optional) Have students write a summary paragraph based on their statements.

Notes

■ Model how to complete the evaluation T.

■ Pluses and wishes may be done as independent or group tasks.

■ Discuss group rules (e.g., you are responsible for your own behavior, you must contribute to the group, you must be willing to help anyone else in your group) prior to the activity. Discussing examples also helps students in completing their evaluation sheets.

■ (Optional) Ask students to divide a certain number of points between themselves, based on the quality and quantity of each member's contributions (e.g., each group earns 20 points total. Group members may decide that one member earned 10 points, one earned 7, and the other earned 3, based on what each contributed to the activity).

Sample Student Work

Plusses	Wishes
My partner helped me understand the paper	I wouldnt fool around

Plusses	Wishes
Agreed on evreything devied the work egwley	I wish we read the diretions more carfuley on page two second part page 2

Plusses	Wishes
Worked well together Everyone understade We cooperated We were bith together on every- thing	we were little slow

Student Self-Assessment

4–6

Outcome

■ To develop and use the language of mathematics.

Materials

■ Paper
■ Pencil

Assessment Activity

1. In this activity students will describe their strengths and weaknesses on the given unit. They will describe ideas or types of problems that are still difficult for them to understand and will indicate whether they are prepared to do the upcoming assessment.

2. Instruct students to write a letter to you before the assessment is given. They should complete statements like the following:

    a. The most important part of this unit was . . .
    b. I really learned how to . . .
    c. It was most difficult for me to learn to . . .
    d. The concept I still do not understand is . . .
    e. What I need to do to learn this is . . .
    f. I am/am not ready to do the assessment because . . .

3. Read the letters, and provide whatever additional learning experiences before giving the assessment.

Note

■ Look at the notes after students do the assessment to see any discrepancies between students thinking they are ready for the assessment and the results of the assessment.

Performance Review

Outcome

■ To assess the student's own performance.

Materials

■ Questions to be answered
■ Pencils

Assessment Activity

1. Ask students to write paragraphs assessing their work on a test or a unit or have students orally respond to questions concerning a test or a unit. (An actual student sample from a test is provided on the next page.)

2. Compare students' self-assessments with your assessments, students' scores, and written work.

3. Hold a conference with each student to compare assessments. The student should try to explain any differences in assessments. Both should plan how to improve the student's awareness and self-assessment skills for the next unit.

Notes

■ Including specific questions you want answered often results in better responses than simply asking students to evaluate their work. It is desirable, however, to reduce the number of prompts as the year progresses.

■ Include an assessment question at the end of tests so students can reflect on their work while it is still in front of them and perhaps make changes as they are thinking about it.

■ Sample questions:
  • Evaluate your work on this test and this unit. How well do you think you did on this test?
  • How many points do you think you will earn? Why do you think you will earn that number of points?
  • What was your best section? Why?
  • What section would you most want to improve? Why?
  • What study habit most helped you as you were preparing to take this test?
  • What will you do differently before the next test?
  • How much time and effort did you put into your assignments in this unit?
  • Do you think your assignments and this test really show what you know? Why or why not?
  • What is the most important thing you learned in this unit?

Sample Student Work

Name _____ Date _____

Evaluate your work on this test and this unit.

How well do you think you did on this test?

How many points do you think you will earn?

Why do you think you will earn that number of points?

What was your best section?

What section would you most want to improve?

What study habit most helped you as you were preparing to take this test?

What will you do differently before the next test?

How much time and effort did you put into your assignments in this unit?

Do you think your assignments and this test really show what you know?

What is the most important thing you learned in this unit?

I think I did great on this test. any where from (85 - 100) is how well I'll do. Because I studied hard and I knew a lot of problems on this test. My best section was multiple choice. Probably on th short answer questions, I would study a section and then my parents would quiz me. I will try and study before I even get the study guide. I put a lot of time and effort into this test. I studied a lot and tried to do my best on the work. Yes, because I used everything I knew to take this test and to do the work sheets. I think the most important thing I learned was to use measurement and weights because I had never learned about things like decimeters and how many millimeters are in a meter. And overall this is probably my favorite unit of all.

Strategies

Interviews

Observations

Portfolios

Student Self-
Assessment

➤ Performance
Tasks

Student
Writing

PERFORMANCE TASKS

DESCRIPTION

Individually or in groups, students are given a task to perform. By observing students as they complete the task and by reviewing their product or completed task (e.g., writing sample, presentation to class, product), you can assess progress on attainment or understanding of outcomes. Student performance may be evaluated by awarding points based on some established criteria (holistic or analytic scoring).

EVALUATION PURPOSES

- To assess students' ability to understand and apply outcomes being studied
- To enhance and evaluate students' ability to use appropriate mathematical presentation and representation

NOTES

1. Performance tasks may involve explaining work done or process used, formulating hypotheses, explaining mathematical situations, writing directions, creating new related problems, making generalizations, describing patterns or solutions, and so on.

2. Reading individual papers generated by students may seem time consuming and burdensome. The results, however, are worth it because you will have greater insight into what students know and do not know, as well as any gaps in their knowledge.

3. Two methods to evaluate the students' work are holistic and analytic scoring. See page 8.

BEGINNING USERS

1. Give an assignment that can be done in a number of ways (e.g., a nonroutine problem), and ask students to record all their work. Sort the papers into stacks that might be labeled "unacceptable," "acceptable," and "exemplary." Judge each piece as a whole, and give it a score. Get a feel for students' work by asking yourself questions. For example,

   - Does it show some outstanding feature? Some spark of originality?
   - What understandings, misconceptions, problems in thinking are evident from the work?
   - What were the features that distinguished unacceptable performance, acceptable performance, and exemplary performance?

2. Start collecting open-ended performance tasks that can help you assess student understanding.

INTERMEDIATE USERS

1. Develop your own bank of performance tasks from which to draw. Try some of them. Use student responses and your observations to generate indicators or criteria that denote the absence, development, or presence of important elements. Then try a holistic or analytic scoring process, using the different criteria you generate. Check the section Performance Indicators, page 3, for scoring ideas.

2. Talk to students about what you are looking for and how you will be evaluating their work. Collect some exemplary models to share with students so they know your target and what you expect of them.

ADVANCED USERS

1. Refine criteria and your record-keeping process until you come up with something you can use effectively and efficiently. Consider ways for communicating the information to both students and parents. Begin involving students in the evaluation of their work.

2. As students improve, introduce increasingly more complex or involved tasks and projects.

EXAMPLES OF PERFORMANCE TASKS

Performance Tasks	Key Concepts
1. Say: We have decided to paint our classroom. What do we need to consider? Make a plan for this painting job.	Problem solving Collection and organization of data Mathematical communication Measurement
2. Say: I have 6 nickels and 2 dimes in my pocket. I put 3 of the coins in my hand. How much money am I likely to have in my hand? Tell me why you think that.	Problem solving Mathematical reasoning Mathematical communication Probability
3. Say: Plan the menu and purchasing of food for your group for the class campout. You have $ _____ to spend on food for each person in your group. Your report needs to explain the process you used to make your decisions, your menu, your grocery list, and the cost.	Problem solving Mathematical connections Mathematical communication Collection and organization of data
4. Two students each have a geoboard. One student's geoboard has a design. Each student is seated so she or he cannot see the other geoboard. The student with the design gives the other student directions on how to make the design.	Mathematical communication Geometry Spatial sense
5. Say: Provide students with a graph. Have them describe two different situations that it could describe. Ask them to write a question for one of your situations.	Mathematical reasoning Mathematical communication Statistics

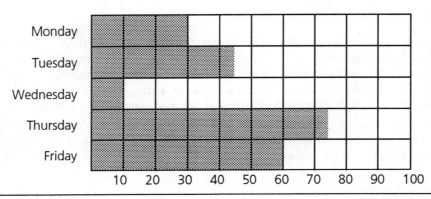

Performance Tasks	Key Concepts
6. Say: Jeff has 2 pair of jeans—1 pair of black jeans and 1 pair of blue jeans. He has 3 T-shirts—1 red,1 blue, and 1 black. Jeff randomly chooses a T-shirt and a pair of jeans. What are his chances of choosing jeans and a T-shirt of the same color? Explain your answer. You may use a chart or drawing.	Problem solving Probability Mathematical communication
7. Without giving students a reference, ask them to list two things in the room they think are about ____ meters (or ____ feet) long. Have them record their guesses. Model the length. Have them list three more things of the same approximate length. Have them measure and record all five objects. Then have them find another object, by measuring, that is about the designated length and list that as well. (Similar tasks can be done with other measurements.)	Estimation Measurement concepts *(Similar tasks can be done with other measurements.)*
8. Say: I am going to flip up a card with a problem. Quickly estimate the answer. Then tell me how you got your estimate. Or, Tell me how many digits are in the answer. Or, Tell me whether the answer is greater or less than ____. How do you know that?	Estimation Mental computation *(This can be done as interviews or observations. Similar tasks can be done for mental computation.)*
9. Have a large box of raisins, containers of different sizes, a balance, and calculators. Have groups • estimate the number of raisins in the box. • use any of the materials to make a better estimate. • check their estimates by different methods. • record results and give an oral report on their work.	Problem solving Estimation Cooperation Mathematical reasoning Mathematical communication

Performance Tasks	Key Concepts
10. Say: You have this much change: 8 pennies, 5 nickels, 11 dimes, and 5 quarters. These items may be purchased: • a poster on sale for $1.95 • a ball for $1.29 • a book for $0.95 • a card game for $0.80 Use this information to write a problem.	Formulation of problems Mathematical communication Measurement—money Decimals
11. Have cooperative groups of students use a scale drawing to present an alternative floor plan for the classroom. Try out the arrangement.	Problem solving Cooperation Mathematical communication Spatial reasoning Measurement
12. Have cooperative groups plan and conduct a survey, compile and organize the data, make interpretive statements, and present their results to the class.	Problem solving Statistics Mathematical communication

Strategies

Interviews

Observations

Portfolios

Student Self-Assessment

Perfomance Tasks

➤ Student Writing

DESCRIPTION

Students are given a prompt to which they respond in writing. This written response helps you assess how students formulate, organize, internalize, explain, and evaluate concepts and processes. Writing provides a good record of students' thinking, an indicator of what students are learning, and how students feel. Writing includes the use of drawings and symbols. Writing may be a separate activity or may be part of a larger project or activity.

EVALUATION PURPOSES

- To provide insight about a student's level of understanding
- To provide a way (closure activity) to assess attainment of instructional goals for the entire class
- To assess attitude toward mathematics by writing about ideas and feelings
- To use as a pretest to ascertain prior knowledge, understanding, misconceptions, questions, and so on
- To demonstrate the student's fluency in the communication of mathematical ideas

NOTES

1. Students need a wide variety of experiences in writing before they develop the skills needed for clear, concise explanations. Early efforts can be group or cooperative discussions, followed by writing activities. What students write, particularly at first, may not be a true indicator of what they know or mean.

2. Respond to students' writing in some way. Students need feedback to stay motivated to write.

3. Mechanics need not be corrected or graded unless the writing is part of a final project or report. Students may be asked to underline words they believe may be spelled incorrectly.

4. Writing assessment samples may take a variety of forms:
   - journal entries
   - reports or products of investigation or class activities
   - explanations of the processes used in reaching a conclusion or solving a problem
   - responses to open-ended questions
   - definitions, concepts, and processes written in students' own words
   - explanations of their own errors (self-correction)
   - expressions of their feelings about the learning experience
   - responses to errors of others
   - connections of the mathematics being studied to real-world examples

5. Writing need not be in sentences. It could be pictures with dictated comments.

6. Students need opportunities to share their writing. Writing allows students to see how they can impact or help others, to see alternative models and explanations, and to raise questions; it encourages reflection and refinement; and it builds a sense of community and trust so students are more willing to take risks.

7. Writing sends a message to students: Clearly communicating mathematical ideas is an important skill.

SAMPLE WRITING QUESTIONS

1. Write a problem that could be solved with the strategy we discussed today.
2. Explain why the answer is right or wrong.
3. What did you learn from today's math lesson?
4. How was your performance? How could you improve it?
5. What would you do differently next time?
6. Write a test problem or question that I might give to see whether students understood today's lesson.
7. What was most difficult for you today? Why?
8. What kinds of errors did you make? Why?
9. Talk to your stuffed bear, and tell it how you felt about math today.
10. What questions do you have about today's lesson?
11. Create a problem using what was learned today.
12. What did you like or dislike about today's lesson? Say why you liked or disliked it.
13. How well did your group cooperate today? Describe any problems and how you managed them.
14. Explain _____ in you own words.
15. Explain the errors you made in the assignment.
16. What do you like or dislike about students sharing their work with the class? Why?
17. How did you do on the lesson? Focus on how you did better or worse than you expected. Try to tell why.
18. What did you learn during the lesson that you did not know before?
19. Explain how you solved the problem.
20. Write a letter to a friend, explaining how to _____ .
21. Find the error in the following problem, and explain why it is an error.
22. Write a story problem to go with this math sentence/picture/graph.
23. Suppose you forgo _____ How could you figure it out?
24. José forgot how to _____ . Write José a letter explaining the steps.

BEGINNING USERS

1. Student writing may be done sporadically, with no attempt on your part to keep records. For example, occasionally have students write brief responses to open-ended questions or have students write about terms or steps that were presented.
2. A starting point might be to have students write during the last five minutes of math time, responding to the activity or to specific questions. If students summarize what they learned or are raise questions, the writing activity will serve as both a closure activity and as a means of checking for understanding.

In the following example students were asked to explain what a fraction is and to give an example of when they used a fraction.

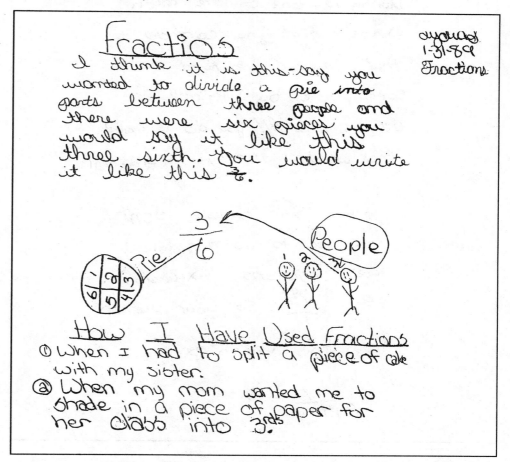

3. At the beginning of a unit, use writing to find out more about what students already know. Ask them to describe what they already know or can do, to list what they remember about the topic or concept, to list all the questions they can, or to explain how to do something.

In the following examples students were asked to tell what division is.

It's a math thing with divededs, goshos and divesers. It is a lessay experyce. The secret is Don't MaSh Sot Chocolate Browinies. D. Divide, M. Multiply, S. Subtract, C. Compare, and B. Bring Down

Divison is one of the math
choices that you can do
that may be hard to
some people but it really is
very simple. All you do is multiply
Backwards Here is a problem

4⟌44 Som people dont
Know How to do This Follow
these drictions 4 x what is
44   44   So your answer
        × 4
        ──
        11
to this Divison problem
is 11.
    4⟌44

4. Ask students or groups to write about a problem or investigation. Have them hand in their work or discuss it with others and then make revisions. This revised version should becomes the paper to be evaluated.

INTERMEDIATE USERS

1. Work with students on refining and improving their written responses. If you are not getting the quality of responses you hoped for, try an evaluation T. (See page 44 for a description.)

2. Have students explain, in writing, their thinking process. Have them write to a third party (e.g., a student in a lower grade, a parent, a favorite stuffed toy).

In the following examples students were asked to explain how they estimated the number of raisins in a box and how they divided the raisins equally among group members.

Well I saw about 13 lieing flat   78
on the top. I X'ed it by 6 cause
~~that~~ it couldrepeat about 6 times
and I got   78

I divided 4 into 104 and we   104
each get 26
but sence noneof us like
Rasins we gave themall
to justen 11

3. Move students toward self-evaluation. The evaluation T works here as well; at least one comment in each column must be on their own performance or behavior.

4. Try limited use of journals or student notebooks. Anticipate that early attempts will be less than desired. Students will need to be taught how to use a journal. Improvement will come with sustained effort, as well as by providing specific feedback and encouragement.

ADVANCED USERS

1. Use student writing frequently in a variety of ways to attain and assess instructional goals. Having students write is an integral part of the mathematics learning experience. Request that students critique their own performance and set goals in writing. Request that students reflect on their thinking and explain it in writing.

2. Use journals as a means of maintaining a long-term record of student learning and progress. If lines of communication are open and students feel comfortable with writing, they may want to share and discuss excerpts from their journals.

3. Use writing samples in the portfolios as a means of showing growth over time.

4. Work on defining criteria to use when reviewing or discussing student growth with the student or parent.

Record Keeping

Teachers continually observe individual, small group, and class performance to assess aspects of student behavior and attitude. A common concern of teachers is finding effective yet efficient ways to record student behavior—strategies that work for you, not overwork you. Some common techniques, with innovative and helpful suggestions, suggested by teachers are described.

PERFORMANCE INDICATOR AND RECORD-KEEPING SHEETS

One technique is to make the performance indicator sheet a record-keeping sheet as well. The top half of the sheet lists performance indicators; the bottom half lists student names. This format helps ensure that you observe each student and make a judgment about the student's performance. The indicators provide criteria for assessing students' understanding and products. The example provided is for a statistics task.

Outcomes

■ To make a graph to record and interpret data.

Performance Sample Indicators for Student Who Is

Not Understanding	Developing	Understanding/Applying
▲ Student cannot complete task ▲ The graph contains more than two errors ▲ The graph is inaccurate or incomplete ▲ Student cannot or does not attempt to communicate results or make interpretive statements	▲ Student needs assistance in constructing graph ▲ The graph contains minor errors ▲ Errors can be corrected if pointed out ▲ Student needs assistance in communicating or interpreting results	▲ Student constructs graph without assistance ▲ Axes, increments, and labels are done correctly ▲ Data are graphed correctly ▲ Student can communicate results and make interpretive statements
Gary Monica Sadeg Juan Linda Mike	June Bo Rebecca Mitchell Jeremy Debra Cathy D. Mark Avery	Miguel Jacob Cathy L. Sarah Sheri Micki Denny DeRonda Chi Li

The form on the next page can be used for record keeping (state the outcome(s), write in the indicators, and record student performance).

Outcome(s)

Sample Indicators for Who Student Is

Not Understanding	Developing	Understanding/Applying

CALENDAR/SEATING CHART MODELS

Use either large calendars or seating charts (see the Observation Form on page 61) to record student information. Write one student's name in each cell. Use this as a space for recording individual student observations. This model helps you identify at a glance which students you have not observed or called on frequently enough to have good data.

As with any model, you can modify it to make it work better in your particular situation:

1. Write your notes on stick-on pads or computer mailing labels and then affix them to the cells at a later time.

2. Develop a simple coding system (e.g., "+" for correct response, "–" for incorrect response, "?" for student-raised question) for recording some responses and then write in specific notes or phrases about observed behaviors.

3. Do a math interview with the student listed on a given day. The mutual benefits are evident: Students enjoy the one-to-one time with you, and you get valuable insights into students' level of understanding. Consider including questions that ascertain how students feel about mathematics and that involve student self-evaluation.

S	M	T	W	Th	F	S
			1 Paul	2 Connie	3 Sammie	4
5	6 Matt	7 Sue	8 Gordie	9 Louise	10 Sally	11
12	13 Kim	14 Bert	15 Juan	16 Pat	17 BJ	18
19	20 Bob	21 Val	22 Ida	23 Mitch	24 Mike	25
26	27 Dave	28 Gayle	29 Janis	30 Maureen		

NOTECARD MODELS

Use individual student notecards in a file. The idea of this system is to have a card on each student. For this model you need index cards, strapping or masking tape, and heavy cardstock. A clipboard is optional. Write a student's name on the bottom of each card. Then tape the cards to the cardstock, overlapping, with each student's name in view. To reinforce the card, put tape on both sides.

Use the cards to record specific behaviors and insights about individual students. Observations may be limited to predetermined outcomes on which you want to collect data. Once a card is full, it can be filed for future reference (e.g., report form information, parent conferences).

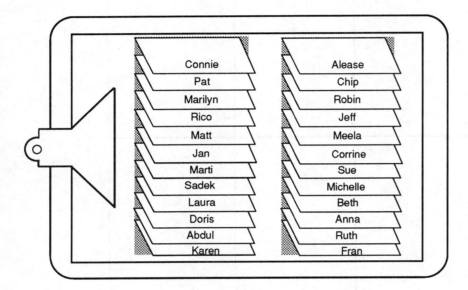

KINDERGARTEN MODEL FOR USING NOTECARDS

Use index cards grouped for A.M. AND P.M. Put name tags on top of each pile. Place a rubber band around them so you can pull out cards or staple a new card to the original one when the card is full on both sides. The top of each card contains essential information such as:
- Name
- Birth Date
- Telephone Number
- Address
- Health Problems

You can take the cards home and think back about the students and note down more information, as well as writing on them during class and break times.

ASSESSMENT NOTEBOOK

Use a three-ring notebook with dividers or tabs that is indexed for each student. Provide several pages for each student. Log and date observations in the notebook regularly. You may want to put student products into the notebook.

The following information describes how you might keep and record information, observations, and samples of work in an organized and portable notebook.

Materials

- 3-ring notebook, 1" or larger
- Tabbed notebook dividers, one for each student in the class plus a few extra
- 15–30 copies of the class list on a boxed chart (see sample)

Assessment Activity

Divide the notebook into two sections.

Record-Keeping Section: In the front of the notebook, set up one divider for each major strand (e.g., multiplication, fractions, place value). Behind each divider place a boxed chart. Keep together the test results and selected observations for each strand to make it easy to see individual and class progress on each strand.

Student Sample Section: Selected examples of individual work and assessment activities can be three-hole punched and placed after each student's divider. Possible student products to keep in the notebook include pretests, summary tests after completing content strands, daily work, and student self-assessment of concept mastery.

Name	Pre Test	Hands-on Lesson	Difficulty with 1000	Difficulty with 10,000	Can model, but not explain	Comments
Tom	☆					
Mary	-2	✓			✓	
Kadessa	-5		✓		✓	wasn't feeling well day of pretest
Brandi	-3	✓	✓	✓	✓	
Randall	-1					
Andrew	-3	✓	✓	✓	✓	

CHECKLIST

Create and use your own checklists (with or without rating scales) and consistently use them to evaluate certain aspects of students' performance or attitudes. Checklists may be done as a matrix to show the entire class, or they may be done as one sheet per student (e.g., similar to a report card).

You may want to include a space for comments, code the date of the observation, or develop a simple coding system to record observations (e.g., "–" does not understand, "✔" developing, "+" mastered.

Name	Rote Counting	One-to-one corresp.	Numeral recognition	Numeral formation				Comments
Billie	19	to 12	1-10	1-10				
Joel	10	to 6	1-10	Revise 2,5,3				
Amy	50	to 12	1-10	1-10				
Rhys	70+	to 12	1-20	1-20				goes beyond other students

Name									Comments

Addition and Subtraction with Regrouping

Outcome

- To recognize errors in addition and subtraction problems.

Materials

- Addition with Regrouping Worksheet
- Subtraction with Regrouping Worksheet
- Pencils

Assessment Activity

1. Distribute Addition with Regrouping or Subtraction with Regrouping Worksheets.

2. Ask students to circle the incorrect problems and to explain in writing why these problems are incorrect and how to do them correctly.

Notes

- Some students may need to explain orally how to do the problems correctly.
- Writing about mathematics prior to this assessment will help students know how to do this type of assessment.

Content Areas

Addition and Subtraction

Activity Type

Manipulative

Representational

➤ Abstract

Strategies

Interviews

Observations

Portfolios

Student Self-Assessment

Performance Tasks

➤ Student Writing

Outcome

■ To recognize errors in addition and subtraction problems.

Sample Performance Indicators for Student Who Is

Not Understanding	Developing	Understanding and Applying
▲ Does not recognize incorrect problems ▲ Does not write an explanation ▲ Writes but does not explain why the problems are incorrect ▲ Cannot tell how to correct the problems	▲ Recognizes some of the incorrect problems ▲ Provides only partial explanation of why the problems are incorrect	▲ Recognizes all of the problems that are incorrect ▲ Writes complete descriptions explaining why problems are incorrect

Addition with Regrouping

Name _____ Date _____

Correct this paper. Circle the problems that are incorrect.

A.
$$
\begin{array}{r}
1 \\
6\,0\,6 \\
+\,2\,8\,9 \\
\hline
9\,8\,5
\end{array}
$$

B.
$$
\begin{array}{r}
1{,}6\,4\,2 \\
+\quad 8\,6\,7 \\
\hline
1\,1\,4{,}1\,0\,9
\end{array}
$$

C.
$$
\begin{array}{r}
1\ \ 1 \\
7\,3\,5 \\
+\,2\,7\,6 \\
\hline
1{,}0\,1\,1
\end{array}
$$

D.
$$
\begin{array}{r}
1\ \ 1 \\
7\,7\,7 \\
+\,4\,3\,8 \\
\hline
1{,}2\,1\,5
\end{array}
$$

1. Explain why these problems are incorrect.

2. Describe how to do the problems correctly.

Subtraction with Regrouping

Name _____ Date _____

Jesse completed this paper. You are his teacher. Circle his mistakes, and write a note to Jesse explaining why they are wrong.

1
```
   672
 − 157
 ─────
   829
```

6 9
```
  7̸ 0̸¹5
 −2 3 7
 ──────
  4 6 8
```

6 12
```
  7̸ 3̸¹0
 −4 5 1
 ──────
  2 7 9
```

3 10 10
```
  4̸ 2̸ 2
 −1 7 7
 ──────
  2 3 3
```

Analyzing Word Problems

Outcomes

- To analyze word problems by identifying needed and not-needed information.
- To determine needed computation for a given problem.
- To solve word problems.

Materials

- Cards with word problems written on them
- Manipulatives
- Paper and pencil

Assessment Activity

1. Read a problem (samples listed below), and place the problem card in front of the student or on the overhead. Ask the student to retell the story problem in his or her own words to determine the student's level of understanding.
2. If a student indicates that he or she can retell the story accurately, ask the student to demonstrate the process with manipulatives, pictures, tables, and so on.
3. Encourage the student to record the equation and the answer on the paper provided.

Notes

- Sample Problems:
  - ▲ Perlita is collecting interesting shells. On Saturday she collected 15 shells; on Sunday, 7 shells; and on Monday, 10 shells. How many shells did she collect on Saturday and Sunday?
  - ▲ Ken had 85¢. He bought a package of baseball cards for 40¢. How much money does he have left?
- If problem solving is done on a routine basis, students can keep their work in journals. This allows you to see student growth over time.

Content Areas

Problem Solving and Logic

Mathematical Thinking

Activity Type

➤ Manipulative
➤ Representational
➤ Abstract

Strategies

➤ Interviews
Observation
➤ Portfolios
Student Self-Assessment
➤ Performance Tasks
Student Writing

Outcomes

- To analyze word problems by identifying needed and not-needed information.
- To determine needed computation for a given problem.
- To solve word problems.

Sample Performance Indicators for Student Who Is

Not Understanding	Developing	Understanding/Applying
▲ Cannot retell in own words the problem ▲ Guesses at answer ▲ Cannot model the problem with materials, pictures, or tables ▲ Is unable to write equation for problem	▲ Retells the problem in own words; some information may be missing or wrong ▲ Chooses the wrong operation ▲ Needs prompts to model problems with materials, pictures, or tables ▲ Writes correct equation, but makes mistake(s) in computation	▲ Retells the problem in own words ▲ Identifies the correct operation ▲ Can model problems with materials, pictures, or tables ▲ Writes and solves the equation correctly

Body Ratios

Outcome

- To use ratio and proportion.
- To use and explain a problem-solving strategy.

Materials

- Rulers
- String (arbitrarily cut)
- Paper and pencil
- Calculators

Assessment Activity

1. Divide the class into cooperative groups of four students.
2. Give each group a ruler, a length of string, and two or more calculators.
3. Say: "The Statue of Liberty has a nose that measures 4 feet 6 inches from the bridge to the tip. Using your rulers, string, calculators, and what you know about your own body, find the length of Miss Liberty's right arm (the one holding the torch)."
4. While you are observing, some will finish and want to know whether they are correct. Do not answer. Tell them to write out how they solved the problem.
5. When all groups have written their steps, call upon individuals in each group to explain how their group went about solving the problem.
6. Miss Liberty's right arm measures 42 feet. If the groups do not get this answer, ask them why.

Notes

- The following are student explanations of why their answers did not match the length of Miss Liberty's right arm:

  - Her body is not in proportion
  - Artistic license
  - Arm and torch would look too long
  - Too long an arm would not hold up well to weather and time
  - People were shorter back then
  - French people may not be as tall as Americans
  - The artist did not know his math

- Students can solve this problem without knowing formal definitions of ratio and proportion.
- This lesson can be used to introduce ratio and proportion.
- The idea for the lesson came from *About Teaching Mathematics* by Marilyn Burns.

Content Areas

Measurement

Problem Solving and Logic

Fractions, Decimals, Ratio, and Percent

Activity Type

➤ Manipulative

  Representational

➤ Abstract

Strategies

  Interviews

➤ Observations

  Portfolios

  Student Self-Assessment

➤ Performance Tasks

➤ Student Writing

Outcome

- To use ratio and proportion.
- To use and explain a problem-solving strategy.

Sample Performance Indicators for Student Who Is

Not Understanding	Developing	Understanding/Applying
▲ Did not know where to begin ▲ Needs prompts to measure nose and arm ▲ Has difficulty seeing a relationship between his or her body and that of the statue ▲ Unsure of reasonableness of answer	▲ Able to measure own nose, but uncertain as to what to do with this information ▲ Multiplies the length of the nose by the length of the arm ▲ Needs prompts to understand the relationship or to set up a proportion between own body and that of statue ▲ Thinks answer is reasonable	▲ Finds the ratio of a nose to an arm ▲ Measures nose and right arm ▲ Understands the relationship or sets up a proportion between own body and that of statue ▲ Confident that answer is reasonable

Building Geometric Shapes
on the Geoboard

Outcomes

■ To make a given shape on a geoboard correctly.

■ To describe attributes of the shape.

Materials

■ 2 geoboards and a few geobands

Assessment Activity

1. Direct the student to make a specific shape on the geoboard (e.g., triangle, four-sided figure that is not a square).

2. Ask the student to describe how to make the shape. As the student describes what to do, follow the instructions exactly and probe to determine whether the student can name attributes (properties) of the shape.

Note

■ If the student has difficulty using the geoboard, have the student explain how to draw the shape. To determine whether the student knows any properties, ask the student to describe what he or she knows about the shape.

Content Areas

Geometry and
 Spatial Sense

Activity Type

➤ Manipulative

Representational

Abstract

Strategies

➤ Interviews

Observations

Portfolios

Student
 Self-Assessment

➤ Performance
 Tasks

Student Writing

Outcomes

■ To make a given shape on a geoboard correctly.

■ To describe attributes of the shape.

Sample Performance Indicators for Student Who Is

Not Understanding	Developing	Understanding/Applying
▲ Is unable to make shapes on the geoboard ▲ Is unable to explain how to build the shapes ▲ Recognizes some shapes but cannot describe properties	▲ Able to make most shapes ▲ Has difficulty explaining how to build the shapes without prompts ▲ Recognizes shapes and can name some properties of some shapes	▲ Correctly makes shapes ▲ Can explain how to build the shapes ▲ Catches and corrects self if errors are made in describing how to build the shapes ▲ Can name some properties for each shape

Calendar

Outcomes

- To sequence months/days/dates.
- To read a calendar and answer questions.

Materials

- Calendar
- List of questions

Assessment Activity

1. Use the following questions during calendar time. Suggested grade levels are noted for each question. Asterisked (*) questions need not be introduced until later (November–December).

Grade Level	Questions
K–2	What day is it today?
K–2	What day was it yesterday?
K–2	What day will it be tomorrow?
*1–2	What day comes before _____?
*1–2	What day comes after _____?
*1–2	What day comes between _____ and _____?
K–2	What is the month?
*1–2	What was last month?
*1–2	What will next month be?
K–2	What are the days of the week? (in order?, grades 1–2).
K–2	What are the months of the year? (in order?, grades 1–2).
1–2	How many days are in a week?
1–2	How many days are in this month?
1–2	What is the first day of the month?
1–2	What is the last day of the month?
2	What date will it be 2 days from today?
2	What date will it be 1 week from today?
2	What was the date 4 days ago?
2	What was the date 2 weeks ago?
2	What is the date of the fourth Wednesday?
2	How many Tuesdays this month?
2	Are there more Mondays or Thursdays?

Content Areas
Measurement

Activity Type
Manipulative
➤ Representational
Abstract

Strategies
➤ Interviews
Observations
Portfolios
Student
Self-Assessment
➤ Performance
Tasks
Student Writing

2. More complicated and interpretive teacher-generated questions may be added later in the year at any grade level.

Notes

- Choose a "student of the day" to answer key (related to those Outcomes being assessed) calendar questions. By rotating this task, all students will have an opportunity to demonstrate what they know about the calendar.

- Questions may be written on cards. The student may choose 2 to 3 key calendar questions to answer each day.

- Write the questions on cards. Make the question cards available to all students to explore informally. When one student can answer all the questions, that student signs a chart "I can answer the 20 calendar questions!" and then reads the questions to another student. If that student is able to answer the questions, she or he signs in and also becomes a questioner. Over a period of time, you will be able to identify students still having problems.

- Kindergarten students will use counting sticks to demonstrate the number of days they have attended school. This number could then be transferred to a number line.

Outcomes

- To sequence months/days/dates.
- To read a calendar and answer questions.

Sample Performance Indicators for Student Who Is

Not Understanding	Developing	Understanding/Applying
▲ Does not look at calendar to determine date	▲ Can tell date by actually touching the calendar	▲ Can tell today's/yesterday's/tomorrow's date
▲ Cannot identify sequences/patterns for days of the week/weeks and/or dates	▲ Can identify some sequences/patterns	▲ Can identify date sequences/patterns on the calendar
▲ Does not know days of the week	▲ Knows some of the days of the week	▲ Knows the days of the week in order
▲ Does not know months of the year	▲ Knows some of the months of the year	▲ Knows months of the year in order
▲ Cannot determine how many days are left in the month	▲ Can determine, with prompting, how many days are left in the month	▲ Can determine how many days are left in the month
▲ Cannot determine how many days are left before a special event	▲ Can determine, with prompting, how many days are left before a special event	▲ Can determine how many days are left before a special event
▲ Confuses months, days, and seasons	▲ Can categorize some months, days, and seasons	▲ Can differentiate between months, days, and seasons
▲ Cannot determine date for the week before today or week after today	▲ Can, with prompting, determine date for the week before today or week after today	▲ Can determine date for the week before today or week after today

Catch Your Breath

Outcome

■ To use a stem and leaf plot to record and describe or interpret data.

Materials

■ Calculators
■ Paper and pencil
■ Clock or watch with a second hand

Assessment Activity

1. Have students have their partners time them as they hold their breath.
2. As they finish, have students post their times on the board.
3. Assign groups of two to organize the data in two ways, one of which must be a stem and leaf plot.
4. Have each student write five descriptive or interpretive statements about his or her stem and leaf plot.
5. Have each student, on the back of the paper, do a self-assessment. Possible questions to be answered are: How comfortable am I in organizing and displaying data? Can I, independently, set up a stem and leaf plot? Can I make descriptive or interpretive statements about the data?

Notes

■ This activity is adapted from a lesson in *Used Numbers: Statistics, The Shape of the Data*, by S. J. Russell and R. B. Corwin.

■ If you have the students collect the data a second time for comparison, have them make a second stem and leaf plot or have them set up a double stem and leaf plot. This often leads to interesting interpretive comments about the data.

■ With the introduction of this extra data you can look for mean, median, mode, and range.

■ Data also can be used to set up using other graphs (e.g., a box and whiskers plot, a line plot).

Content Areas

Statistics and Probability

Activity Type

Manipulative

➤ Representational

➤ Abstract

Strategies

Interviews

➤ Observations

➤ Portfolios

➤ Student Self-Assessment

➤ Performance Tasks

➤ Student Writing

Outcome

■ To use a stem and leaf plot to record and describe or interpret data.

Sample Performance Indicators for Student Who Is

Not Understanding	Developing	Understanding/Applying
▲ Is not able to set up a stem and leaf plot ▲ Is not able to describe or interpret the data ▲ With prompts can make a descriptive statement about the data	▲ May need prompts to create a stem and leaf plot ▲ Creates a stem and leaf plot correctly, but cannot interpret or describe the data ▲ Can interpret or describe the data, but needs prompts in creating a stem and leaf plot ▲ Can make only descriptive statements about the data	▲ Independently creates the stem and leaf plot correctly ▲ Can describe or interpret the data ▲ Can make descriptive and interpretive statements about the data

Checking Division

Outcome

- To divide one-digit into three-digit numbers by using computational algorithm.

Materials

- Jessica's Test Worksheet and pencil

Assessment Activity

1. Give the student the worksheet, and explain that this is a test that Jessica took at Stone School.
2. Ask the student to find the mistakes in Jessica's test, circle them, and then to explain to Jessica what she did wrong.

Notes

- This activity may be used both as a pretest and as a posttest for the division unit to assess whether the student understands the long division algorithm.
- Each problem has one error. Even if the error is early in the problem, it is still counted as only one error. The goal of the assessment is to see whether the student can locate different types of long division errors. Students who demonstrate an understanding of the skill will use written explanations, such as:
  - ▲ Jessica, you can't divide 7 into 5; it goes into 56 so write the 7 above the 6 not the 5.
  - ▲ Jessica, your remainder is bigger than the divisor.
  - ▲ Jessica, 2 goes into thirteen 6 times not 4 times.
  - ▲ Jessica, this problem is right but you don't have to write all the zeros.
  - ▲ Jessica, you subtracted wrong.
  - ▲ Jessica, 3 – 2 is 1 not 2
- This assessment will be difficult for students who have not done much writing in mathematics class. Practice analyzing and writing out the mistakes if necessary.

Content Area

Multiplication and Division

Activity Type

Manipulative

Representational

➤ Abstract

Strategies

Interviews

Observations

Portfolios

Student Self-Assessment

Performance Tasks

➤ Student Writing

Outcome

■ To divide one-digit into three-digit numbers by using computational algorithm.

Sample Performance Indicators for Student Who Is

Not Understanding	Developing	Understanding/Applying
▲ Is unable to locate more than one error ▲ Is unable to explain why Jessica made errors ▲ Asks lots of questions during assessment	▲ Is able to locate some errors ▲ Is able to redo problems correctly but cannot explain why problems are wrong ▲ May view problem 5 as incorrect because of extra numbers that were brought down	▲ Is able to locate all errors ▲ Can clearly explain where mistakes were made ▲ Can rework and explain how to correct problems

Jessica's Test

Name _____ Date _____

Jessica is a student at Stone School. She recently took a division test. Listed below are some of the problems from the test. Circle each of Jessica's mistakes. Explain to her why she got the problem wrong. You may want to use sentences like "Jessica, you got number 1 wrong because. . . ." Write your explanations on the back of this sheet.

1.
```
       8 1 0  R1
   7 | 5 6 8
       5 6
       0 8
         7
         1
```

2.
```
       1 5 4  R5
   2 | 3 1 3
       2
       1 1
       1 0
         1 3
           8
           5
```

3.
```
       2 8 0
   4 | 8 3 2
       8
       0 3 2
         3 2
       0 0 0
```

4.
```
       8 3  R2
   9 | 7 3 9
       7 2
         2 9
         2 7
           2
```

5.
```
       1 6 3  R2
   3 | 4 3 1
       3 0 0
       1 3 1
       1 2 0
         1 1
           9
           2
```

Checking out
Order of Operations

Outcomes

- To simplify an expression using order of operations.
- To use a calculator code to represent entries (optional).
- To compute mentally.

Materials

- Deck(s) of playing cards
- Calculators
- Paper and pencil

Assessment Activity

1. Have students work in pairs or cooperative groups. Review cooperative group rules if necessary.
2. Have the pairs or groups write down what they remember about order of operations. Discuss steps and post them on the overhead or board.
3. If necessary, review calculator codes.
4. Introduce the card activity students will be using to demonstrate their understanding of order of operations and writing calculator codes:

   a. The numerical value of the cards are as follows:

Card	Value
ace	1
2–10	face value
jack	11
queen	12
king	13

   Suit does not matter.

   b. Turn over six cards. The numerical value of the sixth card is the target number. The other five cards are to be used to generate the target number.

   c. Students write the numerical expression, simplify it, and write a calculator code (optional).

Content Areas

Calculators

Algebraic Ideas

Estimation and
  Mental
  Computation

Activity Type

Manipulative

➤ Representational

➤ Abstract

Strategies

Interviews

➤ Observations

Portfolios

Student
  Self-Assessment

➤ Performance
  Tasks

Student Writing

5. Work several examples. Turn over six cards. Give teams time to find a solution. Discuss how they wrote their expression and calculator code.

	Example 1	**Example 2**
	5, 4, jack, 2, 2	queen, 2, 3, 7, 4
5 cards	5	king
target card	$5 \times 2 + 4 - 11 + 2$	$3(2 + 4) - 12 + 7$
expression	$10 + 4 - 11 + 2$	$3 \times 6 - 12 + 7$
	$14 - 11 + 2$	$18 - 12 + 7$
	$3 + 2$	$6 + 7$
	5	13

Calculator code (optional)

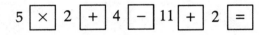

6. Once students are comfortable with the process, deal six cards so teams can start working.

7. Let students know how to get new cards once they complete a problem (e.g., make deck available at front of room; you go to the group and deal new cards).

8. As pairs or groups complete a problem, check their work, coding your observations.

Notes

- Encourage teams to find more than one solution for the target number.
- You may want to introduce the activity with five cards instead of six cards.
- The calculator codes may be difficult to do if students have not worked with the memory keys.
- Problems students could not solve can be posted as challenges.
- Calculators should not have algebraic logic.

Outcomes

- To simplify an expression using order of operations.
- To use a calculator code to represent entries (optional).
- To compute mentally.

Sample Performance Indicators for Student Who Is

Not Understanding	Developing	Understanding/Applying
Mental Computations ▲ Relies on paper and pencil or calculator for computation ▲ Demonstrates frustration with computations ▲ Is uncomfortable playing with various number combinations ▲ Attempts seem random	**Mental Computations** ▲ May check own computations with calculator ▲ Has a feel for how the numbers, particularly the smaller numbers, can go together ▲ Will experiment with different number combinations ▲ Has strategies for trying different combinations	**Mental Computations** ▲ Accurately computes mentally ▲ Demonstrates a sense or intuition about how numbers can go together ▲ Is comfortable experimenting with different number combinations ▲ Has strategies for trying different combinations ▲ May keep a record of what was tried
Order of Operations ▲ Does computations from left to right regardless of operation ▲ Has difficulty generating a correct numerical expression ▲ Struggles with parentheses ▲ May do operations in an order that makes sense to him or her	**Order of Operations** ▲ May not go through left to right ▲ Can write a correct numerical expression ▲ Struggles with parentheses (may not want to drop or move them) ▲ May incorrectly give precedence to one operation	**Order of Operations** ▲ Performs operations in the correct order ▲ Knows how to use parentheses ▲ May have a sense of number properties, using them to perform operations in a different order
Calculators ▲ Is not using memory keys (e.g., writes number on paper) ▲ Makes repeated errors in entries ▲ May be able to read a calculator code ▲ Cannot generate the calculator code	**Calculators** ▲ Will use or try memory keys ▲ Makes correct entries ▲ Can read and enter calculator code ▲ Needs prompts when generating calculator codes	**Calculators** ▲ Can use and explain memory keys ▲ Knows how to clear memory ▲ Makes correct entries

Check It Out

Outcomes

■ To demonstrate how to use a calculator.

■ To demonstrate how to correct a paper by using a calculator.

Materials

■ Calculators

■ Check It Out Worksheet

Assessment Activity

1. Hand out calculators and worksheets.

2. Have students work individually.

3. Problems A and B: Students are to write down their answers for each step.

4. Problems C and D: If students agree with the answer, they are to leave it alone. If they do not agree, they are to cross out the wrong answer and write in the correct answer.

5. Remind students to check their work on problems A to D.

Notes

■ The final answers are provided on problems A and B to help students spot any errors.

■ Depending on the students' age and their comfort level of using calculators, you may want to add another correct answer earlier on problems A and B.

■ Some students may enjoy making up their own problems and incorrect/correct answers for their classmates to try.

■ Calculators should not have algebraic logic.

Content Areas

Calculators

Activity Type

➤ Manipulative

➤ Representational

Abstract

Strategies

Interviews

➤ Observations

Portfolios

Student Self-Assessment

➤ Performance Tasks

Student Writing

Outcomes

- To demonstrate how to use a calculator.
- To demonstrate how to correct a paper by using a calculator.

Sample Performance Indicators for Student Who Is

Not Understanding	Developing	Understanding/Applying
▲ Needs help in entering numbers or commands into calculator ▲ Makes many mistakes when working out problems	▲ Sometimes enters numbers or commands incorrectly ▲ Makes some mistakes when working out problems	▲ Uses calculator correctly and easily ▲ Works problems correctly

Check It Out

Name _____ Date _____

	Answers

A. Multiply 8 by 137 _____
Add 624 _____
Divide by 2 _____
Add 308 _____
Subtract 1,015 _____
Divide by 3 _____51_____

B. Multiply 180 by 35 _____
Divide by 90 _____
Multiply by 13 _____
Divide by 5 _____
Add 2,379 _____
Subtract 523 ____2,038____

C. Divide 3,472 by 4 _____868_____ _____
Multiply by 27 ____23,633____ _____
Subtract 3,018 ____20,418____ _____
Divide by 3 _____6,800_____ _____
Add 7,982 ____14,788____ _____
Subtract 9,145 _____6,543_____ _____

D. Multiply 851 by 38 ____32,038____ _____
Subtract 2,047 ____30,021____ _____
Divide by 3 ____10,097____ _____
Add 2,468 ____12,255____ _____
Divide by 5 _____2,513_____ _____
Multiply by 17 ____42,712____ _____

Circles

Outcomes

■ To recognize and define the properties of a circle.

■ To construct a circle.

Materials

■ Pencils and plain paper

■ Class set of compasses

■ Class set of rulers

Assessment Activity

1. During this activity students will construct a circle and its parts by using a compass and will label each part by using correct notation.

2. Provide each student with a compass, a ruler, a plain sheet of paper, and a pencil.

3. Orally give students the following directions (pause between each direction):

   a. Draw a circle that fills most of the space on your paper. Leave some room at the bottom of your page for writing.

   b. Draw the center of the circle, and label it "A".

   c. Draw a diameter, and label one of its endpoints "B" and the other "C".

   d. Draw a chord, and label one of its endpoints "D" and the other "E".

   e. Write these words at the bottom of the page:

      1. center =

      2. diameter =

      3. radius =

      4. chord =

      5. arc =

   f. Write the correct notation for each of these parts of your circle.

   g. Write the definition of circumference at the bottom or on the back of your page.

Note

■ For grades 4 and 5 this is a postassessment activity at the end of a series of lessons on circles. The activity can be used as a preassessment in grade 6.

Content Areas

Geometry and Spatial Sense

Activity Type

➤ Manipulative

➤ Representational

Abstract

Strategies

Interviews

Observations

Portfolios

Student Self-Assessment

➤ Performance Tasks

Student Writing

Outcomes

- To recognize and define the properties of a circle.
- To construct a circle.

Sample Performance Indicators for Student Who Is

Not Understanding	Developing	Understanding/Applying
▲ Constructs figure that barely resembles a circle ▲ Draws figure in which parts are missing ▲ Draws diameter that does not go through center of circle ▲ Does not know what a chord is ▲ Provides incorrect definition of circumference	▲ Draws all parts but mislabels some of them ▲ Confuses chord and diameter ▲ Confuses radius and chord ▲ Provides partial definition of circumference	▲ Correctly constructs circle ▲ Correctly draws and labels all parts ▲ Gives proper definition of circumference

Sample Key

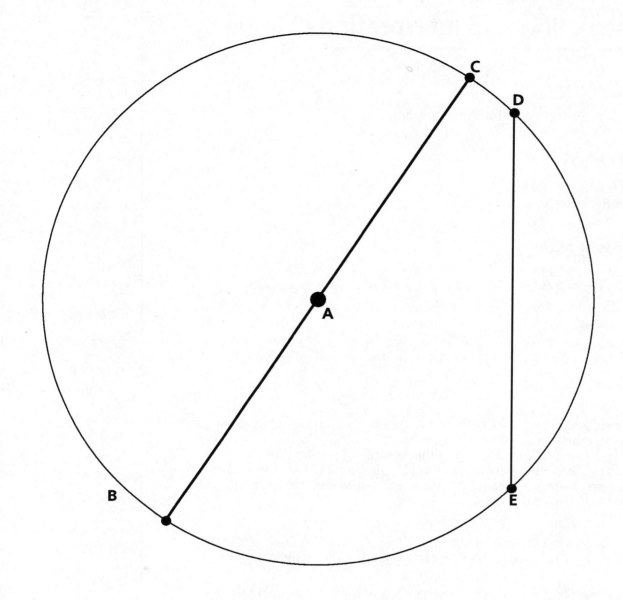

center = A

diameter = $\overline{BC}$ or $\overline{CB}$

radius = $\overline{AB}$ or $\overline{AC}$ or $\overline{BA}$ or $\overline{CA}$

chord = $\overline{DE}$ or $\overline{ED}$

arc = $\overparen{CD}$, $\overparen{DE}$, $\overparen{CE}$, etc.

The circumference is the distance around a circle.

Constructing and Interpreting Graphs

Content Areas

Statistics and
Probability

Activity Type

Manipulative

➤ Representational

➤ Abstract

Strategies

Interviews

Observations

➤ Portfolios

Student Self-
Assessment

➤ Performance
Tasks

➤ Student Writing

Outcome

■ To read, construct, and interpret graphs.

Materials

■ Graph paper and pencils
■ Crayons or markers

Assessment Activity

1. Ask the student to collect data for a topic of his or her choice
   (e.g., favorite food, favorite subject, favorite car, favorite book).

2. Ask the student to construct a bar graph that shows the results of his or
   her survey.

3. Ask the student to write a paragraph that provides at least five pieces of
   information that can be determined from the data on his or her graph.

Notes

■ Some students may need help defining the data to collect. Questions
  with too many variables, such as "What is your favorite food?" may be
  written to include five foods, and the researching student may ask,
  "Which of these foods is your favorite?" Questions with too few variables also create a problem (e.g., How many students live within the city
  limits? and How many students ski?).

■ Ask students to create other graphs.

■ Ask students to display data in two different graphs. Follow-up discussions may include comparisons of advantages and disadvantages of
  each.

■ Have students survey other classes, collect and graph data, and then
  compare data.

■ This activity is appropriate for other graphs as well (e.g., line plot,
  histogram, circle graph, box and whisker plot, stem and leaf plot).

■ Prior to doing tasks independently, have teams cooperatively construct
  surveys and graphs and interpret data.

■ Students' work could be placed into the portfolio.

Outcome

■ To read, construct, and interpret graphs.

Sample Performance Indicators for Student Who Is

Not Understanding	Developing	Understanding/Applying
Independence ▲ Cannot complete task	**Independence** ▲ Needs assistance in collection of data, construction of graph, or interpretation	**Independence** ▲ Is able to work independently on all aspects of task
Collection of Data ▲ Is unable to design survey and collect own data independently	**Collection of Data** ▲ May need minor assistance in phrasing survey or organizing self to collect data	**Collection of Data** ▲ Is able to generate survey and collect data independently
Construction of Graph ▲ Does not have data to construct graph ▲ Creates inaccurate or incomplete graph ▲ Cannot correct errors when pointed out	**Construction of Graph** ▲ Creates graphs but has minor errors or omissions ▲ Can correct errors when pointed out	**Construction of Graph** ▲ Creates correct graph including title, labeled axes, appropriate scale, correctly plotted data
Interpretation ▲ Does not attempt to interpret data or communicate results ▲ Cannot interpret data even with prompts ▲ Can answer only simple questions about data	**Interpretation** ▲ May need assistance in interpreting data and communicating results ▲ Can answer questions about data; may need some prompts	**Interpretation** ▲ Is able to interpret data and clearly communicate results ▲ Can identify trends ▲ Can answer questions about data

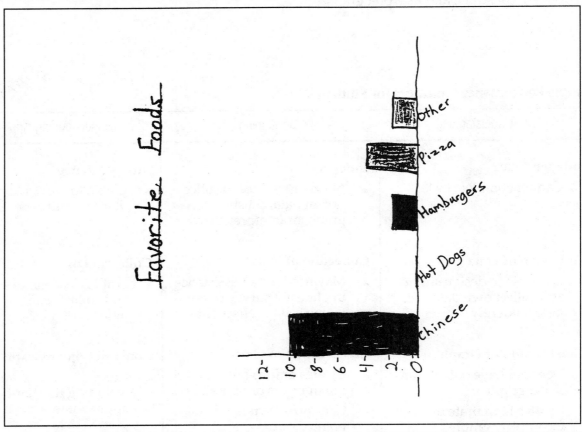

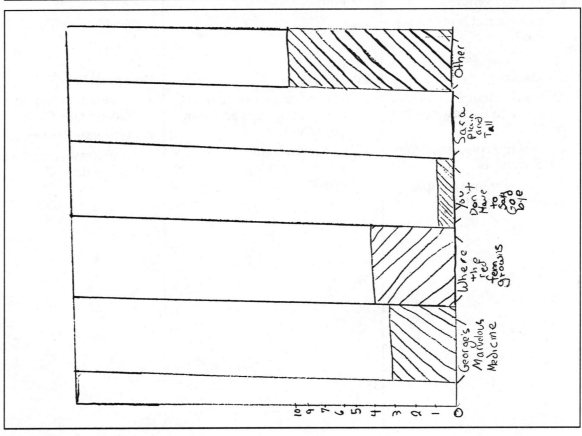

Constructing Tables and Graphs to Solve Equations

Outcomes

- To create tables to solve equations or number sentences.
- To graph ordered pairs on a coordinate grid.

Materials

- Open Sentences Worksheet and pencil

Assessment Activity

1. Give a worksheet to the student.
2. Explain to the student that he or she must complete the tables at the top and then use the ordered pairs from each table to create two lines on the coordinate grid.

Notes

- The two number sentences can be changed easily, or only one can be put on to increase or decrease the level of difficulty.
- Prior to the assessment, students should have practice working with functions (e.g., input/output; What's My Rule?), constructing a table to generate solutions, and plotting number pairs on a grid.

Content Areas

Algebraic Ideas

Activity Type

Manipulative

➤ Representational

Abstract

Strategies

Interviews

Observations

Portfolios

Student
Self-Assessment

➤ Performance
Tasks

Student Writing

Outcomes

- To create tables to solve equations or number sentences.
- To graph ordered pairs on a coordinate grid.

Sample Performance Indicators for Student Who Is

Not Understanding	Developing	Understanding/Applying
▲ Does not know what to do; cannot follow example or ask questions ▲ Generates number pairs that do not match given sentence ▲ Creates graph that does not match table ▲ Cannot explain or has difficulty expressing what was done	▲ Can fill out table or graph but not both ▲ Can supply second number, with prompts ▲ Can tell whether suggested number pairs match the sentence ▲ Can continue pattern once it is started ▲ Can solve for one type of number sentences but not others	▲ Can generate number pairs from sentence ▲ Can graph pairs on a grid accurately and see the pattern ▲ Extension: Can translate sentence into algebraic sentence using x, y ▲ Can use process to solve for x and y on graph

Open Sentences

Name _____ Date _____

1. The first number is
one-half of the second number.

2. $x + y = 12$

x	y

x	y

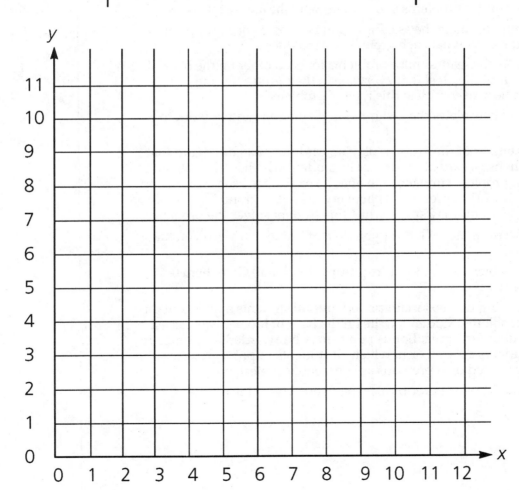

...ask

...erative and responsible group member.

Materi... /

- Decks of playing cards
- Pencil and plain paper
- Assignment sheets you have elected to use for this activity (not provided)

Assessment Activity

1. In this cooperative activity, student groups will complete an assignment, will create and solve similar problems as necessary to ensure that every-one in the group understands how the work should be done, and will be able to solve similar problems and explain why the answer is correct.

2. Have students complete the assignment in heterogeneous groups of four. Observe and record what each group says and does.

3. Direct students to create similar problems for each other on the back of their papers until they feel that everyone in their group thoroughly understands how to complete this type of problem.

4. As each group completes the assignment, they bring written work to you.

5. Give each member of the group a playing card that matches a card that you hold. Choose a card at random. The student who has the matching card solves a problem similar to the ones he or she has been working on. This student's work represents what everyone in the group knows. No one else in the group may speak while this student solves the problem.

6. Ask such questions as, "Why did you do that?" and "How do you know that is correct?"

7. Review the problem with the entire group. (Optional) Give them 0–10 points for the answer.

8. (Optional) During the next math period give all students a quiz contain-ing similar problems. Students write on the back of it what was easiest and hardest about the quiz. Bonus points may be awarded for groups in which all students do well or in which all students improve from the scores they received on a previous assignment or pretest.

9. Indicators should reflect group rules that were stressed in class.

Content Areas
All

Activity Type
Manipulative

Representational

➤ Abstract

Strategies
Interviews

➤ Observations

Portfolios

Student Self-Assessment

➤ Performance Tasks

Student Writing

Outcome

■ To be a cooperative and responsible group member.

Sample Performance Indicators for Student Who Is

Not Understanding	Developing	Understanding/Applying
▲ Copies answers ▲ Does not know how to get started ▲ Needs step-by-step prompts during reporting process ▲ Does not work with group ▲ May watch but not contribute or ask questions	▲ Solves problem but cannot explain procedure ▲ Needs occasional prompts during reporting process ▲ Understands underlying concepts but makes careless mistakes due to inattention or lack of experience ▲ Mixes up sequence or procedure ▲ May be comfortable with some rules, but not others	▲ Confidently solves problem and can explain work ▲ Works cooperatively with others in group ▲ Contributes to group and encourages and supports others ▲ Can assume different roles

Creating and Interpreting Graphs

Outcomes

■ To create a graph using concrete objects.
■ To make descriptive statements about the graph.

Materials

■ Unifix® cubes (7 orange, 5 green, 3 red, 2 brown)
■ 1-in. graph paper with color labels (see Notes)

Assessment Activity

1. Give the student directions: "Here is a sheet of graph paper and some Unifix® cubes. Make a color graph by placing the Unifix® cubes on the paper."
2. Ask the student to make descriptive statements about the graph.
3. Ask questions about the graph:
    a. Which color do you have the most of?
    b. Which color do you have the fewest of?
    c. How many more orange cubes than red cubes do you have? How do you know that?

Notes

■ You could meet with the students during free exploration time to complete this task.
■ To create labels for the color graph, color a green box at the bottom of the graph paper. Skip a space. Color the next space red, then orange, and last brown, skipping spaces in between.

Content Areas

Statistics and Probability

Activity Type

➤ Manipulative

Representational

Abstract

Strategies

➤ Interviews

Observations

Portfolios

Student Self-Assessment

➤ Performance Tasks

Student Writing

Outcomes

- To create a graph using concrete objects.
- To make descriptive statements about the graph.

Sample Performance Indicators for Student Who Is

Not Understanding	Developing	Understanding/Applying
Constructing Graph ▲ Does not use one-to-one correspondence to place one cube into each block ▲ Places cubes randomly on the graph ▲ Cannot complete the task even with suggestions and reminders from the teacher	**Constructing Graph** ▲ Needs to be reminded to use all the Unifix® cubes ▲ Needs to be reminded to place cubes on graph according to color ▲ Needs reassurance from the teacher to complete the task even if completing task correctly	**Constructing Graph** ▲ Completes a graph correctly without help from the teacher
Describing Graph ▲ Does not offer statements about the graph ▲ Is unable to answer questions	**Describing Graph** ▲ Can make some descriptive statements ▲ Can answer simple questions with prompts	**Describing Graph** ▲ Offers different types of descriptive statements ▲ Answers questions correctly

Decimal and Whole Number Place Value

Outcome

■ To put twelve place value name and decimal point cards in the correct order.

Materials

■ Place value strips (copy and cut apart)

Assessment Activity

1. Give the student the twelve place value name and decimal point cards.
2. Ask the student to put the cards into order from largest to smallest (or smallest to largest).
3. Ask the student whether he or she is sure the cards are in the correct order. If yes, ask whether he or she sees and can explain a pattern in the cards. If no, have the student make corrections.
4. Record the student's actions and comments.

Note

■ It takes about one minute to interview each student.

Content Areas

Fractions, Decimals, Ratio, and Percent

Activity Type

Manipulative

➤ Representational

Abstract

Strategies

➤ Interviews

Observations

Portfolios

Student Self-Assessment

➤ Performance Tasks

Student Writing

Outcome

- To put twelve place value name and decimal point cards in the correct order.

Sample Performance Indicators for Student Who Is

Not Understanding	Developing	Understanding/Applying
▲ Does not know where to begin ▲ Puts cards in entirely the wrong order ▲ Tries to avoid completing the task	▲ Knows there is a pattern and tries to create it, but struggles in finding it ▲ Places the cards incorrectly, but catches the mistake and corrects it on his or her own	▲ Puts the cards in the correct order confidently and quickly

Place Value Strips

Hundreds

Tens

Ones

Tenths

Hundredths

Thousandths

Hundred Millions

Ten Millions

Millions

Hundred Thousands

Ten Thousands

Thousands

•

Decimals

Outcome

■ To demonstrate the meaning of decimals by using concrete models to build decimal numerals and to demonstrate decimal relationships.

Materials

■ A place value mat with a dot representing the decimal point for each student

■ Set of base 10 blocks for each student

Assessment Activity

Building Decimals

1. Read aloud the following items, have students build on their mats, and note students' responses:

    a. Show me how many tenths it takes to make a whole.

    b. Show me how many hundredths it takes to make a tenth.

    c. How many hundredths does it take to make a whole?

2. Have students build the following decimals on their mats:

    a. 3 tenths   c. 12 hundredths

    b. 1 and 5 hundredths   d. 3 and 6 tenths

Comparing

Have students build 30 hundredths. Ask, "What is another way to build this number?" Try again with 12 tenths.

Ordering

1. Have students build 2 tenths and then 22 hundredths. Ask, "Which one is larger? How do you know?"

2. Have students build 3 tenths and then 13 hundredths. Ask, "Which one is smaller? How do you know?"

Notes

■ In this activity the value of the base 10 blocks will be as follows: each flat will equal a whole number, each rod will equal a tenth, and each cube will equal a hundredth.

■ It may be necessary to ask students to build additional numbers if you need more information to properly assess each member of the class.

■ This activity could be used as an interview.

■ You may want to include whole numbers in this activity.

Content Areas

Fractions, Decimals, Ratio, and Percent

Activity Type

➤ Manipulative

Representational

Abstract

Strategies

Interviews

➤ Observations

Portfolios

Student Self-Assessment

➤ Performance Tasks

Student Writing

Outcome

■ To demonstrate the meaning of decimals by using concrete models to build decimal numerals and to demonstrate decimal relationships.

Sample Performance Indicators for Student Who Is

Not Understanding	Developing	Understanding/Applying
▲ Cannot show how many tenths make a whole ▲ Cannot show how many hundredths make a tenth ▲ Cannot show how many hundredths make a whole ▲ Copies other students ▲ Has difficulty adjusting to new values of base 10 blocks	▲ Knows value of each block but has difficulty building decimal ▲ Interchanges values of blocks when building decimal	▲ Understands value of each block ▲ Is able to build, compare, and order decimals ▲ Is able to explain what he or she has built

Defining Lines, Rays, Segments, and Angles

Outcome

■ To define lines, line segments, rays, and angles.

Materials

■ A Mathematical Argument Worksheet
■ Pencil

Assessment Activity

1. Instruct the student to pretend to hear Larry the Line, Robin the Ray, Sarah the Segment, and Andrew the Angle arguing about who is the best.

2. Ask the student to record how he or she thinks the argument would sound.

Notes

■ Make sure the student understands that he or she must have the characters give specific reasons, relating to their attributes, for being the best. Simply stating that one is the best and then resorting to name calling is not acceptable.

■ This is a good assessment to use after geometry lessons on these concepts. It will show which students need extra review work before moving on to more complex topics.

Sample Student Work

They are fighting.

Larry → I am best! because I can go all the way forever.

Robin → I am the most. than all the rest! One end is stop, but the other end never stop!

Sarah = I am better than You! both end is stoped, never move.

Andrew = You know why I am best? my middle is stopped and my both end will go all the way up to space.

Content Areas

Geometry and Spatial Sense

Activity Type

Manipulative

Representational

➤ Abstract

Strategies

Interviews

Observations

Portfolios

Student Self-Assessment

Performance Tasks

➤ Student Writing

Outcome

■ To define lines, line segments, rays, and angles.

Sample Performance Indicators for Student Who Is

Not Understanding	Developing	Understanding/Applying
▲ Uses name calling ▲ Does not mention specific attributes	▲ Does not mention attributes for all figures ▲ Confuses attributes ▲ May not respond to all the questions	▲ Gives correct attributes for each figure ▲ Provides a good argument ▲ Responds to all the questions

A Mathematical Argument

Name _____ Date _____

Larry the Line, Robin the Ray, Sarah the Segment, and Andrew the Angle
were having an argument. Each one thought he or she was better than all
the rest. Write how you think their arguments might sound. Why does each
one think he or she is the best? Why would the others disagree?

Division Chart

Outcome

- To understand and model division (one-digit divisor) of whole numbers.

Materials

- Poster sheet with boxes in which to put the problem and a multiplication table (optional)
- Color-coded set of numerals from 0 to 9 (each numeral is on a card of a different color and there are several cards for each numeral)

Assessment Activity

1. Choose a divisor and dividend for the student, and place the numerals in the correct spaces on the poster. The number of digits in the dividend should be determined by the student's developmental level.
2. Ask the student to solve the problem by using the numeral cards and while "thinking aloud" each step that he or she takes.
3. Ask the student to explain why each step was omitted, if necessary.
4. Ask how the student feels about the task (confident, successful, nervous).
5. Record the student's actions and comments.

Notes

- If necessary, allow the student to model the problem with base 10 materials.
- Students may need to be taught how to "think aloud" before they are asked to do this independently.
- If you also want to test a student's knowledge of multiplication facts without giving division clues, omit the multiplication table.
- Numerals are color coded to make finding specific numerals and sorting easier.

Content Areas

Multiplication and Division

Activity Type

Manipulative

Representational

➤ Abstract

Strategies

➤ Interviews

Observations

Portfolios

Student Self-Assessment

➤ Performance Tasks

Student Writing

Outcome

■ To understand and model division (one-digit divisor) of whole numbers.

Sample Performance Indicators for Student Who Is

Not Understanding	Developing	Understanding/Applying
▲ Takes a long time getting started	▲ Tries several strategies before using one that works	▲ Knows how to perform each step and can explain why each step was taken
▲ Asks for help before trying	▲ Completes task with assistance	▲ Does not look at multiplication table
▲ Says feels nervous, uncomfortable, upset with performance task	▲ Fills blank spaces in with zeros	▲ Leaves blank spaces
	▲ Gets correct answer but puts quotient over incorrect numerals in dividend	▲ Says feels confident that answer is correct one
	▲ Makes careless mistakes	
	▲ Makes mistakes but can identify and correct them	
	▲ Does not understand what to do with remainder	
	▲ Says is reasonably successful	

Sample Poster

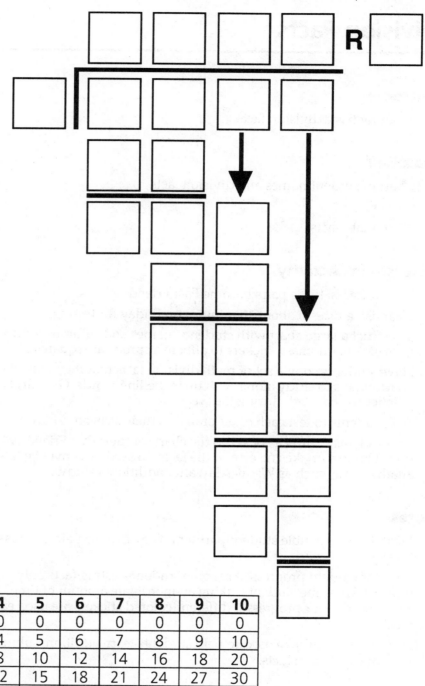

x	0	1	2	3	4	5	6	7	8	9	10
0	0	0	0	0	0	0	0	0	0	0	0
1	0	1	2	3	4	5	6	7	8	9	10
2	0	2	4	6	8	10	12	14	16	18	20
3	0	3	6	9	12	15	18	21	24	27	30
4	0	4	8	12	16	20	24	28	32	36	40
5	0	5	10	15	20	25	30	35	40	45	50
6	0	6	12	18	24	30	36	42	48	54	60
7	0	7	14	21	28	35	42	49	56	63	70
8	0	8	16	24	32	40	48	56	64	72	80
9	0	9	18	27	36	45	54	63	72	81	90
10	0	10	20	30	40	50	60	70	80	90	100

Division Facts

Outcome

■ To know basic division facts.

Materials

■ Chart of student names and division facts
■ Stickers
■ Set of math facts

Assessment Activity

1. Pair students; these pairs become Fact Friends.
2. Establish a time of about 10 minutes on Friday for testing.
3. Construct a large chart with students' names and columns for division facts (0–10). Purchase stickers to affix in appropriate squares of the chart.
4. Have students copy a set of math division facts that they will take home on Mondays to study along with their spelling words. Give drill and practice as seatwork during the week.
5. Ask students to test each other orally on their facts on Friday.
6. Tell students to affix a sticker to the chart for their Fact Friend only if the friend knows (makes no errors) the facts. Missed facts may be retested at another time, such as Wednesday, after additional study.

Notes

■ Establish compatible student partners. They may be paired across grade levels.
■ Monitor student progress. Are some students testing facts only "in order"? Are some students taking an inordinate amount of time? It is easier to monitor progress if different-colored stickers are used each week.
■ Fact Friends could be used to help students learn addition, subtraction, and multiplication facts.

Content Areas

Multiplication and Division

Estimation and Mental Computation

Activity Type

Manipulative

Representational

➤ Abstract

Strategies

Interviews

Observations

Portfolios

➤ Student Self-Assessment

➤ Performance Tasks

Student Writing

Outcome

■ To know basic division facts.

Sample Performance Indicators for Student Who Is

Not Understanding	Developing	Understanding/Applying
▲ Gives incorrect answer to more than half of facts tested ▲ Does not have immediate recall of facts	▲ Misses one or two of the tested facts ▲ Has immediate recall of facts if given "in order"	▲ Gives correct answers to all facts ▲ Has immediate recall of facts given in random order

Division Pictures

Outcome

■ To divide one-digit into two- and three-digit numbers by using pictorial models and computational algorithms.

Materials

■ Paper and pencil

Assessment Activity

1. Give students several division problems (e.g., 67 ÷ 5, 135 ÷ 6).

2. Instruct students to solve the problems. Ask them to show each step with pictures.

3. After students have drawn the pictures, instruct them also to solve the problems by using the division algorithm.

Notes

■ This assessment may be used to determine which students have a good understanding of division and are ready to begin using the algorithm to solve division problems. Students who do not demonstrate understanding may be given more instruction and practice at the "draw it" level.

■ You may want to modify this activity to include use of manipulatives, then pictures of manipulatives, and then the algorithm.

■ This activity can also be done for addition, subtraction, and multiplication.

Content Areas

Multiplication and Division

Activity Type

Manipulative

➤ Representational

➤ Abstract

Strategies

Interviews

Observations

Portfolios

Student Self-Assessment

➤ Performance Tasks

Student Writing

Outcome

■ To divide one-digit into two- and three-digit numbers by using pictorial models and computational algorithms.

Sample Performance Indicators for Student Who Is

Not Understanding	Developing	Understanding/Applying
▲ Has no idea where to begin ▲ Does not know how many bins are needed or does not divide the number into equal groups	▲ Establishes correct number of bins on drawing, but needs prompts to draw the picture correctly ▲ Correctly draws picture of division problem but makes errors in using the division algorithm ▲ Draws bins correctly, draws number correctly, but may require assistance when regrouping is required	▲ Correctly draws picture for division problems, including regrouping ▲ Correctly computes problem using the division algorithm

Sample Student Work

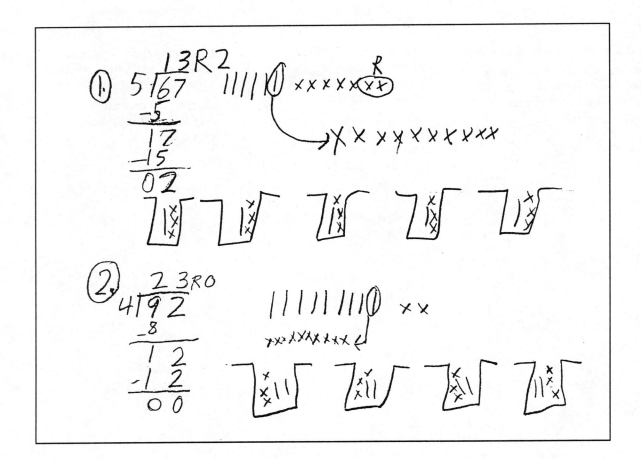

Estimation and Mental Computation in Addition

Outcome

■ To use strategies for estimation and mental computation.

Materials

■ Estimation and Mental Computation Worksheet
■ Pencil

Assessment Activity

1. Distribute worksheets to students.
2. Go over the directions with the class, emphasizing that all the addition should be done mentally.

Notes

■ Some students many need to give explanations orally before they are able to write out explanations.
■ Problems may be adapted to address different abilities and strategies.

Strategies

Interviews

Observations

Portfolios

Student Self-Assessment

➤ Performance Tasks

➤ Student Writing

Outcome

- To use strategies for estimation and mental computation.

Sample Performance Indicators for Student Who Is

Not Understanding	Developing	Understanding/Applying
▲ Adds numbers without rounding ▲ Does not know how to round numbers ▲ Cannot add rounded numbers ▲ Cannot explain or has difficulty expressing what was done	▲ Adds first and then rounds off sum ▲ May round incorrectly ▲ Needs prompting to write explanation	▲ Rounds each addend mentally ▲ Mentally adds rounded numbers correctly and quickly ▲ Can clearly explain each step

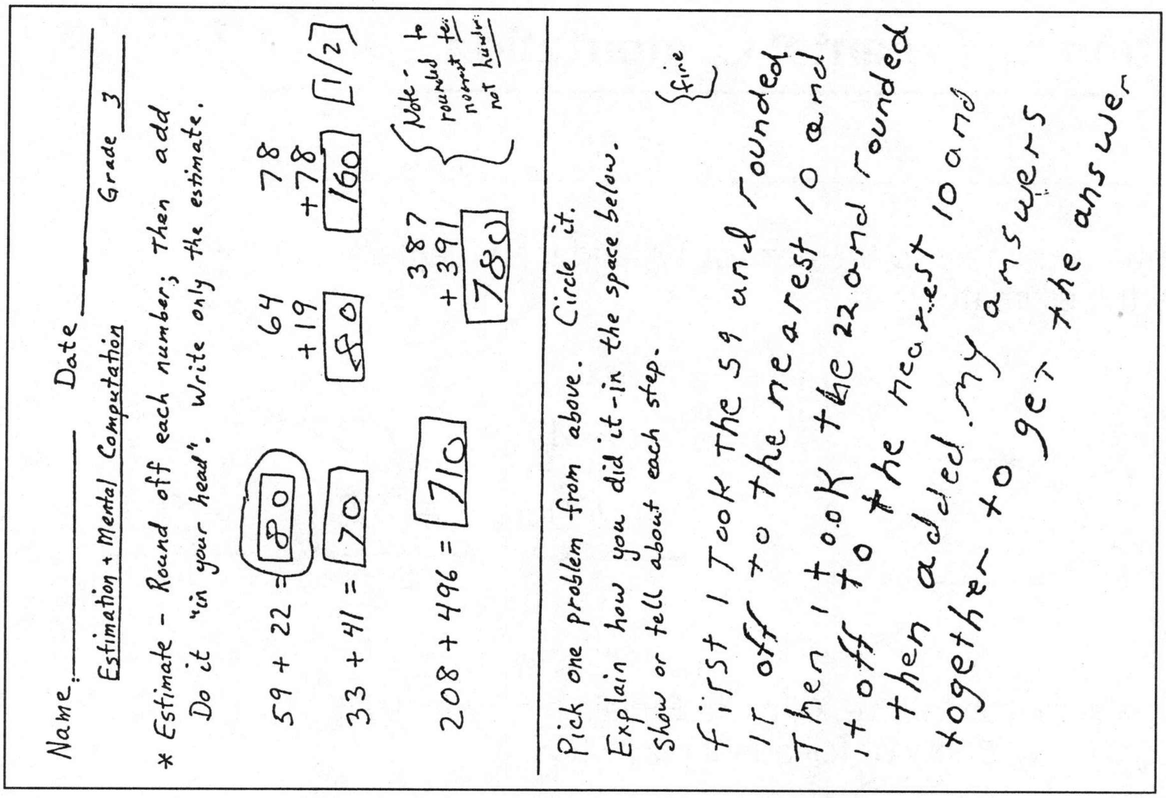

Sample Student Work

Worksheet 1 (top right)

Name: _____ Date _____

Estimation + Mental Computation   Grade 3

*Estimate – Round off each number; then add
Do it "in your head". Write only the estimate.

59 + 22 = (80)

64
+19
[80]

78
+78
[160]   [1/2]

33 + 41 = [70]

387
+391
[780]

{ Note – rounded to nearest ten not hundreds }

Pick one problem from above. Circle it.
Explain how you did it—in the space below.
Show or tell about each step.

First I took the 59 and rounded it off to the nearest 10 and Then I took the 22 and rounded it off to the nearest 10 and then added my answers together to get the answer.

Fine

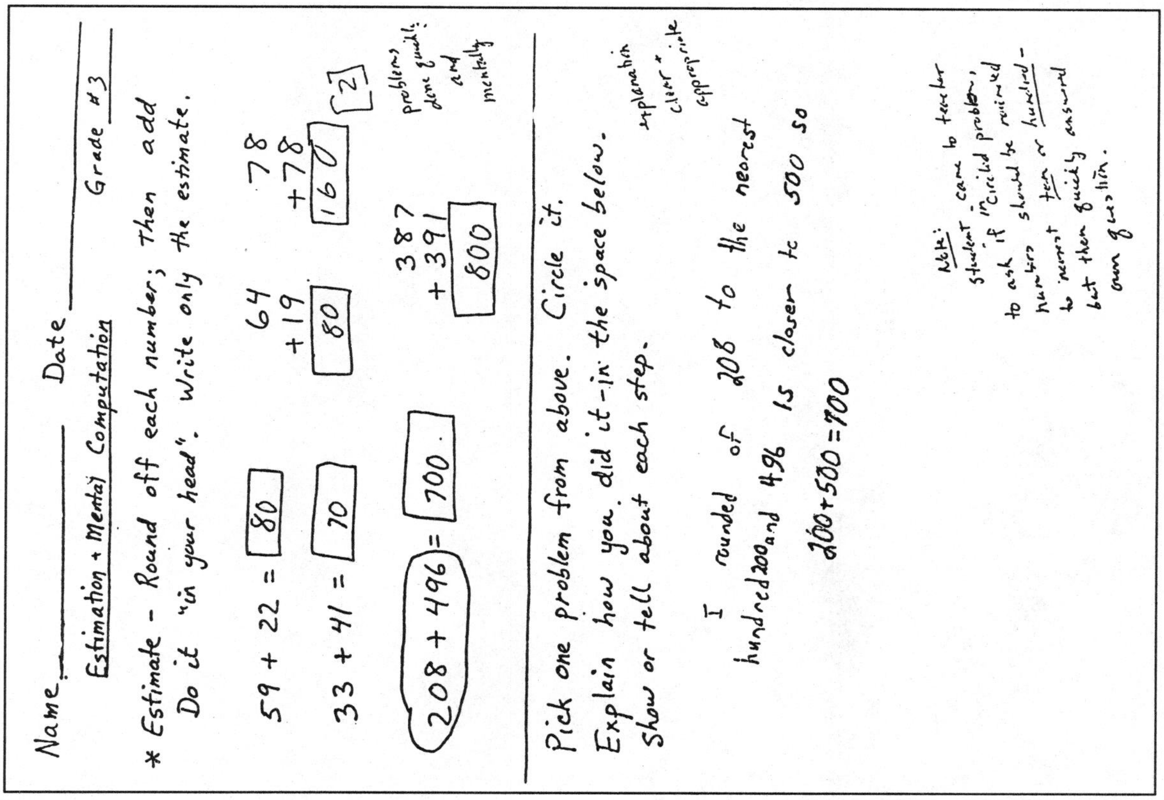

Worksheet 2 (bottom left)

Name: _____ Date _____

Estimation + Mental Computation   Grade #3

*Estimate – Round off each number; then add
Do it "in your head". Write only the estimate.

59 + 22 = [80]

64
+19
[80]

78
+78
[160]   [2]

33 + 41 = [70]

387
+391
[800]

problems done quickly and mentally

208 + 496 = (700.)

Pick one problem from above. Circle it.
Explain how you did it—in the space below.
Show or tell about each step.

explanation clear & appropriate

I rounded of 208 to the nearest hundred 200 and 496 is closer to 500 so

200+500=700

NEXT: student came to teacher to ask if circled problem should be reviewed – hundreds to nearest ten or hundred but then quickly answered own question.

Estimation and Mental Computation in Addition

Estimation and Mental Computation

Name _____ Date _____

Round off each number to the nearest 10, and then mentally add.
Write only the estimate.

59 + 22 = _____

33 + 41 = _____

28 + 96 = _____

```
  6 4        7 8        8 7
+ 1 9      + 7 8      + 9 1
———        ———        ———
```

Pick one problem from above. Circle it. Explain how you did it
in the space below. Show or tell about each step.

Estimation in Multiplication

Outcome

■ To estimate an answer by using a variety of strategies.

Materials

■ Index card with estimation problem (e.g., $89 \times 47 =$)

Assessment Activity

1. Ask the student to estimate the answer without using paper and pencil.
2. Have the student explain his or her strategy.
3. Ask the student to suggest a different strategy.
4. Record the student's responses or name on the Sample Performance Indicators sheet

Notes

■ This activity may be done as a 1- to 2-minute interview.
■ Depending on the problems you select and the developmental level of students, allow students to use paper and pencil.
■ Do an activity similar to this for mental computation.

Content Areas

Estimation and Mental Computation

Activity Type

Manipulative

Representational

➤ Abstract

Strategies

➤ Interviews

➤ Observations

Portfolios

Student Self-Assessment

Performance Tasks

Student Writing

Outcome

- To estimate an answer using a variety of strategies.

Sample Performance Indicators for Student Who Is

Not Understanding	Developing	Understanding/Applying
▲ Begins by multiplying the ones ▲ Does not know where to begin	▲ Uses some estimation strategy but may not recognize more efficient ones (multiplies 9×7 and rounds 63 to 60) ▲ Uses a correct strategy but cannot do work mentally ▲ May have only one strategy	▲ Knows he or she can round first ▲ Can multiply mentally ▲ Knows how many zeros are needed to make the answer correct ▲ Knows which strategies are efficient ▲ Can suggest alternative strategies

Estimation of Quantity

Outcome

- To make reasonable estimates of quantity.

Materials

- 70 pennies
- 3 identical transparent containers (e.g., transparent pill bottles, baby food jars)

Assessment Activity

1. Label the containers A, B, and C. Put 10 pennies into A, 20 into B, and 40 into C.
2. Have the containers out of sight. Tell the student, "I'm going to show you some pennies. Your job is to guess how many pennies are in the container. Do not count the pennies, just guess."
3. Show the student container A for 5 seconds. Then remove the container from sight. Ask, "How many pennies do you think are in this container?"
4. Show the student container B for 5 seconds. Remove the container from sight, and repeat the question.
5. Show the student container C for 5 seconds. Remove the container from sight, and repeat the question.
6. Note the student's answers.

Notes

- Bring out one container at a time.
- Do not empty the pennies out of the container.
- Be sure to show the containers in order from the smallest to the largest number of pennies.
- An extension is to ask, "How many pennies do you think there are altogether?"
- Let the student count the pennies but not until you have finished steps 1 through 5.
- If 10, 20, and 40 are too large, move back to 5, 10, and 20.
- You may vary quantities or objects.
- This activity is adapted from *Mathematics Their Way* by Mary Baratta-Lorton.

Content Areas

Estimation and Mental Computation

Activity Type

➤ Manipulative

Representational

Abstract

Strategies

➤ Interviews

Observations

Portfolios

Student Self-Assessment

➤ Performance Tasks

Student Writing

Outcome

■ To make reasonable estimates of quantity.

Sample Performance Indicators for Student Who Is

Not Understanding	Developing	Understanding/Applying
▲ Provides no response ▲ Estimates are very large (1,000) or very small (6) ▲ Does not use prior knowledge (estimates more in containers A or B than in C)	▲ Estimates most for container C, least for container A ▲ Estimates improve over time	▲ Makes reasonable estimates ▲ Estimate is close to actual amount (e.g., A between 7 and 13, B between 15 and 25, C between 35 and 45) ▲ Uses first estimate to estimate numbers in containers B and C

Explaining Patterns in the Environment

Outcome

■ To explain patterns in the environment.

Materials

■ A model pattern (e.g., AABAABAAB pattern with buttons)

Assessment Activity

1. Present the sample pattern to the student.
2. Ask the student to tell about the pattern: "How would you describe this pattern?" The student may use letters, colors, numbers, or rhythm to explain the pattern.
3. Present more difficult patterns, and ask the student to explain them.
4. Ask the student to locate patterns in the room (environment). After the student identifies a pattern, ask him or her to describe the pattern and to explain why it is a pattern. Sample patterns:
   a. Patterns in student clothing
   b. Patterns in floor tiles
   c. Repetitious border prints
   d. Calendar patterns
   e. Scheduling patterns

Notes

■ This activity may be done as a mini interview.
■ For certain students, you may be able to start by asking them to find patterns in the environment.

Content Areas

Problem Solving and Logic

Algebraic Ideas

Activity Type

➤ Manipulative

Representational

Abstract

Strategies

➤ Interviews

Observations

Portfolios

Student Self-Assessment

Performance Tasks

Student Writing

Outcome

- To explain patterns in the environment.

Sample Performance Indicators for Student Who Is

Not Understanding	Developing	Understanding/Applying
▲ Says, "What do you mean?" ▲ Gives no response ▲ Takes apart the pattern to free explore with the cubes ▲ Demonstrates avoidance behavior ▲ Gives quick, wrong response ▲ Cannot identify patterns in the environment ▲ Cannot explain why something is a pattern	▲ Misinterprets part of the pattern ▲ Can describe by using color, numbers, or letters but cannot explain why it is a pattern ▲ Asks questions about pattern presented ▲ Can identify and describe patterns in the environment but has difficulty explaining what makes something a pattern	▲ Describes the pattern presented, using colors, numbers, or letters to explain it ▲ Can explain pattern and wants to tell how to extend it or show it in a different way ▲ Uses correct verbal language to explain patterns ▲ Can identify and describe patterns in the environment and explain what makes them a pattern

Facts Through Ten

Outcome

■ To provide rote responses to addition and subtraction facts (for facts through 10 within a given time period).

Materials

■ Fact Worksheet (Use the Subtraction and Addition Facts Worksheet or prepare your own using one of the blank worksheets)

Assessment Activity

1. Hand out the worksheets, blank side up.
2. Provide students with a target (a certain number of correct facts in a certain amount of time).
3. When all students are ready, tell them to turn over their papers and to begin.
4. Stop after the target time, and collect the worksheets.

Notes

■ A sample worksheet is provided.
■ Two different blank forms are provided so you can create your own worksheets.
■ Students should be given as many chances as needed.
■ If students have not mastered the facts, they should have opportunities to practice facts, to play games using facts, and so on.
■ Worksheets may be adapted as needed (e.g., could be given orally).

Content Areas

Addition and Subtraction

Activity Type

Manipulative

Representational

➤ Abstract

Strategies

Interviews

Observations

Portfolios

Student Self-Assessment

➤ Performance Tasks

Student Writing

Outcome

- To provide rote responses to addition and subtraction facts (for facts through 10 within a given time period).

Sample Performance Indicators for Student Who Is

Not Understanding	Developing	Understanding/Applying
▲ Is easily frustrated by time constraint	▲ Completes between 50 and 100% of problems	▲ Completes 100% of problems
▲ Completes fewer than 50% of problems	▲ Relies on fingers or other counters	▲ Does not use fingers or other counters
▲ Makes many computational errors	▲ Makes a few computational errors	▲ Makes no computational errors
		▲ Provides immediate responses

Subtraction and Addition Facts

Name _____ Date _____

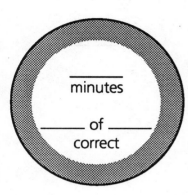

minutes
of
correct

$1 + 0 =$ _____ $8 - 7 =$ _____ $9 - 6 =$ _____
$4 + 4 =$ _____ $5 + 5 =$ _____ $8 + 1 =$ _____
$6 + 4 =$ _____ $4 - 0 =$ _____ $5 + 2 =$ _____
$7 - 5 =$ _____ $8 - 3 =$ _____ $2 + 0 =$ _____
$9 + 1 =$ _____ $9 - 7 =$ _____ $7 - 7 =$ _____

$8 - 5 =$ _____ $7 - 3 =$ _____ $9 - 5 =$ _____ $9 - 4 =$ _____
$7 + 2 =$ _____ $8 - 4 =$ _____ $8 - 6 =$ _____ $8 + 0 =$ _____
$0 - 0 =$ _____ $3 + 2 =$ _____ $7 + 1 =$ _____ $9 - 2 =$ _____
$3 + 1 =$ _____ $2 - 2 =$ _____ $5 + 3 =$ _____ $7 - 6 =$ _____
$6 - 3 =$ _____ $4 + 1 =$ _____ $3 - 0 =$ _____ $9 + 0 =$ _____

$9 - 9 =$ _____ $4 + 2 =$ _____ $2 + 1 =$ _____ $8 - 8 =$ _____
$7 - 4 =$ _____ $1 - 1 =$ _____ $5 + 0 =$ _____ $9 - 3 =$ _____
$6 + 0 =$ _____ $5 + 4 =$ _____ $4 - 3 =$ _____ $6 + 1 =$ _____
$3 + 3 =$ _____ $7 - 0 =$ _____ $6 - 6 =$ _____ $5 - 1 =$ _____
$6 - 5 =$ _____ $8 + 2 =$ _____ $9 - 8 =$ _____ $6 + 2 =$ _____

Fact Worksheet Number_____

Name _____ Date _____

_____ minutes

_____ of _____ correct

= _____ 　　　 = _____ 　　　 = _____

= _____ 　　　 = _____ 　　　 = _____

= _____ 　　　 = _____ 　　　 = _____

= _____ 　　　 = _____ 　　　 = _____

= _____ 　　　 = _____ 　　　 = _____

= _____ 　　 = _____ 　　 = _____ 　　 = _____

= _____ 　　 = _____ 　　 = _____ 　　 = _____

= _____ 　　 = _____ 　　 = _____ 　　 = _____

= _____ 　　 = _____ 　　 = _____ 　　 = _____

= _____ 　　 = _____ 　　 = _____ 　　 = _____

= _____ 　　 = _____ 　　 = _____ 　　 = _____

= _____ 　　 = _____ 　　 = _____ 　　 = _____

= _____ 　　 = _____ 　　 = _____ 　　 = _____

= _____ 　　 = _____ 　　 = _____ 　　 = _____

= _____ 　　 = _____ 　　 = _____ 　　 = _____

Fact Worksheet Number _____

Name _____ Date _____

Fraction Models

Outcome

■ To model fractions using objects and drawings.

Materials

■ One Fraction Models Worksheet for each student
■ One plain sheet of paper, a pair of scissors, and a pencil for each student

Assessment Activity

1. Distribute the worksheet to students, and ask them to cut out the shapes on the sheet.

2. **Activity One**

    a. Ask students to fold one circle into halves, to label each part of the shape, and to set it aside.

    b. Ask students to fold another circle into fourths, to label each part of the shape, and to set it aside.

    c. Do the same for eighths.

3. **Activity Two**

    a. Hand out a plain sheet of paper to each student, and ask the class to fold them into thirds and to number the sections 1, 2, and 3.

    b. Direct students to look at the rectangle. Tell them to pretend that this is one-third of a candy bar and to draw the whole candy bar in section 1 of their papers. When the shape is drawn, ask students to label each section of the bar with its fractional name.

    c. Ask students to pretend that the rectangle is one-sixth of a candy bar and to draw the whole candy bar in section 2 of their papers. When the shape is drawn, ask students to label each section of the bar with its fractional name.

    d. Finally ask students to pretend the rectangle is one-fifth of a candy bar and to draw the whole candy bar in section 3 of their papers. Ask students to label each section of the bar with its fractional name.

Notes

■ This activity may be used before or after instruction to see whether students understand that the whole needs to be divided into equal parts and that the number of those parts depends on the denominator, and know the fractional symbols for one-half, one-fourth, one-eighth, one-third, one-sixth, and one-fifth.

■ As an extension, ask students to pretend that the rectangle is two-fifths of the candy bar and to draw the whole.

Content Areas

Fractions, Decimals, Ratio, and Percent

Activity Type

➤ Manipulative

Representational

Abstract

Strategies

Interviews

➤ Observations

Portfolios

Student Self-Assessment

➤ Performance Tasks

Student Writing

Outcome

- To model fractions by using objects and drawings.

Sample Performance Indicators for Student Who Is

Not Understanding	Developing	Understanding/Applying
▲ Cannot fold circles without help	▲ Needs help to label sections of circles or rectangles correctly	▲ Can fold circles into equal parts and label them correctly
▲ Makes no attempt to fold circles into equal parts	▲ Can fold other circles after being shown how to fold first circle	▲ Knows fractional symbols for one-half, one-fourth, one-eighth, one-third, one-sixth, and one-fifth
▲ Does not know fractional symbols for one-half, one-fourth, one-eighth, one-third, one-sixth, or one-fifth	▲ Needs additional directions to complete folding or drawing tasks	▲ Can use rectangle to draw correctly the whole and fractional parts of whole candy bar
▲ Cannot get whole from unit fraction (candy bar)	▲ Does not use rectangle to draw equal parts of candy bars	▲ Can label each part of candy bars with correct fraction
	▲ Uses rectangle to draw parts of candy bar but gets wrong number of parts	

Fraction Models

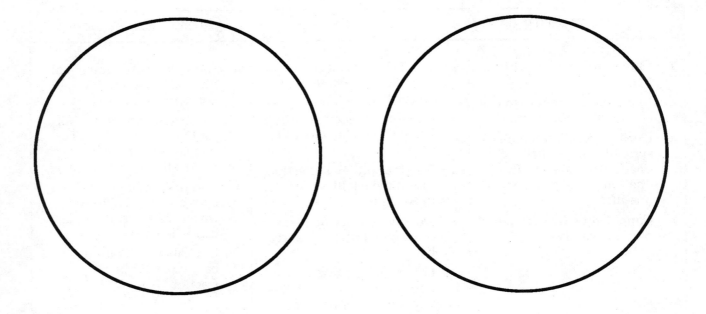

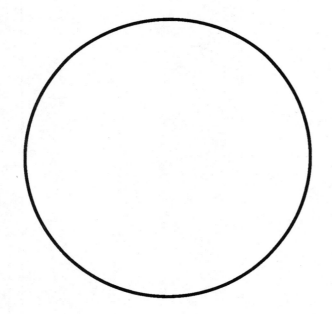

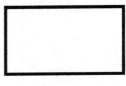

Hands-on Geometry and Measurement Test

Outcomes

Measurement

- To measure and estimate length by using metric and customary units.
- To measure area and perimeter.
- To measure surface area and volume.
- To measure an angle to the nearest degree.

Geometry

- To recognize and define two-dimensional figures and their properties.
- To understand symmetry and congruence.
- To identify and construct lines, line segments, rays, and angles.
- To identify three-dimensional shapes and some of their properties.

Materials

- Performance Tasks: Constructing Geometric Figures Worksheets
- Pencils
- Class sets of compasses, rulers, and protractors

Assessment Activity

Day 1

1. Provide each student with the materials.
2. Have students complete the task at their own pace.
3. When correcting, circle problems for which students have received partial or no credit.

Day 2

1. Discuss the questions (without the questions in front of the students).
2. Let students take their worksheets home to correct mistakes and to earn more points. (Assigning points is optional.)

Notes

- Because of the diversity of the tasks, no Performance Indicators table is given.
- This type of "test" can reveal more about students' conceptions (and misconceptions) than a "traditional" test. The second opportunity to complete the problems provides students with another hands-on experience to help them understand that learning is continuous and does not end with a final unit test.
- Add or delete test items as appropriate for your grade level.

Content Areas

Geometry and Spatial Sense

Measurement

Activity Type

➤ Manipulative

➤ Representational

➤ Abstract

Strategies

Interviews

Observations

Portfolios

Student Self-Assessment

➤ Performance Tasks

Student Writing

Performance Tasks:
Constructing Geometric Figures   60 points

Name _____ Date _____

Directions: You will need a ruler, a protractor, and a compass to complete these sheets. All figures must be as exact as you can make them. Use the side of your ruler to make edges straight.

1. Draw a pair of **intersecting lines.** (4 points)

2. Draw a pair of **parallel line segments.** (4 points)

3. Draw a square that has an **area** of 9 sq cm. (3 points)

4. Draw a **150-degree angle** using the given ray as one of the rays in the angle. (2 points)

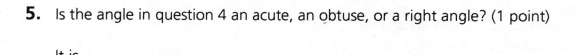

5. Is the angle in question 4 an acute, an obtuse, or a right angle? (1 point)

It is_____ .

6. Draw the **line of symmetry** in the following figure. (3 points)

7. Draw a pair of **perpendicular lines.** (4 points)

8. Draw a **flip** of the following figure. (3 points)

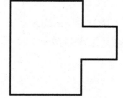

9. Draw a **line segment** that is 15 mm long. (2 points)

10. Look at the indicated **line of symmetry**, and imagine what should be on the blank side of the line. Draw what should be on the blank side of the line of symmetry. (4 points)

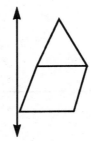

11. Turn the following figure 90 degrees.
Draw a picture of the 90-degree turn. (3 points)

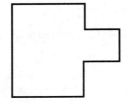

12. Draw a **rectangle** that has a **perimeter** of 10 cm. (4 points)

13. Draw a **ray.** Label the endpoint A. Label another point on the ray, B. (3 points)

14. Draw a **circle.** (It should fill most of the space below.) Label the **center** of the circle, A. Draw a **radius,** and label the endpoint that is on the outside of the circle, B. Start at point B, and draw a **chord.** Label the other endpoint of the chord, C. Start at point C, and draw a **diameter.** Label the other endpoint of the diameter, D. (8 points)

15. Use the circle you just created to find the names of each of the following parts of a circle. Use the correct **notation** for each one. (4 points)

diameter ——————   center ——————

chord ——————   radius ——————

16. In the circle above, the distance around the outside of the circle **from B to C** is called an _____ . (1 point)

17. In the circle above, the distance around the **entire circle** is called the _____ . (1 point)

18. Draw a **75-degree angle** using the given ray as one of the rays in the angle. (2 points)

————————————————————▶

19. Is the angle in question 18 an acute, an obtuse, or a right angle? (1 point)

It is _____ .

20. Draw a **line segment** that is $4\frac{3}{16}$ in. long. (1 point)

21. Draw two **congruent line segments.** (2 points)

High Five: Telling Time

Outcome

■ To tell the time to the nearest 5 minutes.

Materials

■ Telling Time Record Sheet
■ Demonstration clock

Assessment Activity

1. Ask the student to use the clock to "Show me 5:25." If the student correctly shows 5:25, put a check in the correct space on the record sheet. If the student shows another time, record that time.

3. Continue with 3:05, 2:30, 1:50, 6:40. Record the responses.

4. Put 5:00 on the clock, and ask the student the time.

5. Continue with 7:20, 6:15, 2:45, and 4:10. Record the responses.

Notes

■ It takes about 3 minutes to assess each student.

■ This activity is insightful as a preassessment activity that will help in planning for instruction.

Content Areas

Measurement

Activity Type

➤ Manipulative

➤ Representational

   Abstract

Strategies

➤ Interviews

   Observations

   Portfolios

   Student
   Self-Assessment

➤ Performance
   Tasks

   Student Writing

Outcome

- To tell the time to the nearest 5 minutes.

Sample Performance Indicators for Student Who Is

Not Understanding	Developing	Understanding/Applying
▲ Is unable to correctly identify time ▲ Confuses the hour hand with the minute hand ▲ Says "I don't know"	▲ Is able to tell the time on the hour and the half-hour ▲ Has difficulty telling time to the nearest 5 minutes ▲ Takes a long time to show or tell the time ▲ Finds times that are close but not exact ▲ Can recognize but cannot reproduce the time ▲ Counts by fives and points to the numbers as the hands are being moved	▲ Can tell time to the nearest 5 minutes ▲ Responds quickly and accurately to each task

Telling Time Record Sheet

Student Names	Show me:					What time is it?				
	5:25	3:05	2:30	1:50	6:40	5:00	7:20	6:15	2:45	4:10

How Does It Feel?

Outcomes

- To estimate the mass of an object.
- To find the mass of an object to the nearest gram.
- To demonstrate how to use a metric scale.

Materials

- Balance scale and masses (100 g, 10 g, 1 g)
- 6 to 8 objects of various masses

Assessment Activity

1. Meet with each student individually.
2. Place four of the objects in front of the student.
3. Direct the student to pick up the objects to get a sense of each object's mass.
4. Ask the student to estimate each object's mass.
5. Have the student use his or her estimates to place the objects in order from lightest to heaviest.
6. Then tell the student to use the scale to determine, in order, the actual mass of the objects.
7. If the student discovers an object incorrectly placed, ask him or her to explain why this misplacement might have occurred.

Notes

- Use objects that can easily fit into a student's hand (e.g., roll of cellophane tape, roll of masking tape, paperweight, box of paper clips).
- It is possible to have two or three students do this assessment at the same time. Place the students, their objects, and scales into a semicircle with you at the center. Have different objects for each student.

Content Areas

Problem Solving
and Logic

Measurement

Activity Type

➤ Manipulative

Representational

Abstract

Strategies

➤ Interviews

Observations

Portfolios

Student
Self-Assessment

➤ Performance
Tasks

Student Writing

Outcomes

- To estimate the mass of an object.
- To find the mass of an object to the nearest gram.
- To demonstrate how to use a metric scale.

Sample Performance Indicators for Student Who Is

Not Understanding	Developing	Understanding/Applying
▲ Places objects randomly ▲ Does not know how to use a balance scale to determine mass ▲ Has difficulty explaining why an object is out of order	▲ Places objects with one out of order ▲ Needs some help in using a balance scale to determine mass ▲ Has difficulty explaining why an object is out of order	▲ Places objects in correct order by mass ▲ Finds correct mass using a balance scale ▲ Can offer plausible explanation for an object out of order

How Long Does It Take?

Outcome

■ To show an awareness of the time involved for a specific task.

Materials

■ Activity cards

Assessment Activity

1. Photocopy and cut apart the activity cards.
2. Have the student pick two cards. Ask the student which of the activities on the cards takes longer. Ask the student to explain how he or she knows one task takes longer than another.
3. Give the student the stack of activity cards. Ask the student to sort the cards in order from what would take the least amount of time to what would take the most amount of time to complete.

Notes

■ Remove some of the cards for students who are having difficulty.

■ Ask the student how much time he or she thinks it takes to do one or more of the activities.

■ If you wish to use this activity as a performance task, underline a key word on each card. Direct the student to record the key words in sequence of time (least to greatest).

■ Make additional cards or have students create some cards for you.

Content Areas

Measurement

Activity Type

Manipulative

➤ Representational

Abstract

Strategies

➤ Interviews

Observations

Portfolios

Student Self-Assessment

➤ Performance Tasks

Student Writing

Outcome

■ To show an awareness of the time involved for a specific task.

Sample Performance Indicators for Student Who Is

Not Understanding	Developing	Understanding/Applying
▲ Demonstrates no concept of time (e.g. putting "sneeze" in seventh box) ▲ Does not provide an explanation for choices	▲ Sorts most of the activities correctly ▲ Gives minimal explanation for choices	▲ Sorts activity cards correctly ▲ Provides complete explanation for choices

count to 100 by 2s

62-64-66-68-70

smile

ride a bike around a block

return your school library book

walk around the classroom

eat lunch

sneeze

put together a puzzle

152

How's It Going?

Outcome

- To assess how well one solves a problem.

Materials

- Problem Solving Worksheet
- Red and green crayons
- Paper and pencil
- Transparency of story problem of teacher's choice

Assessment Activity

1. Hand out to the class the Problem Solving Worksheets.
2. Show and read aloud a story problem of your choice.
3. Now read aloud, one scale at a time, the problem-solving worksheet. Ask students to use red crayon to mark where they feel they are on each scale.
4. Ask students to work the problem.
5. Tell students that, on finding the solution to the problem, they are to use green crayon to score themselves on the same scale.
6. Have students answer the question at the bottom of their worksheets.

Notes

- This activity assumes previous lessons introducing the problem solving process and different problem-solving strategies have been done.
- When teaching how to use the scale, you may want to introduce them one at a time until students are familiar with the idea and the format.
- Model how to use the scale, and provide much initial discussion and support.
- The scales are intended to be used routinely so that students can monitor their own growth.
- Samples of students' best work, including the scale, may be included in students' portfolios.
- Older students may not need you to read aloud the story or scales.

Content Areas

Problem Solving and Logic

Activity Type

Manipulative

➤ Representational

➤ Abstract

Strategies

Interviews

Observations

Portfolios

➤ Student Self-Assessment

Performance Tasks

Student Writing

Outcome

■ To assess how well one solves a problem.

Sample Performance Indicators for Student Who Is

Not Understanding	Developing	Understanding/Applying
Ability to Solve the Problem (teacher assessment)	**Ability to Solve the Problem (teacher assessment)**	**Ability to Solve the Problem (teacher assessment)**
▲ Misinterprets the problem completely	▲ Misinterprets part of problem	▲ Understands problem completely
▲ Makes no attempt or uses a totally inappropriate strategy	▲ Chooses a correct strategy but gets an incorrect answer	▲ Chooses strategy that solves the problem
▲ Demonstrates avoidance behavior	▲ Needs prompting to select an appropriate strategy	▲ Solves problem correctly
▲ Creates quick solution unrelated to problem		▲ Explains how the problem is solved with the strategies
Ability to Solve the Problem (self-assessment)	**Ability to Solve the Problem (self-assessment)**	**Ability to Solve the Problem (self-assessment)**
▲ Marks scale unrealistically	▲ Marks scale realistically but has variance on scores	▲ Marks scale realistically
▲ Demonstrates lack of confidence in abilities	▲ Demonstrates increasing confidence in abilities	▲ Demonstrates confidence in abilities
▲ Is not aware of how to use self-assessment to help solve problem	▲ May require or request assistance in using self-assessment to help solve problem	▲ Is able to use self-assessment to help solve problems
▲ Demonstrates little understanding of strengths and weaknesses in problem solving	▲ Demonstrates some understanding of strengths and weaknesses in problem solving	▲ Demonstrates understanding of strengths and weaknesses in problem solving

Problem Solving

Name _____ Date _____

1. **Mark the scales using this key:**
   Red—Right after you hear the problem.
   Green—As you complete the problem.

    1 _____ 3 _____ 5
    I do not   I can retell
    understand   the problem
    the problem.   in my own words

    1 _____ 3 _____ 5
    I cannot sort out the   I can sort out
    important and unimportant   the important and
    information.   unimportant imformation.

    1 _____ 3 _____ 5
    I do not know   I
    a strategy or   know a
    where to start.   strategy.

    1 _____ 3 _____ 5
    I do not know   I can explain
    where to start.   the steps I used
                                          to solve it.

2. How difficult was the problem? (please circle)

    Very hard   Okay   Very easy

Identifying Geometric Shapes and Solids

Outcome

■ To recognize geometric shapes and solids and describe their properties.

Materials

■ Plastic bag with draw string, or grocery bag (one bag for every two students)
■ Geometric shapes and solids

Assessment Activity

1. Have partners take turns choosing one object from the bag.
2. Without looking, the student feels it, describes its characteristics, and names the solid.
3. The student shows the object to the partner.

Notes

■ The following describes an alternative procedure for assessing one student:

   ▲ Put each geometric object into a separate bag.
   ▲ Have the student reach in, describe the characteristics of the object, and identify the object.

■ The focus of this task is to assess students' knowledge of two-dimensional shapes. The task is performed, however, with three-dimensional solids.

Content Areas

Geometry and Spatial Sense

Activity Type

➤ Manipulative
➤ Representational
Abstract

Strategies

Interviews
➤ Observations
Portfolios
Student Self-Assessment
➤ Performance Tasks
Student Writing

Outcome

■ To recognize geometric shapes and solids and describe their properties.

Sample Performance Indicators for Student Who Is

Not Understanding	Developing	Understanding/Applying
▲ Incorrectly states characteristics of object ▲ Describes object but cannot name it	▲ Correctly relates characteristics of some solids ▲ Knows some names	▲ Correctly describes all solids and names them

Identifying Shapes
in the Environment

Outcome

- To recognize geometric shapes/solids found in common objects in the environment.

Materials

- Magazine with pictures
- Scissors
- Paste
- Plain paper

Assessment Activity

1. Have the student cut out pictures that contain the shapes/solids being assessed.
2. Tell the student to find at least five examples of each shape/solid.
3. Have the student paste the pictures onto paper.
4. Have the student write or orally describe why he or she has included each object (this should include all of the attributes of the shape/solid students can identify).

Notes

- Shapes/solids may vary by grade level.
- An alternative assessment activity includes the following:
  - ▲ Give the student a set amount of time to walk around the school to locate five examples of identified shapes/solids found in the school environment.
  - ▲ Have the student record findings by writing about or drawing a picture of each shape/solid.

Content Areas

Geometry and
    Spatial Sense

Activity Type

➤ Manipulative

➤ Representational

Abstract

Strategies

Interviews

➤ Observations

Portfolios

Student
    Self-Assessment

➤ Performance
    Tasks

Student Writing

Outcome

■ To recognize geometric shapes/solids found in common objects in the environment.

Sample Performance Indicators for Student Who Is

Not Understanding	Developing	Understanding/Applying
▲ Is unable to locate shapes/solids independently ▲ Is unable to justify his or her choice ▲ Reason for choosing does not include attributes of shapes/solids	▲ Is able to locate and identify some shapes/solids in pictures or environment ▲ Reasons for including objects include some attributes of shapes/solids	▲ Locates and identifies shapes/solids in pictures or environment ▲ Is able to identify all attributes that pertain to each shape/solid

Is It or Isn't It?

Outcomes

■ To recognize a shape by its attributes.

■ To identify attributes of a shape.

Materials

■ Is It or Isn't It? Worksheet

Assessment Activity

1. Give each student a copy of the worksheet, which has examples and nonexamples of a triangle shape.

2. Tell students to circle the examples. Then tell them to respond to the writing prompt that asks them to write a letter about the properties of the shape.

Notes

■ The sample writing prompt came from Mumme and Shepherd's article "Communication in Mathematics" in the September 1990 issue of *Arithmetic Teacher*.

■ Similar writing prompts can be used for other polygons.

■ This activity works well as a preassessment.

Content Areas

Geometry and Spatial Sense

Activity Type

Manipulative

Representational

➤ Abstract

Strategies

Interviews

Observations

Portfolios

Student Self-Assessment

Performance Tasks

➤ Student Writing

Outcomes

- To recognize a shape by its attributes.
- To identify attributes of a shape.

Sample Performance Indicators for Student Who Is

Not Understanding	Developing	Understanding/Applying
▲ Has difficulty distinguishing examples and non-examples ▲ May know whether shape is or is not an example but does not know why	▲ Can identify examples and nonexamples ▲ Identifies some properties ▲ May have a few misconceptions	▲ Correctly identifies examples and nonexamples ▲ Identifies properties of the shape

Is It or Isn't It?

Name _____ Date _____

1. Circle the figures that are triangles.

A. 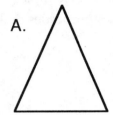 B.  C.  D.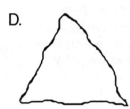

2. James circled figure A only. He says figures B, C, and D are not triangles. Write a letter to James telling him whether you agree with him. Tell him how you answered the question and why.

Sample Student Work

Dear James I think C is a triangle to.
D isn't a triangle because the lines arn't straigt.
B isn't a triangle because the lines arn't conected.
A. is a triangle.

this is a triangle.   this isn't a triangle.   this isn't a triangle.   this is a triangle

To James,

   I dissagree with you because C is still a triangle even though it is upside down. I agree that b and d are not triangles though, because b's lines are not connected and d. does not have strait lines.

Linear Measurement

Outcome

■ To measure linear distance in centimeters and inches.

Materials

■ Items from the classroom (books, erasers, desks, chairs)
■ Linear Measurement Worksheet
■ Performance Indicator sheet
■ Ruler in inches and centimeters

Assessment Activity

1. Direct students to measure classroom items to the nearest inch. (Some explanation of the words *height, length,* and *width* may be needed.)
2. Direct students to measure the items to the nearest centimeter.
3. As students complete the task, observe and record results on the Performance Indicator sheet.

Note

■ You may want to ask students to estimate the measurements of various objects.

Content Areas

Measurement

Activity Type

➤ Manipulative
Representational
Abstract

Strategies

Interviews
➤ Observations
Portfolios
Student Self-Assessment
➤ Performance Tasks
Student Writing

Outcome

- To measure linear distance in centimeters and inches.

Sample Performance Indicators for Student Who Is

Not Understanding	Developing	Understanding/Applying
▲ Does not begin measuring with end of ruler ▲ Cannot measure something longer than ruler (30 cm or 12 in.) ▲ Writes length as long as ruler is less than 12 in. long ▲ Uses incorrect unit or unit label (e.g., measures centimeters but calls it inches)	▲ Starts measuring at 1-inch mark rather than at end of ruler but does not account for this in reporting the measurement ▲ Cannot measure something longer than ruler ▲ Does not know what to do with partial units	▲ Measures accurately to nearest whole unit ▲ Knows what to do with partial units ▲ Can measure items longer than ruler ▲ Uses labels correctly

Linear Measurement

Name _____ Date _____

Measure in inches (in.):

    1. length of spelling book   _____

    2. length of chalk eraser   _____

    3. width of your desk   _____

    4. height of chair   _____

Measure in centimeters (cm):

    1. width of math book   _____

    2. length of chalk eraser   _____

    3. width of spelling book   _____

    4. height of chair   _____

Line Plots

Outcome

- To construct and interpret line plots.

Materials

- Line Plots Worksheet
- Pencil

Assessment Activity

1. Distribute worksheets.
2. Explain that students must use the given data about shoes to construct a line plot.
3. Tell students they must analyze the data by answering the questions at the bottom of the page.

Notes

- This is a good tool to use as a pre- or postassessment to evaluate what needs to be taught or who needs to be re-taught.
- Students' work can be included in their portfolios, particularly if a final graphing product is also included.
- With a magnetic chalkboard, line plots can be drawn on the board and magnets can be used as data points. Some teachers like to model this with square self-adhesive notepads.

Content Areas

Statistics and Probability

Activity Type

Manipulative

➤ Representational

➤ Abstract

Strategies

Interviews

Observations

➤ Portfolios

Student Self-Assessment

➤ Performance Tasks

➤ Student Writing

Outcome

■ To construct and interpret line plots.

Sample Performance Indicators for Student Who Is

Not Understanding	Developing	Understanding/Applying
▲ Is not able to set up line plot ▲ Is not able to analyze the data ▲ Is not able to create a line plot without step-by-step instructions ▲ Does not know what a line plot is	▲ Creates line plot correctly and independently but cannot interpret significance of data it represents ▲ Sets up line plot correctly and analyzes significant aspects of data with prompts ▲ Independently sets up line plot but needs prompts to interpret some of data that it represents ▲ Independently sets up line plot and discusses significant aspects of the data but interpretation of data is incomplete	▲ Creates line plot correctly and independently ▲ Accurately transfers data to line plot ▲ Includes clumps, bumps, holes, and range in discussion of data ▲ Gives a reasonable response for the "typical" number with justification for answer

Line Plots

Name _____ Date _____

This collection of data tells how many pairs of shoes each person in fourth grade at Adams School owns.

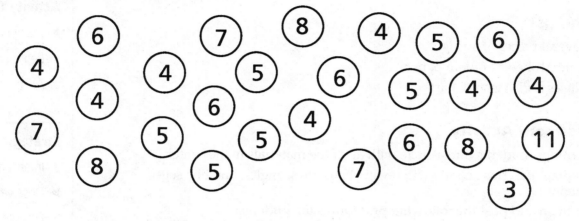

Your job is to construct a line plot from the data.

Now that you have constructed the line plot, analyze the data. What is the typical number of pairs of shoes? Tell what you know about bumps, clumps, and holes. How about outliers and range?

Lines, Rays, Angles, and Line Segments

Suggested Grades

5–6

Outcomes

- To understand the concepts of lines, rays, angles, and line segments.
- To work cooperatively with others, self-evaluating performance.

Materials

- Several pieces of string
- Several sheets of plain paper
- Pluses and Wishes Charts

Assessment Activity

1. Arrange students into a circle with all of the materials in the center.
2. Explain that this activity will review lines, rays, angles, and line segments.
3. Explain and post the following procedures for students:
   a. Students will use string, their bodies, and the paper, if necessary, to create a geometric figure.
   b. They will represent endpoints of figures by standing with their arms at their sides.
   c. They will represent rays by extending one of their arms straight out to the side.
   d. String will be used for line segments.
   e. Paper will be used to check right angles.
4. Ask for some volunteers to model the procedure. The class then critiques the performance.
5. Students then decide what steps to follow when they are asked to create a figure and to write them on the board. This list might include the following:
   a. listening to directions
   b. talking to partners
   c. picking up string
   d. following directions
   e. checking that directions have been followed
   f. saying, "We're done"
6. A second group then models the procedure. Students use the procedural steps to critique the performance.

Content Areas

Geometry and Spatial Sense

Activity Type

➤ Manipulative

Representational

Abstract

Strategies

Interviews

➤ Observations

Portfolios

Student Self-Assessment

➤ Performance Tasks

Student Writing

7. Call on various groups of students, and ask them to form the following figures:
   a. right angle
   b. acute angle
   c. obtuse angle
   d. ray
   e. line
   f. line segment
   g. parallel lines
   h. perpendicular lines

8. As each group performs, record students' actions on the Performance Indicators sheet.

9. Students each assess their own ability to work in small groups by looking at the board and choosing one characteristic that they see as their greatest strength and one that needs improvement:

do it right	pay attention
respect	listen
polite	hold string without dropping it
everyone participates	don't fidget
help each other	hold string straight

   Students complete a Pluses and Wishes Chart and then write a short paragraph elaborating on these two characteristics. (An explanation of the chart is in Student Self-Assessment, page 41.)

Notes

- Students need some practice in using strings, people, arms, and so on to model figures before doing this assessment.

- This lesson serves as both a review for students and as an assessment tool for you to tell whether students are ready to begin working more abstractly with geometrical concepts.

- Students need extensive critiquing lessons before they can be successful. This will be difficult if the class has no previous experience.

Outcomes

- To understand the concepts of lines, rays, angles, and line segments.
- To work cooperatively with others, self-evaluating performance.

Sample Performance Indicators for Student Who Is

Not Understanding	Developing	Understanding/Applying
Perpendicular/Parallel ▲ Confuses the two or cannot form either	**Perpendicular/Parallel** ▲ Forms them with prompts ▲ Does not use paper corner	**Perpendicular/Parallel** ▲ Uses paper corner to ensure perpendicular/parallel lines
Ray ▲ Forms line or line segment	**Ray** ▲ Forms it with prompts	**Ray** ▲ Forms it immediately
Right Angle ▲ Forms any angle	**Right Angle** ▲ Forms angle that looks to be 90° but does not check it with paper	**Right Angle** ▲ Uses paper corner to form angle
Line ▲ Forms wiggly line or forms line segment	**Line** • Forms line segment or ray	**Line** ▲ Forms line, both endpoints showing that line goes on continuously
Line Segment ▲ Interchanges line and line segment	**Line Segment** ▲ Can form it with prompts	**Line Segment** ▲ Forms it immediately
Acute/Obtuse ▲ Confuses the two	**Acute/Obtuse** ▲ Can form them with prompts	**Acute/Obtuse** ▲ Forms them immediately
Group Work ▲ Does not get to the task ▲ Is rude ▲ Uses loud voice ▲ Is uncommunicative	**Group Work** ▲ Asks for assistance to resolve conflicts ▲ Talks before working	**Group Work** ▲ Resolves own conflicts ▲ Gets right to the task ▲ Is respectful ▲ Is cooperative

Pluses and Wishes

Name _____ Date _____

Pluses	Wishes

Math in Everyday Life

Outcome

- To write examples showing the application and the role of mathematics in daily life

Assessment Activity

1. Ask students to write a paragraph giving specific examples of how they daily use math and math skills other than in math class. Use a prompt such as, "How does math come in handy every day?"

2. Ask students to be specific and to cite examples that are current in their own lives (not as adults).

Notes

- This activity may be given to students of any grade and at any time to emphasize mathematical connections and to assess whether students are able to make connections.

- Older students will give more sophisticated answers.

- The following are actual student responses.

  - When you are in like a science club you have to know your math. If you wanted to be a teacher you have to know your math to teach math. If you want to get out of school you have to know math—you don't want to flunk. If you are a banker you have to count the money right.

  - Math comes in handy when you count how long you can stay outside. When you count how many books you have. When you count how many days in June.

  - Math comes in handy when you buy milk at the lunchroom you might buy milk for 50¢ when it only costs 40¢ you want fair change. You would say 50¢ – 40¢ = 10¢. If you sell lemonade with your friends you want to split the money you would divide.

Strategies

Interviews

Observations

Portfolios

Student
Self-Assessment

Performance
Tasks

➤ Student Writing

Outcome

- To write examples showing the application and the role of mathematics in daily life.

Sample Performance Indicators for Student Who Is

Not Understanding	Developing	Understanding/Applying
▲ Gives general or unclear examples ▲ Cites only math class examples	▲ Gives only one example ▲ Gives examples of use of math as an adult ▲ Gives several uses of same concept (e.g., counting books, counting days, counting time)	▲ Gives several different situations with examples ▲ Uses numbers to illustrate example

Measuring and Estimating Length

Outcomes

- To estimate length in a nonstandard unit.
- To measure length in a nonstandard unit.

Materials

- Materials to use as nonstandard unit (e.g., chalk, paper clips, pencils)
- Measurement Record Worksheets
- Pencils
- Objects to measure (e.g., books, table, shelf)

Assessment Activity

1. Tell students that they will be working with partners. Assign partners.
2. Explain that Activity 1 has three parts.

   Activity 1

   a. Each student is to estimate the length of a designated object using _____ as the measurement unit. Each partner should record his or her estimate on the worksheet.

   b. Together the partners should then measure the object using _____ as the measurement unit. The actual measurement in this nonstandard unit should be recorded, including the unit label.

   c. Partners should compare and discuss the estimated and actual measurements. Tell students that this discussion may be used to help them do a better job of estimating the length of the next object.

3. Model the activity and the use of the recording sheet.
4. Tell students that they will do this activity for three objects; list them so that students can record them on their record sheets.
5. **Activity 2**

   a. Partners are to select three additional items to estimate and measure length.

   b. They should use the same measurement unit.

6. **Activity 3**

   a. Still using _____ as the measurement unit, partners are to predict three items that they think are about _____ units long.

   b. Partners then should measure to check the prediction.

Activity Type

➤ Manipulative

Representational

Abstract

Strategies

Interviews

Observations

Portfolios

Student
Self-Assessment

➤ Performance
Tasks

Student Writing

Notes

- Be sure students include unit names when they record their measurements and estimates.
- Allow students to decide how to handle fractional parts of units.
- This activity may be repeated with different objects as standard units.
- This activity may be modified for other measurements (e.g., weight, volume).
- The activity may be repeated with standard units (inches/feet and centimeters/meters).
- If you have students measure the same objects using different units, they should discuss how the unit affects the measurement.

Outcomes

- To estimate length in a nonstandard unit.
- To measure length in a nonstandard unit.

Sample Performance Indicators for Student Who Is

Not Understanding	Developing	Understanding/Applying
▲ Plays with objects ▲ Makes inappropriate estimates throughout activities ▲ Appears to make guesses without using any strategy ▲ Does not use measurement unit correctly ▲ May have difficulty counting units	▲ Uses first estimate and measurement to refine and improve later estimates ▲ Can use an estimation strategy if told how ▲ May make minor errors in measuring objects ▲ Counts and records actual measurement	▲ Makes appropriate estimates ▲ Uses estimation strategies ▲ Uses measurement unit correctly ▲ Counts and records actual measurement accurately

Measurement Record

Name _____ Date _____

Object used as unit _____

ACTIVITY 1

OBJECT	PARTNER 1's GUESSES	PARTNER 2's GUESSES	ACTUAL MEASUREMENT
_____ _____ _____	_____ _____ _____	_____ _____ _____	_____ _____ _____

ACTIVITY 2

OBJECT	PARTNER 1's GUESSES	PARTNER 2's GUESSES	ACTUAL MEASUREMENT
_____ _____ _____	_____ _____ _____	_____ _____ _____	_____ _____ _____

ACTIVITY 3

Predict three things that are about _____ long. Measure them.

Object Predicted	Actual Measurement
_____	_____
_____	_____
_____	_____

INCHES 0 1 2 3 4 5 INCHES 6

Missing Addends

Outcomes

- To identify a missing addend.
- To justify and describe the process used to get a solution to the problem.

Materials

- Number sentences (on cards or papers)
- Counters
- Container

Assessment Activity

1. *(Concrete)* Choose a number to work with (e.g., 7). Display 7 counters and write 7. Cover three of the counters with the container, and ask, "How many are hidden? How do you know?" Repeat the process several times, placing a different number of counters under the container. Always encourage the student to explain how she or he got an answer.

2. *(Symbolic)* Present the student with facts that she or he has shown mastery with (e.g., 5 + ☐ = 7). Ask, "Five plus what number equals 7? How do you know ☐ is the correct answer? Why? What did you do first to solve this problem?"

3. Present the student with a problem that is not a fact problem, (e.g., 22 + ☐ = 30). Ask, "Twenty-two plus what number equals 30? How do you know ☐ is the correct answer? Why? What did you do first to solve this problem?"

4. Present the student with a set of addition equations:

4 + ☐ = 9	4 + ☐ = 15	4 + ☐ = 13
4 + ☐ = 11	4 + ☐ = 17	

5. Ask, "Four plus what number equals 9? What do you need to do to keep answering? Can you suggest a pattern that might help you solve these problems? Can you describe your solutions?" (pattern) "Are you sure these are the correct answers? Why?"

Notes

- Problems may be modified to fit the developmental level of the student.
- Allow students to use counters if they wish.
- Students may use a written assessment to justify and describe the process used.

Content Areas

Algebraic Ideas

Activity Type

➤ Manipulative

Representational

➤ Abstract

Strategies

➤ Interviews

Observations

Portfolios

Student Self-Assessment

➤ Performance Tasks

Student Writing

Outcomes

■ To identify a missing addend.

■ To justify and describe the process used to get a solution to the problem.

Sample Performance Indicators for Student Who Is

Not Understanding	Developing	Understanding/Applying
▲ Gets confused and does not understand what is being asked ▲ Is confused by number missing from equation	▲ Can solve at concrete level by only giving answer ▲ Can give answer to missing addend fact card but cannot explain answer ▲ Activity step 4: Can work each equation but does not use idea of pattern to solve	▲ Can solve at concrete level and can explain answer ▲ Gives answer to missing addend fact card and can explain answer ▲ Activity step 4: Solves first two or three equations and then solves rest of equations using pattern and can explain it

Modeling Addition
and Subtraction

Outcomes

- To read an addition (subtraction) problem that involves regrouping.
- To manipulate materials to solve an addition (subtraction) problem that requires regrouping.
- To solve an addition (subtraction) problem that requires regrouping.
- To demonstrate and explain the solution with manipulatives.

Materials

- Place value materials (e.g., base 10 blocks, beans, cups)
- Place value board
- Equation cards
- Paper and pencil

Assessment Activity

1. **Activity One** (Concept Level)
   a. Work with a group of up to five students, giving each student a different problem in which regrouping occurs (e.g., 19 + 6).
   b. State the problem as the student models the problem with manipulatives on a place value board.

2. **Activity Two** (Connecting Level)
   a. Give a group of up to five students different cards containing addition (subtraction) problems that require regrouping.
   b. Ask each student to show you how to solve the problem by using manipulatives and a place value board.

3. **Activity Three** (Symbolic Level)
   a. Work with a group of up to five students. Orally give each student a different addition (subtraction) problem that requires regrouping.
   b. Have the student solve the problem on paper.
   c. Ask the student to "prove" the answer using manipulatives and a place value board.

Content Areas

Addition and Subtraction

Activity Type

➤ Manipulative

➤ Representational

➤ Abstract

Strategies

Interviews

➤ Observations

Portfolios

Student Self-Assessment

➤ Performance Tasks

Student Writing

Outcomes

- To read an addition (subtraction) problem that involves regrouping.
- To manipulate materials to solve an addition (subtraction) problem that requires regrouping.
- To solve an addition (subtraction) problem that requires regrouping.
- To demonstrate and explain the solution with manipulatives.

Sample Performance Indicators for Student Who Is

Not Understanding	Developing	Understanding/Applying
▲ Regroups when not necessary ▲ Does not realize when needs to regroup ▲ Builds numbers incorrectly ▲ Does not add correctly ▲ Has difficulty explaining process	▲ Realizes a trade has to be made but does not know how ▲ Is able to work through process with prompts ▲ Builds original addends incorrectly but adds correctly ▲ May have difficulty explaining process	▲ Completes task successfully ▲ Is able to explain process ▲ Can relate the paper-and-pencil algorithm to the manipulative model

Modeling Division

Outcome

■ To model division by a one-digit divisor using base 10 blocks.

Materials

■ Pencil and writing paper
■ A personal set of base 10 blocks, inclusive of ones, tens, and hundreds blocks
■ Paper folded into fourths or four paper plates per student

Assessment Activity

1. Give a division problem that uses 4 as a divisor.
2. Then say the following aloud:
   ▲ What place do we look at first when dividing?
   ▲ Distribute your hundreds blocks.
   ▲ How many hundreds blocks ended up in each square?
   ▲ Where does that get recorded?
   ▲ How many total hundreds blocks got distributed?
   ▲ Where does that get recorded?
   ▲ How many hundreds blocks are left over?
   ▲ Where does that get recorded?
   ▲ What do we do with the leftover hundreds blocks?
3. Continue the same dialogue for the tens and ones places.
4. Observe student performance, completing the Performance Indicator sheet.
5. Do as many problems as needed to assess students.

Notes

■ This assessment may be used early in a division unit to assess understanding of long division. Provide prompts. Later in the unit, use the same assessment without prompts.
■ This task may be done with groups of four to six students to make it easier to complete observations.

Content Areas

Multiplication and Division

Activity Type

➤ Manipulative

Representational

Abstract

Strategies

➤ Interviews

Observations

Portfolios

Student Self-Assessment

➤ Performance Tasks

Student Writing

Outcome

■ To model division by a one-digit divisor using base 10 blocks.

Sample Performance Indicators for Student Who Is

Not Understanding	Developing	Understanding/Applying
▲ Cannot distribute blocks ▲ Can write out problem correctly but has no correlation between written problem and tens block activity ▲ Looks confused when you ask questions ▲ Asks lots of questions about where blocks should be placed ▲ Is watching what other students do and is copying	▲ Can distribute numbers that do not require exchanging ▲ Can write out some steps of problem but gets stuck at various points ▲ Can distribute blocks correctly but cannot write out algorithm ▲ Is sometimes able to assist other students who do not understand the process ▲ Can answer some prompts but most often waits for answer from another student before distributing blocks	▲ Can correctly distribute the hundreds, tens, and ones blocks ▲ Able to correctly write out the problem ▲ Is able to answer lead questions you ask ▲ Is able to explain to another student what to do in the problem ▲ Is often ahead of the teacher during the lesson

Money Counts!

Outcomes

- To identify the value of a coin.
- To give the total value of a set of coins (less than $1.00).

Materials

- Set of overhead coins or transparencies of sets of coins
- Money Counts! Worksheet
- Student coin sets (optional)
- Overhead projector

Assessment Activity

1. To determine whether the student can recognize coins, show individual coins (heads or tails) and then have the student record the values on the worksheet.
2. On the overhead projector, show a set of coins (e.g., 1 nickel and 3 dimes). The student is to figure out the total and record the total on the worksheet.

Notes

- You could give the student a coin set to model what is on the transparency.
- This assessment may be done as an activity station by stamping coin faces on numbered index cards.
- As an extension, give the names of coins and have the student state the total value (e.g., say, "penny, dime, quarter, and 2 nickels").
- Consider having the student create a story situation to go with one of the problems.
- The process could be reversed, with you providing the total values and the student generating possible combinations.

Content Areas

Measurement

Activity Type

Manipulative

➤ Representational

Abstract

Strategies

Interviews

Observations

Portfolios

Student Self-Assessment

➤ Performance Tasks

Student Writing

Outcomes

■ To identify the value of a coin.

■ To give the total value of a set of coins (less than $1.00).

Sample Performance Indicators for Student Who Is

Not Understanding	Developing	Understanding/Applying
▲ Has difficulty telling the difference between coins ▲ Cannot assign correct value of coins	▲ Can name coin by looking at the head side only ▲ States values of coins with some prompting ▲ May have difficulty computing total value	▲ Identifies coins from both sides ▲ States values of coins ▲ Adds coins of value less than $1.00 ▲ May mentally total values

Money Counts!

Name _____ Date _____

1. _____ ¢	6. _____ ¢
2. _____ ¢	7. _____ ¢
3. _____ ¢	8. _____ ¢
4. _____ ¢	9. _____ ¢
5. _____ ¢	10. _____ ¢

Money Counts!

Name _____ Date _____

1. _____ ¢	6. _____ ¢
2. _____ ¢	7. _____ ¢
3. _____ ¢	8. _____ ¢
4. _____ ¢	9. _____ ¢
5. _____ ¢	10. _____ ¢

Money Values

Outcome

■   To determine the value of groups of coins totaling less than $5.00.

Materials

■   Money Record Sheet
■   Coins and dollars

Assessment Activity

Task 1

1.   Say to the student, "Show me a dime. How much money is that?" (10¢)
     "Show me a quarter. How much money is that?" (25¢) Continue this
     questioning with a nickel and a penny.

2.   Record the student's responses on the Money Record Sheet. Put each
     correct answer into the designated space.

Task 2

3.   Continue with the "Counting Groups of Coins" section. Ask the student,
     "How much is in front of you?" (12¢, 37¢, 58¢).

4.   If the answer is correct, put a check in the space. If the answer is
     incorrect, write down the amount the student gives.

Task 3

5.   For the section "Demonstrating Money Combinations," ask the student
     to make $1.00, 35¢, and 79¢. Record the coins the student uses to make
     each amount.

Notes

■   Each interview should take three to four minutes.
■   Tasks may be modified as appropriate.

Content Areas

Measurement

Activity Type

➤ Manipulative

Representational

Abstract

Strategies

➤ Interviews

Observations

Portfolios

Student
Self-Assessment

➤ Performance
Tasks

Student Writing

Outcome

■ To determine the value of groups of coins totaling less than $5.00.

Sample Performance Indicators for Student Who Is

Not Understanding	Developing	Understanding/Applying
▲ Cannot identify values of coins ▲ Cannot correctly count groups of coins ▲ Cannot create money combinations	▲ Can identify coins but cannot combine them ▲ Can count groups of coins but cannot create groups of coins ▲ Makes errors in addition	▲ Can identify values of coins and dollar ▲ Can correctly count groups of coins ▲ Can create money combinations

Money Record Sheet

Student Names	Show me a				Counting Groups of Coins			Demonstrating Money Combinations		
	dime	quarter	nickle	penny	12¢	37¢	58¢	$1.00	35¢	79¢

Multi-digit Multiplication

Outcome

■ To multiply three-digit by two-digit numbers using computational algorithms.

Materials

■ Multiplication Test, Parts A and B
■ Pencil
■ Base 10 materials (optional)

Assessment Activity

1. Give the student Multiplication Tests A and B.
2. Direct the student to solve the problems on Part A and to explain how to correct any incorrect problems on Part B.

Notes

■ Part A will show which students can correctly determine the product of two multi-digit whole numbers.
■ Part B will show which students understand the concept of multiplication and which students are just "going through the motions."
■ In Part A, have students draw a picture of the multiplication problems.
■ In Part A, ask students to create a story problem to match one or more of the problems.
■ Students who have difficulty with Part B may benefit from drawing a picture or using base 10 materials to model the problem.

Content Areas

Multiplication and Division

Activity Type

Manipulative

➤ Representational

➤ Abstract

Strategies

Interviews

Observations

Portfolios

Student Self-Assessment

➤ Performance Tasks

➤ Student Writing

Outcome

■ To multiply three-digit by two-digit numbers using computational algorithms.

Sample Performance Indicators for Student Who Is

Not Understanding	Developing	Understanding/Applying
▲ Gets most or all of problems in Part A incorrect ▲ Makes errors that indicate he or she does not know steps in solving a multi-digit multiplication problem ▲ Is unable to correctly identify all problems that are correct/incorrect ▲ Is unable to explain why any problems are incorrect	▲ Correctly completes most problems in Part A ▲ Makes careless errors (e.g., incorrect multiplication facts, errors in addition) ▲ Is unable to explain or incorrectly explains why some problems are incorrect	▲ Correctly completes all problems in Part A ▲ Can identify incorrect problems and explain errors

Multiplication Test

Part A

Name _____ Date _____

Solve:

A. $\begin{array}{r} 649 \\ \times\ 36 \\ \hline \end{array}$

B. $\begin{array}{r} 903 \\ \times\ 54 \\ \hline \end{array}$

C. $\begin{array}{r} 747 \\ \times\ 68 \\ \hline \end{array}$

D. $\begin{array}{r} 560 \\ \times\ 69 \\ \hline \end{array}$

E. $\begin{array}{r} 486 \\ \times\ 27 \\ \hline \end{array}$

F. $\begin{array}{r} 95 \\ \times\ 83 \\ \hline \end{array}$

Multiplication Test

Part B

Name _____   Date _____

José also took a multiplication test. Check José's work. Do you agree with his answers? If not, tell what he did wrong for each incorrect problem.

A.
```
    3 6 4
  ×   2 9
  3 2 7 6
  7 2 8 0
  10, 5 5 6
```

B.
```
    7 6 3
  ×   4 6
  4 5 7 8
  3 0 5 2
  7, 6 3 0
```

C.
```
    6 1 9
  ×   6 3

  18, 6 2 4
```

D.
```
    8 4 1
  ×   6 3
  2 5 2 3
  5 0 4 6 0
  52, 9 8 3
```

E.
```
    4 0 3
  ×   2 5
  2 0 5 5
  8 0 6 0
  10, 1 1 5
```

F.
```
    5 1 8
  ×   2 6
  3 1 0 2
  1 0 3 6 0
  13, 4 6 2
```

Multiplication/Division Facts

Outcome

■ To know basic multiplication and division facts.

Materials

■ Multiplication/Division flash cards (optional)
■ Multiplication/Division Facts—Teacher Record-Keeping Sheets
■ Multiplication/Division Facts—Student Goal-Setting Sheets

Assessment Activity

1. Meet with each student individually to pretest quick recall of facts. Ask facts from the Teacher Record-Keeping Sheets in random order. (It is helpful to work from easy to difficult.) If the student knows a fact, cross it out on the sheet. If the student does not know a fact, leave it as is. Have the student read the facts and tell the answers, or you read the facts to the student.

2. When all of the facts are tested, look at the Student Goal-Setting Sheets with the student. Fill in the information, determine which facts the student will learn and when he or she will be tested on these facts. These sheets stay with the student, so mark the problems to be learned (with a dot) and the date on the Teacher Record-Keeping Sheets.

3. Retest students on the dates indicated on their sheets. Keep a permanent record of known facts on the Teacher Record-Keeping Sheets.

4. Set a new goal for each student.

Notes

■ Teacher Record-Keeping Sheets are provided in place of a Performance Indicators table.

■ Set aside a certain time for testing each day, and have certain students assigned to each day of the week.

■ Award certificates to students who have mastered all of the facts.

■ Let parents and guardians know about the Student Goal-Setting Sheets so that they can work with the students at home.

■ You may want to date and color-code the Teacher Record-Keeping Sheets.

■ Many thanks to LeAnn Corkins for contributing this idea.

Content Areas

Multiplication and Division

Estimation and Mental Computation

Activity Type

Manipulative

Representational

➤ Abstract

Strategies

➤ Interviews

Observations

Portfolios

➤ Student Self-Assessment

Performance Tasks

Student Writing

Multiplication Facts
Student Goal-Setting Sheet

Name _____

1 x 1	2 x 1	3 x 1	4 x 1	5 x 1	6 x 1	7 x 1	8 x 1	9 x 1	10 x 1
1 x 2	2 x 2	3 x 2	4 x 2	5 x 2	6 x 2	7 x 2	8 x 2	9 x 2	10 x 2
1 x 3	2 x 3	3 x 3	4 x 3	5 x 3	6 x 3	7 x 3	8 x 3	9 x 3	10 x 3
1 x 4	2 x 4	3 x 4	4 x 4	5 x 4	6 x 4	7 x 4	8 x 4	9 x 4	10 x 4
1 x 5	2 x 5	3 x 5	4 x 5	5 x 5	6 x 5	7 x 5	8 x 5	9 x 5	10 x 5
1 x 6	2 x 6	3 x 6	4 x 6	5 x 6	6 x 6	7 x 6	8 x 6	9 x 6	10 x 6
1 x 7	2 x 7	3 x 7	4 x 7	5 x 7	6 x 7	7 x 7	8 x 7	9 x 7	10 x 7
1 x 8	2 x 8	3 x 8	4 x 8	5 x 8	6 x 8	7 x 8	8 x 8	9 x 8	10 x 8
1 x 9	2 x 9	3 x 9	4 x 9	5 x 9	6 x 9	7 x 9	8 x 9	9 x 9	10 x 9
1 x 10	2 x 10	3 x 10	4 x 10	5 x 10	6 x 10	7 x 10	8 x 10	9 x 10	10 x 10

Date I set goal: _____

I have _____ days to study.

Date when I'll be tested next: _____

_____	Facts I have learned since last time.
_____	Facts I've decided to learn for next time.
_____	Facts I still need to practice a little more.

1 x 1	2 x 1	3 x 1	4 x 1	5 x 1	6 x 1	7 x 1	8 x 1	9 x 1	10 x 1
1 x 2	2 x 2	3 x 2	4 x 2	5 x 2	6 x 2	7 x 2	8 x 2	9 x 2	10 x 2
1 x 3	2 x 3	3 x 3	4 x 3	5 x 3	6 x 3	7 x 3	8 x 3	9 x 3	10 x 3
1 x 4	2 x 4	3 x 4	4 x 4	5 x 4	6 x 4	7 x 4	8 x 4	9 x 4	10 x 4
1 x 5	2 x 5	3 x 5	4 x 5	5 x 5	6 x 5	7 x 5	8 x 5	9 x 5	10 x 5
1 x 6	2 x 6	3 x 6	4 x 6	5 x 6	6 x 6	7 x 6	8 x 6	9 x 6	10 x 6
1 x 7	2 x 7	3 x 7	4 x 7	5 x 7	6 x 7	7 x 7	8 x 7	9 x 7	10 x 7
1 x 8	2 x 8	3 x 8	4 x 8	5 x 8	6 x 8	7 x 8	8 x 8	9 x 8	10 x 8
1 x 9	2 x 9	3 x 9	4 x 9	5 x 9	6 x 9	7 x 9	8 x 9	9 x 9	10 x 9
1 x 10	2 x 10	3 x 10	4 x 10	5 x 10	6 x 10	7 x 10	8 x 10	9 x 10	10 x 10

Division Facts
Student Goal-Setting Sheet

I keep getting CLOSER to knowing all my facts!

Name _____

1 ÷ 1	2 ÷ 2	3 ÷ 3	4 ÷ 4	5 ÷ 5	6 ÷ 6	7 ÷ 7	8 ÷ 8	9 ÷ 9	10 ÷ 10
2 ÷ 1	4 ÷ 2	6 ÷ 3	8 ÷ 4	10 ÷ 5	12 ÷ 6	14 ÷ 7	16 ÷ 8	18 ÷ 9	20 ÷ 10
3 ÷ 1	6 ÷ 2	9 ÷ 3	12 ÷ 4	15 ÷ 5	18 ÷ 6	21 ÷ 7	24 ÷ 8	27 ÷ 9	30 ÷ 10
4 ÷ 1	8 ÷ 2	12 ÷ 3	16 ÷ 4	20 ÷ 5	24 ÷ 6	28 ÷ 7	32 ÷ 8	36 ÷ 9	40 ÷ 10
5 ÷ 1	10 ÷ 2	15 ÷ 3	20 ÷ 4	25 ÷ 5	30 ÷ 6	35 ÷ 7	40 ÷ 8	45 ÷ 9	50 ÷ 10
6 ÷ 1	12 ÷ 2	18 ÷ 3	24 ÷ 4	30 ÷ 5	36 ÷ 6	42 ÷ 7	48 ÷ 8	54 ÷ 9	60 ÷ 10
7 ÷ 1	14 ÷ 2	21 ÷ 3	28 ÷ 4	35 ÷ 5	42 ÷ 6	49 ÷ 7	56 ÷ 8	63 ÷ 9	70 ÷ 10
8 ÷ 1	16 ÷ 2	24 ÷ 3	32 ÷ 4	40 ÷ 5	48 ÷ 6	56 ÷ 7	64 ÷ 8	72 ÷ 9	80 ÷ 10
9 ÷ 1	18 ÷ 2	27 ÷ 3	36 ÷ 4	45 ÷ 5	54 ÷ 6	63 ÷ 7	72 ÷ 8	81 ÷ 9	90 ÷ 10
10 ÷ 1	20 ÷ 2	30 ÷ 3	40 ÷ 4	50 ÷ 5	60 ÷ 6	70 ÷ 7	80 ÷ 8	90 ÷ 9	100 ÷ 10

Date I set goal: _____

I have _____ days to study.

Date when I'll be tested next: _____

[ ] Facts I have learned since last time.

[ ] Facts I've decided to learn for next time.

[ ] Facts I still need to practice a little more.

1 ÷ 1	2 ÷ 2	3 ÷ 3	4 ÷ 4	5 ÷ 5	6 ÷ 6	7 ÷ 7	8 ÷ 8	9 ÷ 9	10 ÷ 10
2 ÷ 1	4 ÷ 2	6 ÷ 3	8 ÷ 4	10 ÷ 5	12 ÷ 6	14 ÷ 7	16 ÷ 8	18 ÷ 9	20 ÷ 10
3 ÷ 1	6 ÷ 2	9 ÷ 3	12 ÷ 4	15 ÷ 5	18 ÷ 6	21 ÷ 7	24 ÷ 8	27 ÷ 9	30 ÷ 10
4 ÷ 1	8 ÷ 2	12 ÷ 3	16 ÷ 4	20 ÷ 5	24 ÷ 6	28 ÷ 7	32 ÷ 8	36 ÷ 9	40 ÷ 10
5 ÷ 1	10 ÷ 2	15 ÷ 3	20 ÷ 4	25 ÷ 5	30 ÷ 6	35 ÷ 7	40 ÷ 8	45 ÷ 9	50 ÷ 10
6 ÷ 1	12 ÷ 2	18 ÷ 3	24 ÷ 4	30 ÷ 5	36 ÷ 6	42 ÷ 7	48 ÷ 8	54 ÷ 9	60 ÷ 10
7 ÷ 1	14 ÷ 2	21 ÷ 3	28 ÷ 4	35 ÷ 5	42 ÷ 6	49 ÷ 7	56 ÷ 8	63 ÷ 9	70 ÷ 10
8 ÷ 1	16 ÷ 2	24 ÷ 3	32 ÷ 4	40 ÷ 5	48 ÷ 6	56 ÷ 7	64 ÷ 8	72 ÷ 9	80 ÷ 10
9 ÷ 1	18 ÷ 2	27 ÷ 3	36 ÷ 4	45 ÷ 5	54 ÷ 6	63 ÷ 7	72 ÷ 8	81 ÷ 9	90 ÷ 10
10 ÷ 1	20 ÷ 2	30 ÷ 3	40 ÷ 4	50 ÷ 5	60 ÷ 6	70 ÷ 7	80 ÷ 8	90 ÷ 9	100 ÷ 10

Student _____

1 × 1	2 × 1	3 × 1	4 × 1	5 × 1	6 × 1	7 × 1	8 × 1	9 × 1	10 × 1
1 × 2	2 × 2	3 × 2	4 × 2	5 × 2	6 × 2	7 × 2	8 × 2	9 × 2	10 × 2
1 × 3	2 × 3	3 × 3	4 × 3	5 × 3	6 × 3	7 × 3	8 × 3	9 × 3	10 × 3
1 × 4	2 × 4	3 × 4	4 × 4	5 × 4	6 × 4	7 × 4	8 × 4	9 × 4	10 × 4
1 × 5	2 × 5	3 × 5	4 × 5	5 × 5	6 × 5	7 × 5	8 × 5	9 × 5	10 × 5
1 × 6	2 × 6	3 × 6	4 × 6	5 × 6	6 × 6	7 × 6	8 × 6	9 × 6	10 × 6
1 × 7	2 × 7	3 × 7	4 × 7	5 × 7	6 × 7	7 × 7	8 × 7	9 × 7	10 × 7
1 × 8	2 × 8	3 × 8	4 × 8	5 × 8	6 × 8	7 × 8	8 × 8	9 × 8	10 × 8
1 × 9	2 × 9	3 × 9	4 × 9	5 × 9	6 × 9	7 × 9	8 × 9	9 × 9	10 × 9
1 × 10	2 × 10	3 × 10	4 × 10	5 × 10	6 × 10	7 × 10	8 × 10	9 × 10	10 × 10

(This multiplication fact grid, 1 × 1 through 10 × 10, is repeated in eight identical blocks on the page, each headed by a blank "Student _____" line.)

Student _____

Student _____

Student _____

Student _____

Student _____

Student _____

Student _____

Student________________

1 ÷ 1	2 ÷ 2	3 ÷ 3	4 ÷ 4	5 ÷ 5	6 ÷ 6	7 ÷ 7	8 ÷ 8	9 ÷ 9	10 ÷ 10	12 ÷ 12
2 ÷ 1	4 ÷ 2	6 ÷ 3	8 ÷ 4	10 ÷ 5	12 ÷ 6	14 ÷ 7	16 ÷ 8	18 ÷ 9	20 ÷ 10	24 ÷ 12
3 ÷ 1	6 ÷ 2	9 ÷ 3	12 ÷ 4	15 ÷ 5	18 ÷ 6	21 ÷ 7	24 ÷ 8	27 ÷ 9	30 ÷ 10	36 ÷ 12
4 ÷ 1	8 ÷ 2	12 ÷ 3	16 ÷ 4	20 ÷ 5	24 ÷ 6	28 ÷ 7	32 ÷ 8	36 ÷ 9	40 ÷ 10	48 ÷ 12
5 ÷ 1	10 ÷ 2	15 ÷ 3	20 ÷ 4	25 ÷ 5	30 ÷ 6	35 ÷ 7	40 ÷ 8	45 ÷ 9	50 ÷ 10	60 ÷ 12
6 ÷ 1	12 ÷ 2	18 ÷ 3	24 ÷ 4	30 ÷ 5	36 ÷ 6	42 ÷ 7	48 ÷ 8	54 ÷ 9	60 ÷ 10	72 ÷ 12
7 ÷ 1	14 ÷ 2	21 ÷ 3	28 ÷ 4	35 ÷ 5	42 ÷ 6	49 ÷ 7	56 ÷ 8	63 ÷ 9	70 ÷ 10	84 ÷ 12
8 ÷ 1	16 ÷ 2	24 ÷ 3	32 ÷ 4	40 ÷ 5	48 ÷ 6	56 ÷ 7	64 ÷ 8	72 ÷ 9	80 ÷ 10	96 ÷ 12
9 ÷ 1	18 ÷ 2	27 ÷ 3	36 ÷ 4	45 ÷ 5	54 ÷ 6	63 ÷ 7	72 ÷ 8	81 ÷ 9	90 ÷ 10	108 ÷ 12
10 ÷ 1	20 ÷ 2	30 ÷ 3	40 ÷ 4	50 ÷ 5	60 ÷ 6	70 ÷ 7	80 ÷ 8	90 ÷ 9	100 ÷ 10	120 ÷ 12

Student________________

1 ÷ 1	2 ÷ 2	3 ÷ 3	4 ÷ 4	5 ÷ 5	6 ÷ 6	7 ÷ 7	8 ÷ 8	9 ÷ 9	10 ÷ 10	12 ÷ 12
2 ÷ 1	4 ÷ 2	6 ÷ 3	8 ÷ 4	10 ÷ 5	12 ÷ 6	14 ÷ 7	16 ÷ 8	18 ÷ 9	20 ÷ 10	24 ÷ 12
3 ÷ 1	6 ÷ 2	9 ÷ 3	12 ÷ 4	15 ÷ 5	18 ÷ 6	21 ÷ 7	24 ÷ 8	27 ÷ 9	30 ÷ 10	36 ÷ 12
4 ÷ 1	8 ÷ 2	12 ÷ 3	16 ÷ 4	20 ÷ 5	24 ÷ 6	28 ÷ 7	32 ÷ 8	36 ÷ 9	40 ÷ 10	48 ÷ 12
5 ÷ 1	10 ÷ 2	15 ÷ 3	20 ÷ 4	25 ÷ 5	30 ÷ 6	35 ÷ 7	40 ÷ 8	45 ÷ 9	50 ÷ 10	60 ÷ 12
6 ÷ 1	12 ÷ 2	18 ÷ 3	24 ÷ 4	30 ÷ 5	36 ÷ 6	42 ÷ 7	48 ÷ 8	54 ÷ 9	60 ÷ 10	72 ÷ 12
7 ÷ 1	14 ÷ 2	21 ÷ 3	28 ÷ 4	35 ÷ 5	42 ÷ 6	49 ÷ 7	56 ÷ 8	63 ÷ 9	70 ÷ 10	84 ÷ 12
8 ÷ 1	16 ÷ 2	24 ÷ 3	32 ÷ 4	40 ÷ 5	48 ÷ 6	56 ÷ 7	64 ÷ 8	72 ÷ 9	80 ÷ 10	96 ÷ 12
9 ÷ 1	18 ÷ 2	27 ÷ 3	36 ÷ 4	45 ÷ 5	54 ÷ 6	63 ÷ 7	72 ÷ 8	81 ÷ 9	90 ÷ 10	108 ÷ 12
10 ÷ 1	20 ÷ 2	30 ÷ 3	40 ÷ 4	50 ÷ 5	60 ÷ 6	70 ÷ 7	80 ÷ 8	90 ÷ 9	100 ÷ 10	120 ÷ 12

Student________________

1 ÷ 1	2 ÷ 2	3 ÷ 3	4 ÷ 4	5 ÷ 5	6 ÷ 6	7 ÷ 7	8 ÷ 8	9 ÷ 9	10 ÷ 10	12 ÷ 12
2 ÷ 1	4 ÷ 2	6 ÷ 3	8 ÷ 4	10 ÷ 5	12 ÷ 6	14 ÷ 7	16 ÷ 8	18 ÷ 9	20 ÷ 10	24 ÷ 12
3 ÷ 1	6 ÷ 2	9 ÷ 3	12 ÷ 4	15 ÷ 5	18 ÷ 6	21 ÷ 7	24 ÷ 8	27 ÷ 9	30 ÷ 10	36 ÷ 12
4 ÷ 1	8 ÷ 2	12 ÷ 3	16 ÷ 4	20 ÷ 5	24 ÷ 6	28 ÷ 7	32 ÷ 8	36 ÷ 9	40 ÷ 10	48 ÷ 12
5 ÷ 1	10 ÷ 2	15 ÷ 3	20 ÷ 4	25 ÷ 5	30 ÷ 6	35 ÷ 7	40 ÷ 8	45 ÷ 9	50 ÷ 10	60 ÷ 12
6 ÷ 1	12 ÷ 2	18 ÷ 3	24 ÷ 4	30 ÷ 5	36 ÷ 6	42 ÷ 7	48 ÷ 8	54 ÷ 9	60 ÷ 10	72 ÷ 12
7 ÷ 1	14 ÷ 2	21 ÷ 3	28 ÷ 4	35 ÷ 5	42 ÷ 6	49 ÷ 7	56 ÷ 8	63 ÷ 9	70 ÷ 10	84 ÷ 12
8 ÷ 1	16 ÷ 2	24 ÷ 3	32 ÷ 4	40 ÷ 5	48 ÷ 6	56 ÷ 7	64 ÷ 8	72 ÷ 9	80 ÷ 10	96 ÷ 12
9 ÷ 1	18 ÷ 2	27 ÷ 3	36 ÷ 4	45 ÷ 5	54 ÷ 6	63 ÷ 7	72 ÷ 8	81 ÷ 9	90 ÷ 10	108 ÷ 12
10 ÷ 1	20 ÷ 2	30 ÷ 3	40 ÷ 4	50 ÷ 5	60 ÷ 6	70 ÷ 7	80 ÷ 8	90 ÷ 9	100 ÷ 10	120 ÷ 12

Student________________

1 ÷ 1	2 ÷ 2	3 ÷ 3	4 ÷ 4	5 ÷ 5	6 ÷ 6	7 ÷ 7	8 ÷ 8	9 ÷ 9	10 ÷ 10	12 ÷ 12
2 ÷ 1	4 ÷ 2	6 ÷ 3	8 ÷ 4	10 ÷ 5	12 ÷ 6	14 ÷ 7	16 ÷ 8	18 ÷ 9	20 ÷ 10	24 ÷ 12
3 ÷ 1	6 ÷ 2	9 ÷ 3	12 ÷ 4	15 ÷ 5	18 ÷ 6	21 ÷ 7	24 ÷ 8	27 ÷ 9	30 ÷ 10	36 ÷ 12
4 ÷ 1	8 ÷ 2	12 ÷ 3	16 ÷ 4	20 ÷ 5	24 ÷ 6	28 ÷ 7	32 ÷ 8	36 ÷ 9	40 ÷ 10	48 ÷ 12
5 ÷ 1	10 ÷ 2	15 ÷ 3	20 ÷ 4	25 ÷ 5	30 ÷ 6	35 ÷ 7	40 ÷ 8	45 ÷ 9	50 ÷ 10	60 ÷ 12
6 ÷ 1	12 ÷ 2	18 ÷ 3	24 ÷ 4	30 ÷ 5	36 ÷ 6	42 ÷ 7	48 ÷ 8	54 ÷ 9	60 ÷ 10	72 ÷ 12
7 ÷ 1	14 ÷ 2	21 ÷ 3	28 ÷ 4	35 ÷ 5	42 ÷ 6	49 ÷ 7	56 ÷ 8	63 ÷ 9	70 ÷ 10	84 ÷ 12
8 ÷ 1	16 ÷ 2	24 ÷ 3	32 ÷ 4	40 ÷ 5	48 ÷ 6	56 ÷ 7	64 ÷ 8	72 ÷ 9	80 ÷ 10	96 ÷ 12
9 ÷ 1	18 ÷ 2	27 ÷ 3	36 ÷ 4	45 ÷ 5	54 ÷ 6	63 ÷ 7	72 ÷ 8	81 ÷ 9	90 ÷ 10	108 ÷ 12
10 ÷ 1	20 ÷ 2	30 ÷ 3	40 ÷ 4	50 ÷ 5	60 ÷ 6	70 ÷ 7	80 ÷ 8	90 ÷ 9	100 ÷ 10	120 ÷ 12

Student________________

1 ÷ 1	2 ÷ 2	3 ÷ 3	4 ÷ 4	5 ÷ 5	6 ÷ 6	7 ÷ 7	8 ÷ 8	9 ÷ 9	10 ÷ 10	12 ÷ 12
2 ÷ 1	4 ÷ 2	6 ÷ 3	8 ÷ 4	10 ÷ 5	12 ÷ 6	14 ÷ 7	16 ÷ 8	18 ÷ 9	20 ÷ 10	24 ÷ 12
3 ÷ 1	6 ÷ 2	9 ÷ 3	12 ÷ 4	15 ÷ 5	18 ÷ 6	21 ÷ 7	24 ÷ 8	27 ÷ 9	30 ÷ 10	36 ÷ 12
4 ÷ 1	8 ÷ 2	12 ÷ 3	16 ÷ 4	20 ÷ 5	24 ÷ 6	28 ÷ 7	32 ÷ 8	36 ÷ 9	40 ÷ 10	48 ÷ 12
5 ÷ 1	10 ÷ 2	15 ÷ 3	20 ÷ 4	25 ÷ 5	30 ÷ 6	35 ÷ 7	40 ÷ 8	45 ÷ 9	50 ÷ 10	60 ÷ 12
6 ÷ 1	12 ÷ 2	18 ÷ 3	24 ÷ 4	30 ÷ 5	36 ÷ 6	42 ÷ 7	48 ÷ 8	54 ÷ 9	60 ÷ 10	72 ÷ 12
7 ÷ 1	14 ÷ 2	21 ÷ 3	28 ÷ 4	35 ÷ 5	42 ÷ 6	49 ÷ 7	56 ÷ 8	63 ÷ 9	70 ÷ 10	84 ÷ 12
8 ÷ 1	16 ÷ 2	24 ÷ 3	32 ÷ 4	40 ÷ 5	48 ÷ 6	56 ÷ 7	64 ÷ 8	72 ÷ 9	80 ÷ 10	96 ÷ 12
9 ÷ 1	18 ÷ 2	27 ÷ 3	36 ÷ 4	45 ÷ 5	54 ÷ 6	63 ÷ 7	72 ÷ 8	81 ÷ 9	90 ÷ 10	108 ÷ 12
10 ÷ 1	20 ÷ 2	30 ÷ 3	40 ÷ 4	50 ÷ 5	60 ÷ 6	70 ÷ 7	80 ÷ 8	90 ÷ 9	100 ÷ 10	120 ÷ 12

Student________________

1 ÷ 1	2 ÷ 2	3 ÷ 3	4 ÷ 4	5 ÷ 5	6 ÷ 6	7 ÷ 7	8 ÷ 8	9 ÷ 9	10 ÷ 10	12 ÷ 12
2 ÷ 1	4 ÷ 2	6 ÷ 3	8 ÷ 4	10 ÷ 5	12 ÷ 6	14 ÷ 7	16 ÷ 8	18 ÷ 9	20 ÷ 10	24 ÷ 12
3 ÷ 1	6 ÷ 2	9 ÷ 3	12 ÷ 4	15 ÷ 5	18 ÷ 6	21 ÷ 7	24 ÷ 8	27 ÷ 9	30 ÷ 10	36 ÷ 12
4 ÷ 1	8 ÷ 2	12 ÷ 3	16 ÷ 4	20 ÷ 5	24 ÷ 6	28 ÷ 7	32 ÷ 8	36 ÷ 9	40 ÷ 10	48 ÷ 12
5 ÷ 1	10 ÷ 2	15 ÷ 3	20 ÷ 4	25 ÷ 5	30 ÷ 6	35 ÷ 7	40 ÷ 8	45 ÷ 9	50 ÷ 10	60 ÷ 12
6 ÷ 1	12 ÷ 2	18 ÷ 3	24 ÷ 4	30 ÷ 5	36 ÷ 6	42 ÷ 7	48 ÷ 8	54 ÷ 9	60 ÷ 10	72 ÷ 12
7 ÷ 1	14 ÷ 2	21 ÷ 3	28 ÷ 4	35 ÷ 5	42 ÷ 6	49 ÷ 7	56 ÷ 8	63 ÷ 9	70 ÷ 10	84 ÷ 12
8 ÷ 1	16 ÷ 2	24 ÷ 3	32 ÷ 4	40 ÷ 5	48 ÷ 6	56 ÷ 7	64 ÷ 8	72 ÷ 9	80 ÷ 10	96 ÷ 12
9 ÷ 1	18 ÷ 2	27 ÷ 3	36 ÷ 4	45 ÷ 5	54 ÷ 6	63 ÷ 7	72 ÷ 8	81 ÷ 9	90 ÷ 10	108 ÷ 12
10 ÷ 1	20 ÷ 2	30 ÷ 3	40 ÷ 4	50 ÷ 5	60 ÷ 6	70 ÷ 7	80 ÷ 8	90 ÷ 9	100 ÷ 10	120 ÷ 12

Student________________

1 ÷ 1	2 ÷ 2	3 ÷ 3	4 ÷ 4	5 ÷ 5	6 ÷ 6	7 ÷ 7	8 ÷ 8	9 ÷ 9	10 ÷ 10	12 ÷ 12
2 ÷ 1	4 ÷ 2	6 ÷ 3	8 ÷ 4	10 ÷ 5	12 ÷ 6	14 ÷ 7	16 ÷ 8	18 ÷ 9	20 ÷ 10	24 ÷ 12
3 ÷ 1	6 ÷ 2	9 ÷ 3	12 ÷ 4	15 ÷ 5	18 ÷ 6	21 ÷ 7	24 ÷ 8	27 ÷ 9	30 ÷ 10	36 ÷ 12
4 ÷ 1	8 ÷ 2	12 ÷ 3	16 ÷ 4	20 ÷ 5	24 ÷ 6	28 ÷ 7	32 ÷ 8	36 ÷ 9	40 ÷ 10	48 ÷ 12
5 ÷ 1	10 ÷ 2	15 ÷ 3	20 ÷ 4	25 ÷ 5	30 ÷ 6	35 ÷ 7	40 ÷ 8	45 ÷ 9	50 ÷ 10	60 ÷ 12
6 ÷ 1	12 ÷ 2	18 ÷ 3	24 ÷ 4	30 ÷ 5	36 ÷ 6	42 ÷ 7	48 ÷ 8	54 ÷ 9	60 ÷ 10	72 ÷ 12
7 ÷ 1	14 ÷ 2	21 ÷ 3	28 ÷ 4	35 ÷ 5	42 ÷ 6	49 ÷ 7	56 ÷ 8	63 ÷ 9	70 ÷ 10	84 ÷ 12
8 ÷ 1	16 ÷ 2	24 ÷ 3	32 ÷ 4	40 ÷ 5	48 ÷ 6	56 ÷ 7	64 ÷ 8	72 ÷ 9	80 ÷ 10	96 ÷ 12
9 ÷ 1	18 ÷ 2	27 ÷ 3	36 ÷ 4	45 ÷ 5	54 ÷ 6	63 ÷ 7	72 ÷ 8	81 ÷ 9	90 ÷ 10	108 ÷ 12
10 ÷ 1	20 ÷ 2	30 ÷ 3	40 ÷ 4	50 ÷ 5	60 ÷ 6	70 ÷ 7	80 ÷ 8	90 ÷ 9	100 ÷ 10	120 ÷ 12

Student________________

1 ÷ 1	2 ÷ 2	3 ÷ 3	4 ÷ 4	5 ÷ 5	6 ÷ 6	7 ÷ 7	8 ÷ 8	9 ÷ 9	10 ÷ 10	12 ÷ 12
2 ÷ 1	4 ÷ 2	6 ÷ 3	8 ÷ 4	10 ÷ 5	12 ÷ 6	14 ÷ 7	16 ÷ 8	18 ÷ 9	20 ÷ 10	24 ÷ 12
3 ÷ 1	6 ÷ 2	9 ÷ 3	12 ÷ 4	15 ÷ 5	18 ÷ 6	21 ÷ 7	24 ÷ 8	27 ÷ 9	30 ÷ 10	36 ÷ 12
4 ÷ 1	8 ÷ 2	12 ÷ 3	16 ÷ 4	20 ÷ 5	24 ÷ 6	28 ÷ 7	32 ÷ 8	36 ÷ 9	40 ÷ 10	48 ÷ 12
5 ÷ 1	10 ÷ 2	15 ÷ 3	20 ÷ 4	25 ÷ 5	30 ÷ 6	35 ÷ 7	40 ÷ 8	45 ÷ 9	50 ÷ 10	60 ÷ 12
6 ÷ 1	12 ÷ 2	18 ÷ 3	24 ÷ 4	30 ÷ 5	36 ÷ 6	42 ÷ 7	48 ÷ 8	54 ÷ 9	60 ÷ 10	72 ÷ 12
7 ÷ 1	14 ÷ 2	21 ÷ 3	28 ÷ 4	35 ÷ 5	42 ÷ 6	49 ÷ 7	56 ÷ 8	63 ÷ 9	70 ÷ 10	84 ÷ 12
8 ÷ 1	16 ÷ 2	24 ÷ 3	32 ÷ 4	40 ÷ 5	48 ÷ 6	56 ÷ 7	64 ÷ 8	72 ÷ 9	80 ÷ 10	96 ÷ 12
9 ÷ 1	18 ÷ 2	27 ÷ 3	36 ÷ 4	45 ÷ 5	54 ÷ 6	63 ÷ 7	72 ÷ 8	81 ÷ 9	90 ÷ 10	108 ÷ 12
10 ÷ 1	20 ÷ 2	30 ÷ 3	40 ÷ 4	50 ÷ 5	60 ÷ 6	70 ÷ 7	80 ÷ 8	90 ÷ 9	100 ÷ 10	120 ÷ 12

Multiplying Fractions

Suggested Grade

6

Outcomes

- To show in picture form how to multiply fractions.
- To write a word problem for multiplying fractions.

Materials

- Paper and pencil

Assessment Activity

1. Write this problem on the board: $\frac{2}{5}$ of $\frac{1}{3}$

2. Tell students you are going to tell them a story and will draw a picture for this expression.

3. "My neighbor's garden is one-third vegetables and two-thirds flowers." (Draw the garden and hash one-third of it.)

4. "Two-fifths of her vegetables are bean plants." (Divide the one-third into fifths. Shade or write in beans in two of the five parts.)

5. "What fraction of the garden is bean plants?" (Divide the remaining two-thirds into fifths so students can see all three parts divided into equal parts.)

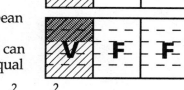

6. Write this problem on the board: $\frac{2}{3}$ of $\frac{2}{5}$. Write a story for it with the students. Have them draw a picture as they create the word problem.

7. Have each student draw a picture and write a word problem for the following expressions: $\frac{1}{5}$ of $\frac{1}{2}$; $\frac{3}{4}$ of $\frac{1}{3}$; $\frac{2}{5}$ of $\frac{3}{4}$.

Notes

- This activity assumes students know how to show fractions with pictures and are comfortable writing their own word problems.

- Point out to those students who try to switch the fractions (commutative property) that they have the same answer but the word problems are not the same.

- This can be used as a self-assessment by having each student tell you his or her comfort level for doing fraction problems in picture and story form.

- Students' work can be put in portfolios.

Content Areas

Fractions, Decimals, Ratio, and Percent

Activity Type

Manipulative
➤ Representational
➤ Abstract

Strategies

Interviews

Observations

➤ Portfolios
➤ Student Self-Assessment
➤ Performance Tasks
➤ Student Writing

Outcomes

- To show in picture form how to multiply fractions.
- To write a word problem for multiplying fractions.

Sample Performance Indicators for Student Who Is

Not Understanding	Developing	Understanding/Applying
▲ Cannot draw a picture for the fractions ▲ Does not know where to begin ▲ Cannot write a word problem	▲ Can draw a picture for each fraction but cannot put them together ▲ Confuses the order of the fractions when drawing and writing about them ▲ Can write a word problem for one fraction but needs help with the other	▲ Can draw a picture for the fractions ▲ Knows the order in which to draw and write about the fractions ▲ Can write a word problem that fits the fractions

Nonstandard Measurement:
Guess and Check

Outcomes

- To estimate length in a nonstandard measurement.
- To measure length in nonstandard units.

Materials

- Book with pictures of things to measure (one per student)
- Unifix® cubes, ice-cream sticks, paper clips, counting bears, or any other objects that can be used as nonstandard units
- Guess and Check Worksheet

Assessment Activity

1. Tell students that they are going to measure each other's length with _____ (a nonstandard unit, e.g., Unifix® cubes).
2. Choose a student to model the activity. Have students estimate that student's length.
3. Have the student lie on the floor. Place a row of _____ (e.g., Unifix® cubes) along the student.
4. Have a different student break the _____ (Unifix® cubes) into groups of 10.
5. Count the _____ (Unifix® cubes) by tens and ones.
6. Show students how to record their answers.

GUESS		CHECK	
tens	ones	tens	ones

7. Tell students that they are going to predict and then use the _____ (Unifix® cubes) to measure things around the room. Give each student a book or a list, and point out the things that they will measure.
8. Have each student work independently.
9. Walk around the room, observing different students.
10. Collect the Guess and Check Worksheets to evaluate students' progress as well.

Notes

- You may want students to record "guesses" in crayon.
- Different nonstandard units (e.g., Unifix® cubes, ice-cream sticks) may be used on different days.

Content Areas

Measurement

Estimation and Mental Computation

Activity Type

➤ Manipulative

Representational

Abstract

Strategies

Interviews

➤ Observations

Portfolios

Student Self-Assessment

➤ Performance Tasks

Student Writing

Outcomes

- To estimate length in a nonstandard measurement.
- To measure length in nonstandard units.

Sample Performance Indicators for Student Who Is

Not Understanding	Developing	Understanding/Applying
▲ Plays with objects used to measure	▲ Can complete task if able to work with another student	▲ Completes task very quickly
▲ Copies from other students	▲ Tries to make reasonable predictions	▲ Can work independently
▲ Cannot make predictions	▲ Needs help with first measurement	▲ Is able to help others
▲ Does not lay units end to end	▲ Lays out units end to end	▲ Makes reasonable predictions
▲ Does not show understanding of a starting point	▲ Counts and records correctly	▲ Lays out units end to end
▲ Records answers incorrectly		▲ Counts and records correctly

Guess and Check

Name _____ Date _____

Object	Guess		Check	
	tens	ones	tens	ones

1. _____

Guess · Check

| | tens | ones | tens | ones |

2. _____

Guess · Check

| | tens | ones | tens | ones |

3. _____

Guess · Check

| | tens | ones | tens | ones |

4. _____

Guess · Check

| | tens | ones | tens | ones |

5. _____

Number Families

Outcome

To demonstrate understanding of number families.

Materials

- Chalkboard
- Large opaque sheet of paper

Assessment Activity

1. Make a line of four large dots on the chalkboard. Write the numeral 4 nearby.
2. Tell the student to cover his or her eyes. Cover two dots with the opaque paper. Tell the student to uncover his or her eyes. Ask, "How many dots are covered?" (Expect an almost instantaneous answer.)
3. Have the student cover his or her eyes again. Cover one dot. Uncover the eyes. Ask, "How many dots are covered?"
4. Repeat the procedure for three, four, and zero dots.

Notes

- The same technique may be used for all other number families.
- Watch for students silently counting.
- The same technique may be followed by using an overhead projector (especially good for whole-class participation).
- Number families may also be assessed by hiding buttons or other objects in your hands. "I have 5 buttons. Here are 2. How many am I hiding?"
- This activity is adapted from *Mathematics Their Way* by Mary Baratta-Lorton.

Content Areas

Addition and Subtraction

Activity Type

Manipulative

➤ Representational

Abstract

Strategies

Interviews

➤ Observations

Portfolios

Student Self-Assessment

➤ Performance Tasks

Student Writing

Outcome

- To demonstrate understanding of number families.

Sample Performance Indicators for Student Who Is

Not Understanding	Developing	Understanding/Applying
▲ Answers incorrectly ▲ Calls the number that is shown	▲ Answers correctly but not immediately ▲ Answers correctly for some questions	▲ Immediately gives the correct answer ▲ Answers correctly for the entire number family

Number Theory Clues

Outcomes

- To apply number theory concepts.
- To create and solve logic puzzles.

Materials

- Paper and pencil

Assessment Activity

1. Have the student solve a number puzzle that uses number theory concepts as clues. Clues for a number puzzle with an answer of 45 follow:
   - ▲ My number is between the thirteenth and sixteenth prime numbers.
   - ▲ Two prime numbers are factors of my number.
   - ▲ The prime factors of my number are less than ten.
   - ▲ My number is an odd number.
2. Do several puzzles if necessary.
3. Have the class write one puzzle together. This shows the process.
4. Have students write number puzzles which use number theory concepts as clues.
5. You may want to direct students to use certain terms in their clues (e.g., one clue must use least common multiple).

Notes

- Puzzles can be tested and critiqued by other students.
- This activity assumes students have worked with logic puzzles.
- If students have not practiced doing logic problems, you may want to work and discuss multiple examples.

Strategies

Interviews

Observations

Portfolios

Student Self-Assessment

Performance Tasks

➤ Student Writing

Outcomes

- To apply number theory concepts.
- To create and solve logic puzzles.

Sample Performance Indicators for Student Who Is

Not Understanding	Developing	Understanding/Applying
▲ Writes clues that indicate the number theory concept is not understood ▲ Writes clues that do not make sense ▲ May write some simple clues, but clues do not form a puzzle ▲ Has difficulty solving puzzles	▲ Can correctly use most number theory concepts in writing clues ▲ May rely on certain concepts in writing clues ▲ Can generate clues, but clues do not necessarily narrow down possible answers ▲ Can solve puzzles, but may have difficulty critiquing or explaining needed changes	▲ Can correctly use number theory concepts in writing clues ▲ Writes coherent clues ▲ Can write clues that narrow down possible answers ▲ May like doing and making more involved or detailed puzzles ▲ Can solve and critique other students' puzzles

Patterns

Outcome

■ To identify, create, extend, and translate patterns.

Materials

■ Unifix® cubes (at least 20 of three different colors)
■ Pattern cards
■ Recorded pattern

Assessment Activity

Identify and Extend Pattern

Create an "AAB" pattern with two colors of Unifix® cubes

A. Ask the student, "What cube would I put next?"

B. Then ask, "Can you extend the pattern the length of your arm?"

Create and Extend Pattern

A. Give the student a pattern description card (e.g., ABCABCABC, ABBABBABB).

B. Ask the student to build the pattern with Unifix® cubes.

C. Have the student describe the pattern.

D. Encourage the student to copy and extend the pattern.

Create and Extend Pattern Two

A. Give the student 20 cubes of two colors.

B. Ask the student to build a pattern.

C. Ask the student to describe his or her pattern and to tell how it would be extended.

Create and Extend Pattern Three

A. Give the student 20 cubes of three colors.

B. Ask the student to build a pattern.

C. Ask the student to describe the pattern and how it would be extended.

Translate Pattern

Have the student use a recorded pattern (his or her own or teacher-generated) and translate (name) it into as many different visual or sound patterns as he or she can (e.g., green, green, white; or AAB or snap, snap, clap).

Content Areas

Algebraic Ideas

Problem Solving and Logic

Activity Type

➤ Manipulative

Representational

Abstract

Strategies

➤ Interviews

➤ Observations

Portfolios

Student Self-Assessment

➤ Performance Tasks

Student Writing

Insert Missing Elements into Pattern

A. Teacher creates a pattern with two colors of Unifix® cubes (not snapped), omitting one and leaving a space in the series.

B. Ask the student what cube would go into the empty space.

Notes

- If Create and Extend Patterns are not challenging enough, introduce a more complicated pattern, increasing the number of elements within the repeated sequence (e.g., AABCCB).

- Similar tasks could be designed to assess students' understanding of growing patterns (e.g., AB, AAB, AAAB, AAAAB, . . . ; 1, 3, 5, 7, 9, . . .).

- Questions for patterning

  a. Can you describe your pattern?

  b. Can you read this pattern?

  c. What is one way to read this pattern? Another?

  d. Can you show me more of this pattern?

  e. Can you explain your pattern?

  f. Can you copy this pattern?

  g. Can you extend the pattern?

  h. Can you create a new pattern?

  i. Can you show this pattern in another way?

  j. Can you explain _____'s pattern?

Outcome

■ To identify, create, extend, and translate patterns.

Sample Performance Indicators for Student Who Is

Not Understanding	Developing	Understanding/Applying
Identify ▲ Is unable to see repetitiveness of pattern (isolate one repetition) ▲ Is unable to read pattern using letter names or attribute names	**Identify** ▲ Sees repetitiveness and can read with prompts	**Identify** ▲ Reads pattern without hesitation in a variety of ways
Create ▲ Randomly places objects and does not create a pattern	**Create** ▲ Creates one or two repetitions of pattern ▲ Can create some patterns	**Create** ▲ Discovers numerous ways to pattern materials
Extend ▲ Extends pattern by randomly placing objects ▲ Cannot tell what comes next	**Extend** ▲ Extends only one repetition ▲ Can extend further with prompts	**Extend** ▲ Extends up to three times without hesitation
Translate ▲ Is unable to read pattern in another way	**Translate** ▲ Reads pattern, with prompts, in another way	**Translate** ▲ Reads pattern in a variety of formats
Insert Missing Element ▲ Cannot determine what is missing from pattern	**Insert Missing Element** ▲ Inserts missing cube into pattern with prompts	**Insert Missing Element** ▲ Inserts cube into pattern

The Assessment Activities

Pattern Cards

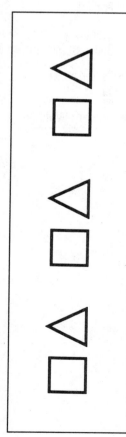

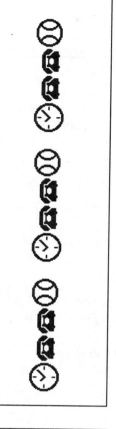

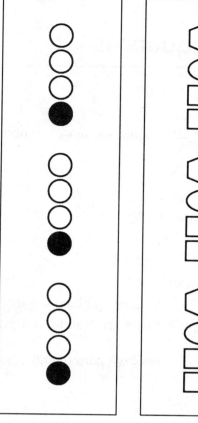

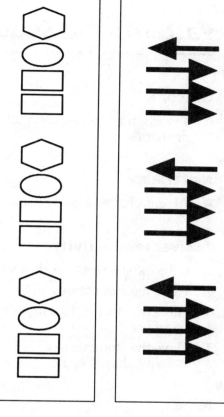

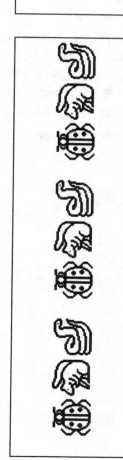

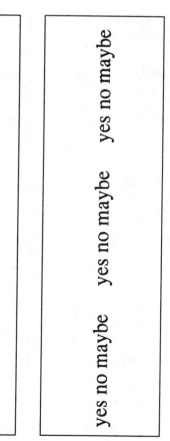

yes no maybe   yes no maybe

yes no maybe   yes no maybe

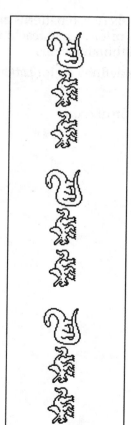

FFVV FFVV FFVV

Patterns and Sequences

Outcome

■ To recognize and extend patterns and sequences composed of numbers or shapes.

Materials

■ Algebra Patterns and Sequences Worksheet

Assessment Activity

1. Give the student a worksheet.
2. Have the student extend first patterns and then sequences.
3. Have the student identify whether a given series comprises a pattern or a sequence.
4. Have the student create his or her own pattern and sequence and describe the difference.

Notes

■ The worksheet presents the difference between patterns and sequences inductively and may be used without prior formal teaching to assess grade-level skills and more advanced thinking skills.

■ For bonus points, students may write definitions for *pattern* and *sequence*.

■ The key word for pattern is "repeat."

■ The key phrase for sequence is "goes on and on."

Content Areas

Algebraic Ideas

Problem Solving and Logic

Activity Type

Manipulative

➤ Representational

Abstract

Strategies

Interviews

Observations

Portfolios

Student Self-Assessment

➤ Performance Tasks

➤ Student Writing

Outcome

- To recognize and extend patterns and sequences composed of numbers or shapes.

Sample Performance Indicators for Student Who Is

Not Understanding	Developing	Understanding/Applying
▲ Cannot extend any or only a few of the sets correctly ▲ For sequences, repeats items to create a pattern ▲ Cannot follow examples provided	▲ Extends most of the sets correctly but cannot identify, distinguish, or create patterns and sequences ▲ Inconsistent; gets 50 to 80% of items in each part correct	▲ Extends nearly every set correctly ▲ Distinguishes between patterns and sequences ▲ Creates own pattern and sequence; does not copy one

Algebra Patterns and Sequences

Name _____ Date _____

A. Continue these **Patterns**

1) ▽ △ ▽ △ ____ ____ ____

2) ○ + □ ○ + □ ____ ____ ____

3) A E I O U A E ____ ____ ____

4) N O O N N O O ____ ____ ____

5) 6 8 6 8 ____ ____ ____

6) 3 4 5 4 3 4 ____ ____ ____

B. Continue these **Sequences**

1) 1 3 5 7 ____ ____ ____

2) 2 12 22 ____ ____ ____

3) C D E F ____ ____ ____

4) A C E G ____ ____ ____

5) L ⊔ ⌐ ____ ____ ____

6) ⬡ ⬡ ⬡ ____ ____ ____

C. Continue each line. Circle whether it is a **Pattern** or **Sequence.**

1) 1 2 3 1 2 3 ____ ____ ____ Pattern / Sequence

2) 2 4 8 16 ____ ____ ____ Pattern / Sequence

3) ╵ ╱ ╶ ╲ ____ ____ ____ Pattern / Sequence

4) O + O - O ____ ____ ____ Pattern / Sequence

D. Create your own:

1) Pattern _____

2) Sequence _____

E. Explain the difference between a pattern and a sequence.

Perimeter and Area
on the Geoboard

Outcomes

- To find shapes for given areas or perimeters.
- To demonstrate that figures with the same area and/or perimeters may have different shapes.

Materials

- Geoboards and geobands
- Geoboard Record Sheet

Assessment Activity

1. Distribute geoboards, geobands, and record sheets to students.
2. Give the following directions:
   a. Make a figure on your geoboard with 7 square units of area.
   b. Record your solution on square 1 on your record sheet, and record the area on the figure (A = 7) next to square 1.
   c. Find the perimeter of this figure. Write the perimeter (P = ?) next to square 1.
   d. Make the perimeter of the figure larger without changing the area. *How do you make the perimeter of a figure larger without changing the area?*
   e. Record your solution on square 2, and write the perimeter and area of this figure next to it.
   f. Make a figure on your geoboard with 12 units of perimeter.
   g. Record your solution on square 3, and record the perimeter of the figure (P = 12) next to square 3.
   h. Find the area of this figure. Write the area (A = ?) next to square 3.
   i. Make the area of this figure larger without changing its perimeter. *How do you make the area of a figure larger without changing the perimeter?*
   j. Record your solution on square 4, and write the perimeter and area of this figure next to it.
   k. Make a figure with 8 square units of area and 12 units of perimeter, and record your solution on square 5. Write the perimeter and area of this figure next to it. *Is there only one possible solution for this problem? Can you show me another?*
   l. Make a figure with 8 square units of area and 14 units of perimeter, and record your solution on square 6. Write the perimeter and area of this figure next to it. *Is there only one possible solution for this problem? Can you show me another?*

Content Areas

Measurement

Activity Type

➤ Manipulative

Representational

Abstract

Strategies

➤ Interviews

➤ Observations

➤ Portfolios

Student Self-Assessment

Performance Tasks

Student Writing

m. Make as many different figures as you can with 16 units of perimeter. Record each solution on a new square on your record sheet. Write the perimeter and area of each solution next to your record of it. *What is the smallest area you can have with a perimeter of 16 units? What is the largest area you can have with a perimeter of 16 units? Can a figure with a perimeter of 16 have 16 square units of area? Why or why not?*

Notes

■ If you are doing this assessment as an interview, ask the questions in italics.

■ Students should have had several opportunities to use geoboards to explore the concepts of perimeter and area before this assessment is used.

■ You may need to demonstrate how to record solutions and label them (A = ?, P = ?) before doing the assessment.

■ Since only three boards are left, offer a second record sheet for P = 16 so students do not assume there are only three or fewer answers.

Outcomes

- To find shapes for given areas or perimeters.
- To demonstrate that figures with the same area and/or perimeters may have different shapes.

Sample Performance Indicators for Student Who Is

Not Understanding	Developing	Understanding/Applying
▲ Cannot make figures with a specific area and/or perimeter ▲ Cannot count area and/or perimeter of figures made by others ▲ Confuses perimeter and area ▲ Does not see any relationship between perimeter and area	▲ Can make figure with specific area and/or perimeter but cannot change one without changing other ▲ Can make required figures on the geoboard but cannot transfer information to record sheet ▲ Cannot make figure when both perimeter and area are defined ▲ Cannot make more than one or two different figures with perimeter of 16 ▲ Can change perimeter and/or area of figure but cannot explain how it is done	▲ Can make figure with specific area and/or perimeter and can change one without changing other ▲ Can easily transfer solutions from geoboard to record sheet ▲ Can explain how perimeter of figure is made larger/smaller without changing area ▲ Can explain how area of figure is made larger/smaller without changing perimeter ▲ Can make at least six different figures with perimeter of 16

Geoboard Record Sheet

Name _____   Date _____

A.

B.

C.

D.

E.

F.

G.

H.

I.

Perusing Perimeter

Outcome

- To draw figures of a specified perimeter.

Materials

- Piece of chalk
- Chalkboard eraser
- Chalkboard
- Centimeter ruler

Assessment Activity

1. Have the student draw three different polygons on the chalkboard. Each polygon must have a perimeter of 80 cm. One of the polygons must have more than four sides.
2. Have the student record the length of each side of each polygon.

Note

- This assessment may be used as a pretest or a posttest.
- For upper grades, relate perimeter to area.

Content Areas

Measurement

Activity Type

Manipulative

➤ Representational

Abstract

Strategies

➤ Interviews

Observations

Portfolios

Student
Self-Assessment

➤ Performance
Tasks

Student Writing

Outcome

■ To draw figures of a specified perimeter.

Sample Performance Indicators for Student Who Is

Not Understanding	Developing	Understanding/Applying
▲ Does not draw a polygon ▲ Draws a polygon but does not measure the sides of the polygon ▲ Measures out a straight line that is 80 cm long	▲ Is able to correctly draw one or two polygons ▲ Draws polygons but randomly places measurements on side to equal 80 cm ▲ Draws polygons that have four sides but cannot create figure that has more than four sides ▲ Is able to complete the task with prompts	▲ Draws, measures, and labels three polygons that have a perimeter of 80 cm

Place Value and Estimation

Outcome

■ To estimate unknown quantities by partitioning into known quantities.

Materials

■ 20 jars, labeled 1 to 20, of beans of varying quantities
■ Portion cups
■ Place value boards
■ Guess and Check Worksheet
■ Pencils

Assessment Activity

1. Divide the class into groups of two. Give each pair portion cups, a place value board, a Guess and Check Worksheet, and pencils.
2. Have each pair examine their jar of beans. Have them estimate how many groups of 10 are in their jar.
3. Have them write their estimate on their Guess and Check Worksheet.

A's GUESS		B's GUESS		ACTUAL	
tens	ones	tens	ones	tens	ones

4. Have them count the beans and separate the beans by 10 into portion cups.
5. Have them place the cups and any remaining beans onto their place value board.
6. Have them record this number and compare it with their estimate.
7. Have them replace the beans into the jars.
8. Have them repeat the task with different jars.

Notes

■ It is helpful to model this activity with the whole class.
■ The quantities should be small initially, increasing as students gain experience.
■ Encourage students to discuss their estimates and counts and to use this information when estimating subsequent quantities.

Activity Type

➤ Manipulative
....
Representational

➤ Abstract
....

Strategies

Interviews

➤ Observations
....
Portfolios

Student
Self-Assessment

➤ Performance
Tasks
....

Student Writing

Outcome

■ To estimate unknown quantities by partitioning into known quantities.

Sample Performance Indicators for Student Who Is

Not Understanding	Developing	Understanding/Applying
▲ Makes an unreasonable guess ▲ Has difficulty counting beans ▲ Has difficulty making groups of 10	▲ Makes appropriate guess, (e.g., if 100 beans are in a jar, a reasonable guess may be 75) ▲ Can count beans but has difficulty placing on place value board ▲ Uses first estimates and counts to improve later estimates	▲ Makes reasonable guess ▲ Is successful in counting and determining the correct answer ▲ Uses first estimates and counts to improve later estimates

Partner A _____

Partner B _____

A's Guess		B's Guess		Actual	
tens	ones	tens	ones	tens	ones

A's Guess		B's Guess		Actual	
tens	ones	tens	ones	tens	ones

A's Guess		B's Guess		Actual	
tens	ones	tens	ones	tens	ones

A's Guess		B's Guess		Actual	
tens	ones	tens	ones	tens	ones

A's Guess		B's Guess		Actual	
tens	ones	tens	ones	tens	ones

Place Value:
Building Numbers

Outcome

■ To build a number in a variety of formats (e.g., 43, 4 tens 3 ones, 40 + 3, forty-three).

Materials

■ Beans, portion cups, Unifix® cubes, or squared material
■ Place value board
■ Several cards with two-digit numerals written on them

Assessment Activity

1. **Activity One** (Concept Level)
   a. Ask the student to build a two-digit number (e.g., 24, 4 tens 7 ones, 20 + 5) with manipulatives and to place it correctly on the place value board.
   b. Ask the student to explain what she or he built.
2. **Activity Two** (Connecting Level)
   a. Show the student a two-digit numeral. Ask him or her to build it with manipulatives.
   b. Ask the student to explain what she or he built. Point to the tens numeral, and ask what it means. Point to the ones numeral, and ask what it means.
3. **Activity Three** (Symbolic Level)
   a. Give the student a two-digit number to record on paper. Then have the student build the number with manipulatives and place it on the place value board.
   b. Ask the student to explain what she or he built.

Note

■ These activities may be done with individual students or with groups of up to five students.

Content Areas

Place Value

Activity Type

➤ Manipulative
➤ Representational
➤ Abstract

Strategies

Interviews
➤ Observations
Portfolios
Student Self-Assessment
➤ Performance Tasks
Student Writing

Outcome

■ To build a number in a variety of formats.

Sample Performance Indicators for Student Who Is

Not Understanding	Developing	Understanding/Applying
▲ Can count to the number (43) but does not have a concept of the number (43) as tens (4) and ones (3) ▲ Does not know ones from tens ▲ Has no idea where to start ▲ Wants to represent 10 with a unit placed on the tens place	▲ Can verbally describe 43 as 4 tens and 3 ones but does not know where to place manipulatives on board ▲ Can build some numbers but has difficulty with others (e.g., those having a 0 in the ones place) ▲ Can build number but has to count each unit in tens place to verify how many tens ▲ Needs prompts like "How many ones? How many tens?" ▲ Puts 43 units on ones side and then realizes the need to trade	▲ Places the correct group of tens and ones on the place value board ▲ Can explain his or her placement of materials ▲ Distinguishes between tens and ones ▲ Recognizes 10 ones and 1 ten as being equivalent

Place Value: Explaining Numbers

Outcome

■ To explain the number on the place value board using expanded and standard numerals and oral/written numbers.

Materials

■ Place value board
■ Beans and portion cups, Unifix® cubes, or base 10 materials
■ Place Value Worksheets (optional)
■ Paper and pencil

Assessment Activity

1. Build a number with manipulatives (e.g., 48, 52, 89).
2. Ask the student to explain the number: "Read the number. How many tens? How many ones?"
3. Ask the student to write the numeral (e.g., 4 tens 8 ones [expanded]; 48 [standard]; forty-eight [oral/written]; 40 + 8).

Notes

■ This activity was adapted from *Mathtime 2* by Olive Fullerton.
■ Between steps 2 and 3, ask the student to complete the written activity on one or both of the worksheets.
■ Ask any students who have difficulty performing step 3 to complete one or both of the worksheets.

Content Areas

Place Value

Activity Type

➤ Manipulative

➤ Representational

➤ Abstract

Strategies

Interviews

➤ Observations

Portfolios

Student Self-Assessment

➤ Performance Task

Student Writing

Outcome

■ To explain the number on the place value board using expanded and standard numerals and oral/written numbers.

Sample Performance Indicators for Student Who Is

Not Understanding	Developing	Understanding/Applying
▲ Gives no answer ▲ Reads board incorrectly ▲ Does not write numeral correctly ▲ Does not know expanded numeral ▲ Cannot write out the oral/written number	▲ Reads board correctly with prompts like: "How many tens; ones?" ▲ Writes numeral correctly with prompt ▲ May not be able to write out oral/written number	▲ Describes the number correctly as ___ tens and ___ ones ▲ Writes numeral correctly in expanded and standard notation ▲ Can write out the oral/written number

Place Value

Name _____ Date _____

Color. Print the numeral.

7 tens and 3	4 tens and 6
_____	_____
2 tens and 8	3 tens and 5
_____	_____
9 tens and 8	5 tens and 2
_____	_____

Place Value

Name _____ Date _____

Complete.

_____ tens and _____ _____	5 tens and 7 _____	_____ tens and _____ 63
8 tens and 4 _____	_____ tens and _____ _____	thirty-four _____
_____ tens and _____ 45	_____ tens and _____ _____	twenty-six _____

Positional Relationships

Outcome

- To demonstrate an understanding of positional relationships.

Materials

- 10 cubes of various colors
- Piece of rope or yarn, 18 in. long
- Positional Relationships Sheet for recording observations

Assessment Activity

1. **Level One** (Assesses understanding of concept)

   Instruct the student as follows:

   A. Right, Left
      1. Put a blue cube on the table (correct color is not important to this task).
      2. Put a red cube on the right side of the blue cube.
      3. Put an orange cube on the left side of the blue cube.

   B. Inside, Outside
      1. Make a loop with the yarn.
      2. Put a cube inside the loop.
      3. Put a cube outside the loop.

   C. Top, Bottom
      1. Make a stack of four cubes. (Correct number is not important to this task.)
      2. What color is on the top?
      3. What color is on the bottom?

   D. First, Next, Last
      1. What color is the first cube in the stack?
      2. What color is the next cube in the stack?
      3. What color is the last cube in the stack?

   E. Under, Over
      1. Put the yarn over the stack of cubes.
      2. Put the yarn under the stack of cubes. (They may fall, but the important observation is whether the student demonstrates an understanding of the concept of under.)

Strategies

➤ Interviews

➤ Observations

Portfolios

Student Self-Assessment

➤ Performance Tasks

Student Writing

F. High, Low
   1. Build a high tower with your cubes. (limit to one that will remain standing)
   2. Build a low tower with your cubes.
G. Above, Below
   1. What color cube is above the red one (or other color of teacher's choice)?
   2. What color cube is below the red one?
H. Middle, Between
   1. Take down your towers.
   2. Put three cubes together in a row.
   3. What color cube is in the middle?
   4. Put a yellow cube between the blue and green cubes (or other colors appropriate to this task).
I. In Front Of, Behind
   1. Put a red cube in front of the blue cube (or other colors appropriate to this task).
   2. Put a green cube behind the orange cube.

2. **Level Two** (Assesses command of the language)

A. Place cubes in the various positions being assessed.

B. Ask the student to describe the position of a designated cube.

Note

■ It will not be necessary to use this entire assessment task formally with all students. Understanding can be assessed informally as students work with materials in a variety of classroom settings. Parts of this instrument may be used as needed.

Outcome

- To demonstrate an understanding of positional relationships.

Sample Performance Indicators for Student Who Is

Not Understanding	Developing	Understanding/Applying
▲ Cannot place cube in designated position ▲ Relies on teacher for cues	▲ Correctly places cube in some of the positions ▲ Is able to do task when direction is repeated once or several times	▲ Correctly places cube in all designated positions ▲ Accurately describes location of cube when teacher places it in various positions ▲ Uses positional words in other contexts

Positional Relationships Sheet

Student Name	Right Left	Inside Outside	Top Bottom	First Next Last	Under Over	High Low	Above Below	Middle Between	In Front of Behind

Primarily
Problem Solving

Outcomes

- To sort and classify objects.
- To read a pattern.
- To create a pattern.
- To insert a missing element into a pattern.

Materials

- 2 sets of junk or treasures, up to 10 objects each, that have not been previously explored
- Sample pattern with elements missing (e.g., adding machine tape with stickers arranged on the tape in a pattern, with some elements missing)

- Items to insert into pattern
- Sorting mat (optional)

Assessment Activity

1. Hand the student one set of treasures, and ask, "What would you do with these?" The student should show and explain what he or she is doing.

2. *(Sorting)* Show the second set of treasures, which you have sorted by some attribute, and say the following:

   a. What is this problem about?

   b. Show me another way to sort these

   c. Explain how you sorted these.

   d. Tell me about another way to sort these.

3. *(Pattern)* Ask the student to make a pattern with one of the treasures and to explain the pattern.

4. Show your sample pattern with the missing elements. Say the following:

   a. What can you tell me about this?

   b. What goes here?

   c. Read the pattern to me.

   d. What do you think comes next? Why?

Content Areas

Problem Solving and Logic

Activity Type

➤ Manipulative

Representational

Abstract

Strategies

➤ Interviews

Observations

Portfolios

Student Self-Assessment

Performance Tasks

Student Writing

Outcomes

- To sort and classify objects.
- To read a pattern.
- To create a pattern.
- To insert a missing element into a pattern.

Sample Performance Indicators for Student Who Is

Not Understanding	Developing	Understanding/Applying
Sorting and Classifying ▲ Plays with materials instead of sorting them ▲ Makes numerous errors ▲ Needs frequent prompts	**Sorting and Classifying** ▲ Can sort if given the attributes ▲ Can correct errors if pointed out	**Sorting and Classifying** ▲ Can sort and classify objects correctly ▲ Can select sorting categories ▲ Can explain how he or she did sorting
Patterning ▲ Is unable to explain pattern ▲ Cannot insert missing elements ▲ Creates random arrangement rather than a pattern	**Patterning** ▲ Can explain the pattern ▲ Cannot insert missing elements ▲ Can create a pattern	**Patterning** ▲ Can explain the pattern ▲ Can insert missing elements ▲ Can create a pattern

Probability
Using Objects

Outcome

■ To use concrete objects to solve a probability problem.

Materials

■ Counters in three different colors (10 to 15 each)

■ Paper and pencil to record solutions (optional)

Assessment Activity

1. For the first task, direct the student to use the counters to make a three-by-three grid (three rows with three counters in each row) so that the same color counter is used only once in any row or column.

2. For the second task, tell the student to pretend that each color of counter is a different flavor of ice cream. Then direct the student to make every different double-dip ice-cream cone he or she can from these three flavors.

3. After the task is completed, ask such questions as

   a. How do you know your answer is correct?

   b. Could you do it another way; a faster way?

   c. If the order of the cones mattered (that is, a cherry/vanilla cone is different from a vanilla/cherry), can you tell from your solution how many more cones you could make?

Notes

■ The second task has an intentional ambiguity. Answer the student's questions if he or she is trying to clarify understanding of the task. Such questions might be, "Can you use the same flavor twice in the same cone?" (yes) or "Does the order of the dips matter?" (no).

■ If the student cannot get started, give a minimal restatement or explanation of the task. Suggest flavors for each color (e.g., red counter is cherry) or show one cone.

■ Rather than conducting an interview (which is preferred), have the student record solutions for each task. A paper with an outline of a three-by-three grid could be supplied for the first task and perhaps a dozen outlined double-dip cones for the second task. If this is done in a group setting, clarify the second task in advance: "You may use the same flavor twice; the order of the cones does not matter."

Content Areas

Statistics and
   Probability

Activity Type

➤ Manipulative
   ....
   Representational

   Abstract

Strategies

➤ Interviews
   ....
   Observations

   Portfolios

   Student
   Self-Assessment

➤ Performance
   Tasks
   ....
   Student Writing

Solutions, Task 1:

A	B	C		A	B	C
B	C	A	or	C	A	B
C	A	B		B	C	A

Solutions, Task 2:

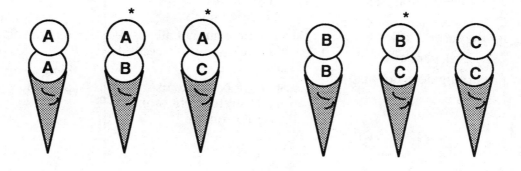

*If order does matter, these may get reversed to get 3 more cones.

Outcome

■ To use concrete objects to solve a probability problem.

Sample Performance Indicators for Student Who Is

Not Understanding	Developing	Understanding/Applying
▲ Cannot solve first task ▲ Gets fewer than four cones for the second task ▲ Asks irrelevant questions ▲ Prompting does not help	▲ Solves just one of the two tasks adequately ▲ Gets most but not all possible combinations in second task ▲ States or begins to use a viable strategy but cannot carry it through	▲ Can do both tasks ▲ Can explain strategy and record solutions ▲ Asks questions that indicate complexity of task and possible variations

Problem-solving Strategies

Outcome

■ To select and apply appropriate problem-solving strategies.

Materials

■ Word/story problem written on a card
■ Manipulatives when appropriate
■ Pencil

Assessment Activity

1. Ask the student to solve a problem and to tell you the steps he or she is using.

   Sample Problem

   LaShanda took five friends to the amusement park. Everyone wanted to take one ride on the roller coaster with every other person. How many rides were taken altogether?

2. Record the student's response on the sample Performance Indicators Sheet.

Note

■ *How to Evaluate Progress in Problem Solving,* by R. Charles et al., provides alternative evaluation strategies and performance criteria.

Content Areas

Problem Solving and Logic

Activity Type

Manipulative

➤ Representational

➤ Abstract

Strategies

➤ Interviews

Observations

Portfolios

Student Self-Assessment

Performance Tasks

Student Writing

Outcome

- To select and apply appropriate problem-solving strategies.

Sample Performance Indicators for Student Who Is

Not Understanding	Developing	Understanding/Applying
▲ Does not understand what question is being asked ▲ Has no idea how to begin working on the problem ▲ Selects inappropriate strategies ▲ Cannot solve problem with prompting ▲ Does not recognize unreasonable answers	▲ May misinterpret part of the problem ▲ Needs prompts or reinforcements ▲ Begins working through the problem but gets wrong answer ▲ Gets correct answer but does not use efficient method ▲ Can solve if told which strategy to use	▲ Understands elements of the problem ▲ Begins problem by setting up a strategy ▲ Stays with task until finds an appropriate strategy ▲ Uses strategies efficiently ▲ Can explain strategy used ▲ Provides correct answer
Example: $2\overline{)5}$ $\begin{array}{r}2\ \text{r}1 \\ 4 \\ \hline 1\end{array}$	Example: 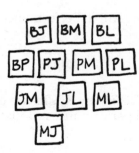	Example: 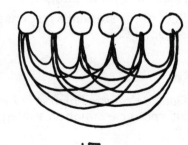 $\begin{array}{r}15 \\ \hline 5 \\ 4 \\ 3 \\ 2 \\ 1\end{array}$

Problem Solving:
Strategies and Process

Outcomes

- To use a variety of problem-solving strategies.
- To use a problem-solving process.

Materials

- Copy of Problem-Solving Evaluation Worksheets, Problem-Solving Scoring Sheet, and Problem-Solving Strategy Inventory for each student
- Pencils

Assessment Activity

1. Hand out copies of Problem-Solving Evaluation Worksheets to the class. Explain the scoring system. Emphasize the importance of writing a clear explanation of how they selected a strategy and got their answer.

2. Allow students as much time as they need to complete all the problems.

3. Score the test by using the answer key. Record separate scores for each of the three sections for each problem.

4. Return tests to students, along with copies of the Problem-Solving Scoring Sheet. Ask students to transfer their scores onto the sheets and to write paragraphs describing their strengths and weaknesses in solving the problems. At this time you may decide to discuss specific problems and solutions.

5. To help students assess which strategies they use and which they do not use, distribute copies of the Problem-Solving Strategy Inventory, and ask students to make a tally of strategies used. Discuss why they rely more heavily on some strategies than on others.

Answer Key

The correct strategies to these problems can be found by using strategies other than those listed for each problem.

1. Answer: Carl's project is on plants.
   Strategy: Make a chart.

2. Answer: Yoshi could make 18 different lunches.
   Strategy: Make an organized list.

3. Answer: Jesse will have read 4 books.
   Strategy: Make a table.

4. Answer: There will be 12 groups of two and 7 groups of three.
   Strategy: Draw a picture or make a table.

5. Answer: It will take Mr. Grand 6 months to lose 36 pounds.
   Strategy: Look for a pattern.

Content Areas

Problem Solving
and Logic

Activity Type

Manipulative

➤ Representational

➤ Abstract

Strategies

Interviews

Observations

➤ Portfolios

➤ Student
Self-Assessment

➤ Performance
Tasks

➤ Student Writing

---

6. Answer: The students made 76 cookies.
   Strategy: Work backward.
7. Answer: Juan read 285 pages and George read 95 pages.
   Strategy: Guess and check or write an equation.

Notes

- Asking students to explain their answers is important for many reasons:
  - ▲ It helps you understand and evaluate students' strengths and weaknesses in problem solving.
  - ▲ It helps students better understand their own thought processes.
  - ▲ It helps students see that problems can be solved in a variety of ways.

- Without a great deal of modeling and practice, students will probably not be able to write complete explanations of how they solve problems. Asking students to write explanations and using student writings as models should become a routine part of problem-solving lessons.

- This evaluation could be used as a pretest to determine students' strengths and weaknesses in problem solving and as a posttest, after all of the strategies have been introduced, to help determine which strategies need to be emphasized in subsequent instruction. Early and late samples can be placed in portfolios to demonstrate growth.

- The Problem-Solving Scoring Sheet could be kept as part of the students' portfolios.

- In selecting problems, look for those that can be solved by using different strategies. Also consider problems from different content strands (e.g., logic problems, probability problems).

- *How to Evaluate Progress in Problem Solving*, by R. Charles et al., provides alternative evaluation strategies and performance criteria.

Outcomes

- To use a variety of problem-solving strategies.
- To use a problem-solving process.

Sample Performance Indicators for Student Who Is

Not Understanding	Developing	Understanding/Applying
Understanding ▲ Does not understand problem ▲ Relies on others to explain problems	**Understanding** ▲ May misinterpret part of problem	**Understanding** ▲ Understands key elements of problem
Planning and Implementing ▲ Makes no attempt to solve problems ▲ Selects inappropriate strategies ▲ Cannot explain answers at all or explanation makes no sense	**Planning and Implementing** ▲ Can solve a problem if told which strategy to use ▲ Knows a strategy to use but does not implement it correctly or completely ▲ Uses a strategy that will work but arrives at wrong answer ▲ Recognizes that an answer is incorrect but does not know how to find correct answer ▲ Uses a limited number of strategies to solve problems ▲ Can name the strategy used to solve a problem and give limited explanation of how that strategy was used	**Planning and Implementing** ▲ Identifies a strategy that will solve problem correctly and implements it correctly and completely ▲ Is able to use more than one strategy to solve problems ▲ Explains strategies and answers logically and coherently
Answering ▲ Does not recognize whether answer is reasonable	**Answering** ▲ Can correct errors when they are pointed out ▲ May have answer but no label ▲ Recognizes unreasonable answers	**Answering** ▲ Recognizes that answer is incorrect and can find correct solution ▲ Writes out complete answer ▲ Recognizes whether answer is reasonable

Problem–solving Evaluation

Name _____ Date _____

Directions: You can earn as many as 4 points for each problem: 1 point for using a strategy that will solve the problem, 1 point for finding the correct answer to the problem, and 2 points for explaining how you decided which strategy to use and how you used it to find a solution to the problem.

1. Four fourth graders are taking part in the school science fair. Their names are Linda, Judy, Carl and Karen. Their projects are on solar energy, plants, gravity, and electricity. Judy's project is on gravity, and Karen's is not on plants. If Linda's is on electricity, what is Carl's on?

Solve the problem:

Answer:

Explain how you got your answer:

2. Yoshi is making a lunch for the school picnic. He could have a peanut butter, cheese, or egg salad sandwich. He could have a bag of potato chips, corn chips, or popcorn. For dessert, he could have an apple or a banana. How many different lunches could Yoshi make?

Solve the problem:

Answer:

Explain how you got your answer:

3. Kenny and Jesse love to read. Kenny reads one book every 3 days and Jesse reads one book every 6 days. How many books will Jesse have read when Kenny has read 8 books?

Solve the problem:

Answer:

Explain how you got your answer:

4. The 45 students in the fifth grade at Dewey Elementary School are in the cafeteria eating lunch. There are 19 tables in the cafeteria. Two or three students are sitting at each table. How many groups of two are there and how many groups of three are there?

Solve the problem:

Answer:

Explain how you got your answer:

5. Mr. Grand is 36 pounds overweight and is going on a diet. If he loses 11 pounds the first month, 9 pounds the second month, and 7 pounds the third month, and he continues losing at this rate, how long will it take him to lose 36 pounds?

Solve the problem:

Answer:

Explain how you got your answer:

6. Five students in Mrs. Travis' class made cookies for the bake sale. Patty made twice as many cookies as Jeremy. Jeremy made 6 more cookies than Karla. Karla made 4 more cookies than Michael. Michael made half as many cookies as Peter. Peter made 12 cookies. How many cookies did the students make altogether for the sale?

Solve the problem:

Answer

Explain how you got your answer:

7. George and Juan read a total of 380 pages for the the Read-a-thon. Juan read 3 times as many pages as George. How many pages did each of them read?

Solve the problem:

Answer:

Explain how you got your answer:

Problem-solving
Scoring Sheet

Name _____ Date _____

Transfer the points you received for each problem to the scorecard below. Use the information on the scorecard to write a paragraph describing your strengths and weaknesses in solving the problems.

Problem Number	Solve the Problem Points	Answer Points	Explanation Points
1			
2			
3			
4			
5			
6			
7			
Total			

Strengths and Weaknesses

Problem-solving Strategy Inventory

Name _____ Date _____

Make tally marks to indicate which strategies you used to solve the problems
on this evaluation.

Guess and check _____

Make a table _____

Look for a pattern _____

Make an organized list _____

Work backward _____

Draw a picture _____

Write an equation _____

Make a chart _____

Other _____

Quarter Time

Outcome

■ To tell time to the hour, half-hour, quarter hour, and minute.

Materials

■ Demonstration clock
■ Time assessment worksheet (see sample below)
■ Time Assessment Record Sheet

Assessment Activity

1. Show the student a clock model. Ask the student to "Show Me" the time indicated on the worksheet. The student should move the clock hands, and you should check the worksheet by using the appropriate key.

2. Ask the student to move the hands of the clock to show a specific time (e.g., 3:27, 9:46).

Notes

■ This is a preassessment activity to determine individual needs.

■ Interviewing may take place during reading or recess and takes only a minute or two per student.

■ Notes regarding a student's knowledge of time may be written on the worksheet as information for you. Writing the incorrect time next to the time asked will help pinpoint a student's specific need.

■ This may be used as a posttest after addressing students' individual needs.

Content Areas

Measurement

Activity Type

➤ Manipulative
➤ Representational
   Abstract

Strategies

➤ Interviews
   Observations
   Portfolios
   Student Self-Assessment
➤ Performance Tasks
   Student Writing

Sample Time Assessment Worksheet

Name _____ Date _____   c = correct response

x = incorrect response

o = no response

Show me:

3:00 _____

2:30 _____   **Telling Time (to the minute)**

1:15 _____   ____ ____ : ____ ____ _____

6:45 _____   ____ ____ : ____ ____ _____

Outcome

■ Tell time to the hour, half-hour, quarter hour, and minute.

Sample Performance Indicators for Student Who Is

Not Understanding	Developing	Understanding/Applying
▲ Is unable to show or tell any of the times asked ▲ Has no idea of number representation on clock ▲ Consistently makes errors	▲ Hesitates before moving the hands ▲ Counts by fives and points to the numbers as the hands are being moved ▲ Makes some errors ▲ Finds times that are close but not exact	▲ Moves the hands quickly and accurately ▲ Can tell time exactly before and after the hour ▲ Is able to verbalize the concept of telling time

Time Assessment Record Sheet

Student Name	3:00	2:30	1:15	6:45			Notes

Ratio

Outcome

■ To understand ratio.

Materials

■ Colored squares (3 yellow, 5 red, 2 blue)
■ Paper and pencil

Assessment Activity

1. Give the student a set of squares.
2. Ask the student to compare the red squares with the yellow squares.
3. Ask the student to write the comparison as a ratio (e.g., 5:3). Ask him/her to write the comparison another way (such as $\frac{5}{3}$)
4. After the ratios are written, ask the student to explain what he or she has written.

Content Areas

Fractions, Decimals, Ratio, and Percent

Activity Type

➤ Manipulative

Representational

➤ Abstract

Strategies

➤ Interviews

Observations

Portfolios

Student Self-Assessment

Performance Tasks

Student Writing

Outcome

■ To understand ratio.

Sample Performance Indicators for Student Who Is

Not Understanding	Developing	Understanding/Applying
▲ Has no idea where to begin ▲ Moves squares without a plan	▲ Writes a ratio incorrectly ▲ Writes a ratio correctly but is not able to explain what it means ▲ Explains how one group relates to another but is not able to write it in ratio form	▲ Writes the correct ratio in $x : y$ form ▲ Writes the correct ratio in $\frac{x}{y}$ form ▲ Correctly explains what ratio means

Reading with Numbers

Outcomes

- To demonstrate how to use a calculator.
- To demonstrate how to check place value problems with a calculator.

Materials

- Calculators
- Reading with Numbers Worksheet
- Overhead projector, and transparency of a calculator

Assessment Activity

1. Tell students they are going to learn how to read with a calculator.
2. Read the following directions slowly, giving the students time to enter each step on their calculators: enter 2,788; add 3 thousands; subtract 8 tens; subtract 2 hundreds
3. Ask this riddle: "What do you call an 8,000-pound hippopotamus who wants your job?"
4. Have the class invert their calculators and read from the display the answer to the riddle. (5508 = BOSS)
5. Hand out the worksheet. Have students work independently.
   Answers: (1) 3045 = SHOE; (2) 7738 = BELL; (3) 618 = BIG;
   (4) 4914 = HIGH; (5) 937 = LEG.

Notes

- This activity was adapted from a lesson in *Exploring Mathematics: Calculator Sourcebook* (4) by Scott, Foresman, and Company.
- If several students did not get the correct answer, use your overhead calculator and repeat the directions. Have the students check that their displays read the same as yours.
- Have students who finish early make up their own riddles to present to the class.
- The letters for the numbers are as follows:
  0 = O, 1 = I, 2 = Z, 3 = E, 4 = h, 5 = S, 6 = g, 7 = L, 8 = B, 9 = G
- You may want to read the worksheet to the class rather than to distribute it.
- Problems may be adjusted to fit your grade level.
- Students can be asked to write the calculator code.

Content Areas

Calculators

Place Value

Activity Type

➤ Manipulative

➤ Representational

Abstract

Strategies

Interviews

➤ Observations

Portfolios

Student Self-Assessment

➤ Performance Tasks

Student Writing

Outcomes

■ To demonstrate how to use a calculator.

■ To demonstrate how to check place value problems with a calculator.

Sample Performance Indicators for Student Who Is

Not Understanding	Developing	Understanding/Applying
▲ Does not know where to begin ▲ Cannot locate the correct calculator keys ▲ Does not know place value ▲ Cannot "read" a calculator number	▲ Needs some prompts to follow directions ▲ Sometimes needs help on locating a calculator key ▲ Needs some help with place value ▲ Needs help "reading" calculator numbers	▲ Can follow directions ▲ Can locate and use correct calculator keys ▲ Knows place value ▲ Can "read" calculator numbers ▲ Can create riddles to fit calculator letters

Reading with Numbers

Name _____ Date _____

	Number	Word

1. Enter 2,635
Add 1 thousand
Subtract 6 hundreds
Add 1 ten
What did the horse put on his hoof?   _____ _____

2. Enter 443
Add 7 thousands
Subtract 5 ones
Add 3 hundreds
What ring won't fit on your hand?   _____ _____

3. Enter 950
Subtract 4 hundreds
Add 6 tens
Add 8 ones
What does a mouse call an elephant?   _____ _____

4. Enter 6,417
Add 7 ones
Subtract 2 thousands
Add 5 hundreds
Subtract 1 ten
What did the villagers say in greeting to Gulliver? _____ _____

5. Enter 3,781
Add 2 hundreds
Subtract 5 tens
Add 6 ones
Subtract 3 thousands
*What stands, walks, and runs but never
goes anywhere without you?*   _____ _____

Regrouping Using Base 10 Blocks

Outcome

■ To use base 10 blocks to show two or more ways to model a given two- or three-digit number.

Materials

■ Base 10 blocks
■ Base 10 mat
■ Paper and pencil to record solutions (optional)

Assessment Activity

1. Tell the student a two-digit number (e.g., 42).
2. Have the student create the number on the mat.
3. If the student answers successfully, ask him or her to find another way to show the same number (or same amount, if the student is not clear about what to do).
4. Repeat with a three-digit number.

Notes

■ If the student cannot trade a ten for 10 ones, start by asking him or her to use just the ones to show a given number (under 25). Then ask for another way to show it.

■ Variation: Put out on a mat more than 10 ones and some tens.

   ▲ Ask what number it represents.

   ▲ Ask the student to show the number another way by using the blocks.

   ▲ Optional: Have the student write the number before it is regrouped.

Content Areas

Place Value

Activity Type

➤ Manipulative

Representational

Abstract

Strategies

Interviews

➤ Observations

Portfolios

Student Self-Assessment

➤ Performance Tasks

Student Writing

Outcome

- To use base 10 blocks to show two or more ways to model a given two- or three-digit number.

Sample Performance Indicators for Student Who Is

Not Understanding	Developing	Understanding/Applying
▲ Cannot accurately build the number using blocks	▲ Builds number only one way; cannot regroup, even when starting with all ones ▲ Cannot do original task but can do tasks under lesson note ▲ Regroups on mat but cannot explain or record what is done ▲ Can do with two-digit but not with three-digit numbers	▲ Does all tasks accurately ▲ Explains and records accurately ▲ Indicates there may be more than one correct response ▲ Regroups either a 10 or a 100 with three-digit numbers

Solid Geometry

Outcomes

- To compare, classify, and analyze geometric solids by their attributes.
- To identify and construct congruent/similar figures.

Materials

- Math Assessment Worksheet
- Paper and pencil
- Set of 5 wooden or plastic geometric solids (cone, sphere, cube, cylinder, rectangular prism), labeled with a letter a to e.

Assessment Activity

1. Read the worksheet directions for each problem with the student.
2. For problem 6, give the student a set of lettered geometric solids, and ask him or her to examine and write about them.
3. Encourage the student to use specific attributes.

Note

- If geometric solids are in short supply, give the assessment in small groups.

Content Areas

Geometry and Spatial Sense

Activity Type

➤ Manipulative

➤ Representational

➤ Abstract

Strategies

Interviews

Observations

Portfolios

Student Self-Assessment

➤ Performance Tasks

➤ Student Writing

Outcomes

- To compare, classify, and analyze geometric solids by their attributes.
- To identify and construct congruent/similar figures.

Sample Performance Indicators for Student Who Is

Not Understanding	Developing	Understanding/Applying
▲ Writes nothing ▲ Uses attribute words incorrectly ▲ Names solid incorrectly ▲ Is unable to match pictures with names ▲ Does not understand congruence and/or similarity	▲ Identifies solids but cannot describe them ▲ Can identify some attributes ▲ Identifies and describes some solids ▲ Is able to match most pictures with names ▲ May have difficulty with similarity	▲ Correctly names each solid ▲ Distinguishes solids by edges, faces, vertices, and curved surfaces ▲ Identifies and describes solids correctly ▲ Matches pictures with names ▲ Understands congruence and similarity

Math Assessment

Name _____ Date _____

1. Draw a line to connect the picture of the geometric solid and its name.

sphere

cone

cube

cylinder

2. Use the word box to answer the following statements.

Figures that have the same size and shape are _____

_____

A straight line with a beginning point and an ending point is a

_____

Figures that are the same shape but a different size are

_____

WORD BOX

congruent	similar	line segment	symmetry

3. Draw a line segment.

4. Draw two congruent shapes.

5. Look at each geometric solid. Name it and describe its attributes.
Use the words in the word box whenever possible.

WORD BOX

| edges | corners | curved surface | faces | angles |

a. _____

_____

_____

b. _____

_____

_____

c. _____

_____

_____

d. _____

_____

_____

e. _____

_____

_____

Sorting and Graphing

Outcome

■ To construct and interpret a real/picture/bar graph.

Materials

■ Bags of fewer than 20 items with as many as four attributes (e.g., 6 red crayons, 4 blue, 5 yellow, 2 green)
■ Graphing mat
■ Sorting mat (if needed)
■ Sorting objects (e.g., crayons)

Assessment Activity

1. Give each student a set of materials.
2. Tell the group, "Use the materials in your bag to make a graph showing what you have."
3. When a student finishes his or her graph, do one of the following:
   a. Have the student tell a partner six things about the graph.
   b. Tell the student to write six statements about the graph.
4. As the students are constructing and discussing their graphs, observe whether each student can construct the graph and make interpretive statements.

Notes

■ At the beginning of the year, go from a real graph to a picture graph; later in the year, assess from a picture graph to a bar graph.
■ Key questions you may want or need to ask include the following:
   a. What title could you give your graph?
   b. What question could you ask about your graph? How should someone answer that?
   c. Can you describe something about your graph?
   d. Can you come up with another statement? A different kind of statement?
   e. What does this graph tell us? What else?
   f. What do we know for sure?
   g. What label would you put in the headings for the columns?

Content Areas

Statistics and
   Probability

Activity Type

➤ Manipulative
....
   Representational

   Abstract

Strategies

   Interviews

➤ Observations
....
   Portfolios

   Student
   Self-Assessment

➤ Performance
   Tasks
....
   Student Writing

Outcome

■ To construct and interpret a real/picture/bar graph.

Sample Performance Indicators for Student Who Is

Not Understanding	Developing	Understanding/Applying
Constructing	**Constructing**	**Constructing**
▲ Plays with materials instead of constructing graph	▲ May want his or her own selection reaffirmed	▲ Determines attributes for labels correctly and independently
▲ Has no idea where to begin	▲ To begin task, needs to have labels for each category provided	▲ Correctly sorts by attributes
▲ Is unable to sort by attributes	▲ May make a few errors in placing objects on the graph	▲ Is able to label each category
▲ Looks to see what others are doing	▲ Wants progress on construction reaffirmed	▲ Records amounts correctly
▲ Does not place objects on graph appropriately	▲ Makes a real graph first before progressing to picture or bar graph	
Interpreting	**Interpreting**	**Interpreting**
▲ Cannot make a statement because graph was not constructed	▲ Needs examples or probing before being able to generate statements	▲ Can independently generate at least three different types of statements
▲ Can answer a question if asked but cannot generate his or her own interpretation	▲ Tends to stay with only a few types of statements	

Sorting by Attributes

Outcome

■ To sort and classify objects by specific attributes.

Materials

■ 5 different sorting collections (e.g., crayons, shells, nuts, farm animals, buttons)

■ Sorting mats with areas of two to four sections

■ Yarn

■ Index cards to record sorting rules

Assessment Activity

1. Give the student a sorting mat. Have the student place one of the collections above the mat and sort the collection by a suggested attribute. Have the student clear the mat and continue to re-sort in many different ways. The student could generate ideas, or you could suggest size, texture, features, holes, color, type, and so on.

2. If the student has successfully completed the creation of sets and has named attributes, have him or her make a sorting rule. Ask the following questions about the student's way of sorting:

   ▲ How are these the same/different?

   ▲ Does this belong in the set? Why?

   ▲ Why does this belong/not belong in the set?

   ▲ Does anything in this set not belong?

   ▲ In which set does this object belong? Why?

   ▲ What is your sorting rule?

   ▲ What name can you give this set?

   ▲ Can you sort this a different way?

3. Say, "Sort this collection into two categories." Write down the student's descriptions of the sorted groups. Have the student do the writing, if able.

4. Give the student two of the slips (attributes) previously generated or teacher-generated and a collection. Ask the student to sort the collection. Include overlapping categories in the activity. Use a Venn diagram or overlapping circles of yarn.

5. Use student- or teacher-generated attribute cards to have the student sort the material. Ask the student to tell the way the material is sorted. The collection should form overlapping groups, and some material may be outside the yarn.

Content Areas

Problem Solving and Logic

Activity Type

➤ Manipulative

Representational

Abstract

Strategies

Interviews

Observations

Portfolios

Student Self-Assessment

➤ Performance Tasks

Student Writing

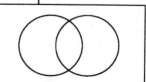

Outcome

■ To sort and classify objects by specific attributes.

Sample Performance Indicators for Student Who Is

Not Understanding	Developing	Understanding/Applying
Sorting with two attributes ▲ Does not know in which string to put an object ▲ Does not know attributes ▲ Does not recognize errors ▲ Needs repeated prompts	**Sorting with two attributes** ▲ Puts a few pieces in correct string ▲ Can name one attribute ▲ Recognizes the difference but cannot explain where to place object	**Sorting with two attributes** ▲ Puts all pieces in correct places ▲ Names attributes ▲ Knows which ones are/are not and why ▲ Can correct errors
Sorting with two to four attributes ▲ Has difficulty sorting, even with prompts, beyond one attribute ▲ Has difficulty identifying the sorting rule for a given set ▲ Does not recognize errors in material sorted	**Sorting with two to four attributes** ▲ Able to sort and re-sort collections beyond one familiar attribute, with prompts ▲ With prompts, can identify the sorting rule ▲ Recognizes but cannot correct errors	**Sorting with two to four attributes** ▲ Is able to sort collections by two or more less-familiar attributes ▲ Has successfully created intersecting sets when objects share the attributes of both sets ▲ Identifies the sorting rule quickly and easily

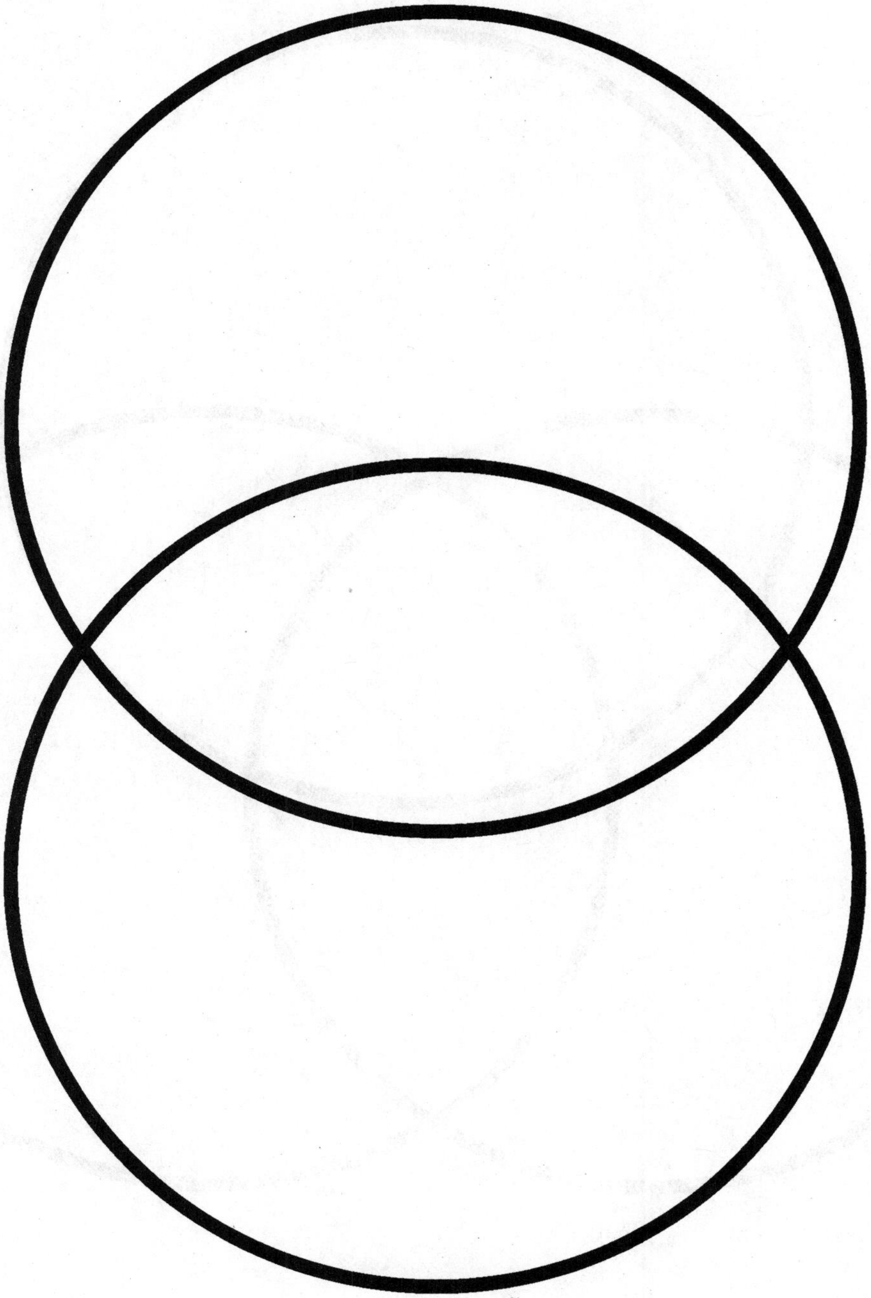

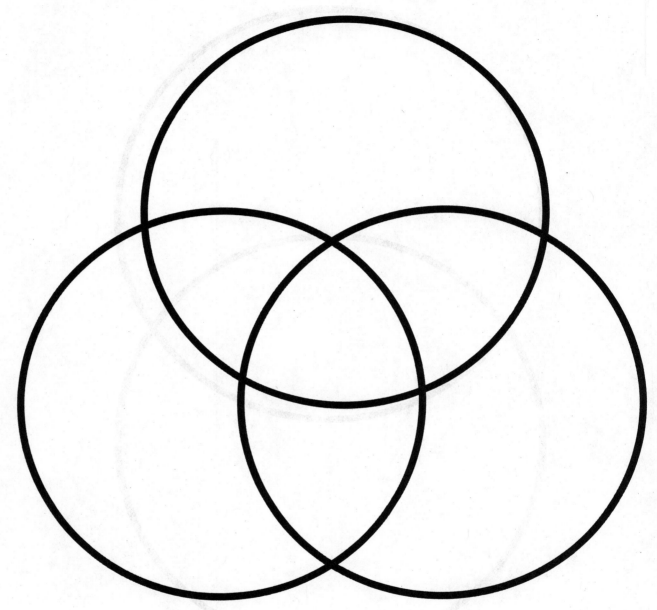

Sorting Geometric Solids

Outcomes

■ To recognize and name geometric solids.

■ To analyze and name attributes of geometric solids.

Materials

■ Two large plastic hoops or circles of string

■ Container of geometric solids

Assessment Activity

Students will be discovering the labels of attributes for two sets, which you have determined in advance. For example, your attribute might be Edges (members include cubes and cones) and No Edges (such as spheres). Other possible attributes: Corners/No Corners; Rolls/Doesn't Roll; Stacks/Doesn't Stack; Slides/Doesn't Slide; Rolls and Stacks/Doesn't Roll and Stack; 8 Corners (Edges)/Less Than 8 Corners (Edges)

1. Spread hoops or string on the floor so that they overlap to form a Venn diagram.

2. Have students sit in a circle around the Venn diagram.

3. Place a geometric solid inside each hoop or string.

4. Ask a student to choose and name a solid and to place it in the appropriate string.

5. If a student places the solid correctly, say "yes" and continue the activity. If the student places the solid incorrectly, say "no," have the student remove the solid and sit down, and ask another student to select and place a solid.

6. Continue until all solids have been placed.

7. Have a student tell what the labels of the sets are.

Notes

■ Choose a student who has decided on his or her own rules to begin a new game.

■ This assessment activity assumes that students have had previous experience sorting and/or classifying solids by using Venn diagrams.

■ Because this is a problem-solving game, correct placement of solids will not occur until some pattern emerges and students begin to test their predictions. Consequently assessment on students' placement of solids should not occur until the pattern begins to take shape.

■ The ability to name a solid can be assessed throughout the activity by having students name the solid before placing it.

Content Areas

Geometry and
Spatial Sense

Activity Type

➤ Manipulative

Representational

Abstract

Strategies

Interviews

➤ Observations

Portfolios

Student
Self-Assessment

➤ Performance
Tasks

Student Writing

Outcomes

- To recognize and name geometric solids.
- To analyze and name attributes of geometric solids.

Sample Performance Indicators for Student Who Is

Not Understanding	Developing	Understanding/Applying
▲ Confuses names of geometric solids ▲ Does not place solids correctly	▲ May need some prompting to name geometric solid ▲ Places one solid correctly	▲ Correctly names geometric solids ▲ Correctly places geometric solid in string and identifies rule

Story to Fit Equation

Outcome

■ To make up a story for a given number sentence.

Materials

■ Bag with equations (written on slips of paper) in it

Assessment Activity

1. Tell the students that they are to choose one equation from the bag.
2. Each student is to write a story for the chosen equation that will meet these two requirements:
   a. The story must end in a question.
   b. The question can be answered by the equation chosen.

Notes

■ Vary the difficulty of the number sentences as abilities change.
■ The complexity of the equation should be appropriate for the developmental level of the students.
■ Grade 1 students may do this orally. They also may be given a number sentence (e.g., $3 + 4 = 7$) and asked to tell or write a story but not to ask or write a question. They also could be asked to draw a picture.
■ Variation: Have the students write their own equations and stories following the two requirements.

Content Areas

Mathematical Thinking

Problem Solving and Logic

Algebraic Ideas

Activity Type

Manipulative

Representational

➤ Abstract

Strategies

Interviews

Observations

Portfolios

Student Self-Assessment

➤ Performance Tasks

➤ Student Writing

Outcome

■ To make up a story for a given number sentence.

Sample Performance Indicators for Student Who Is

Not Understanding	Developing	Understanding/Applying
▲ Does not know where to start	▲ Writes story that fits equation	▲ Can write an appropriate story
▲ Story does not fit equation chosen	▲ Is unable to write an appropriate question	▲ Can write an appropriate question
▲ Confuses operations	▲ Can do task with prompts	

Time and Sequence

Outcome

- To demonstrate an awareness of the passage of time over the course of a day.

Materials

- 6 pictures of events in a child's day (use the sample picture sequences provided, or create your own)

Assessment Activity

1. Say to the student:
   a. These are some things that happen during the day. Look at them, and put them into the order you would do them.
   b. What is the first thing you might do?
   c. Put it here.
   d. Tell me about it.
2. Continue with the rest of the pictures, asking the student what he or she would do next, placing it in order, and having him or her tell you about it.

Content Areas

Measurement

Activity Type

Manipulative

➤ Representational

Abstract

Strategies

➤ Interviews

➤ Observations

Portfolios

Student Self-Assessment

➤ Performance Tasks

Student Writing

Outcome

■ To demonstrate an awareness of the passage of time over the course of a day.

Sample Performance Indicators for Student Who Is

Not Understanding	Developing	Understanding/Applying
▲ Does not understand how to put them in order (what it means to happen first, next, last, etc.) ▲ Arranges pictures haphazardly with no thought to the order ▲ Cannot tell about what activity is occurring in most of the pictures	▲ Knows which events come first or last ▲ May ask questions about some pictures ("Where does this go?") ▲ Has a logical order for some of the events and can tell about it ▲ Can describe what is happening in most of pictures	▲ Uses positional words ▲ Arranges pictures of child's activities during a day in a logical sequence ▲ Can tell (or describe) about events and explain reasons for order ▲ Can give approximate clock times such as "in the morning," "at noon," "in the evening" ▲ May be able to use time vocabulary such as "7 o'clock," "8:30"

Sample Picture Sequences

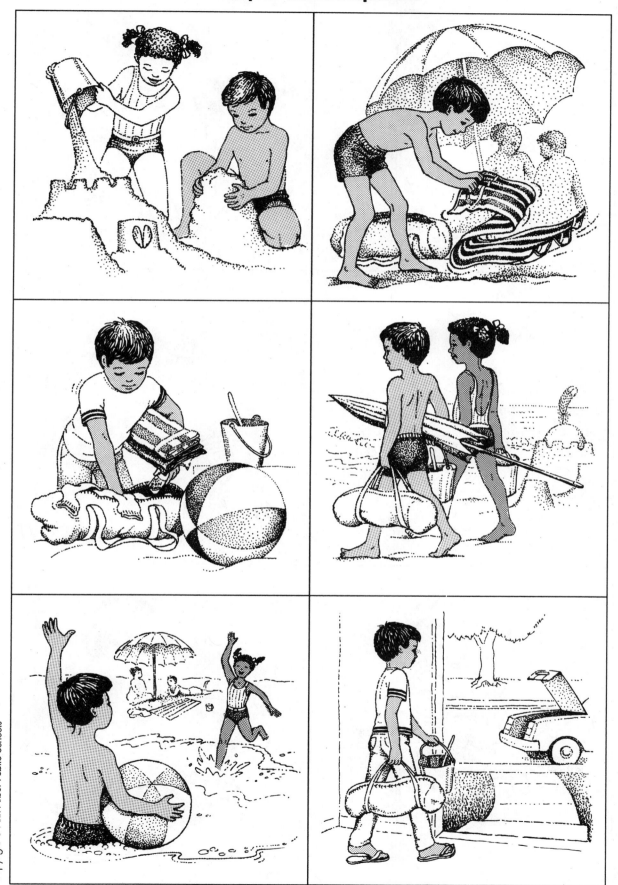

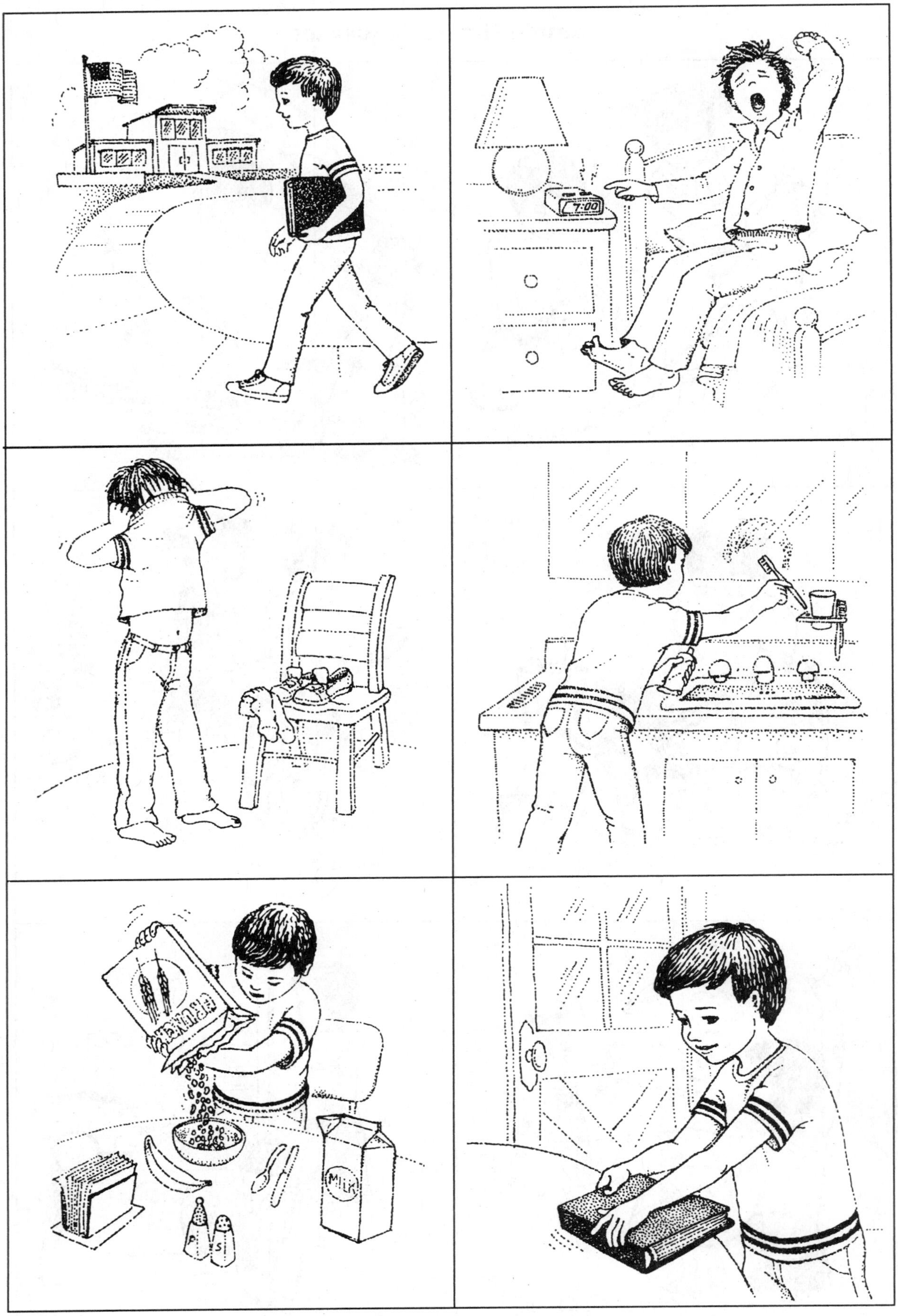
7:00
MILK

Time to Tell Time

Outcome
■ To read and record time to the hour and half-hour on a standard clock and a digital clock.

Materials
■ Time to Tell Time Worksheets
■ Pencils

Assessment Activity
1. Hand out the worksheets.
2. Draw a digital clock on the board.
3. Write in 12:30.
4. Tell students to read the digital time and to draw the hands on clock A to correspond with the time on the board.
5. Repeat, using other times.
6. Say a time. Tell students to draw in the hands to show the time and to write the time below the clock.

Notes
■ To avoid having to redraw the digital clock each time, wet the chalkboard and draw a clock on the wet surface. After the board dries, you can write and erase many times without erasing the clock. To erase the digital clock, use a wet cloth or sponge.
■ The activity may be done as an interview.
■ This task may be extended for fifteen-, five-, and one-minute time intervals.

Content Areas
Measurement

Activity Type
Manipulative
➤ Representational
Abstract

Strategies
➤ Interviews
Observations
Portfolios
Student Self-Assessment
➤ Performance Tasks
Student Writing

Outcome

■ To read and record time to the hour and half-hour on a standard clock and a digital clock.

Sample Performance Indicators for Student Who Is

Not Understanding	Developing	Understanding/Applying
▲ Makes both hands same size ▲ Cannot correctly draw in hour hand	▲ Makes a short and a long hand ▲ Draws hour hand correctly but draws minute hand incorrectly ▲ Draws smaller hand on the hour ▲ Usually records time correctly	▲ Is able to draw both hands correct size ▲ Draws correct time ▲ Records time correctly

Time to Tell Time

Name _____ Date_____

Clock A	Clock B	Clock C
Clock D	Clock E	Clock F
Clock G	Clock H	Clock I

Triangles

Outcome

■ To recognize and define the properties of a triangle.

Materials

■ Chalk and chalkboard

Assessment Activity

1. Ask students to give instructions on how to make a triangle.

2. On the board, follow exactly each student's instructions until the class starts to come to a consensus on the proper way to draw a triangle. Here are some samples of student instructions:

   a. Draw a shape that has three sides.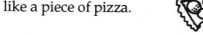

   b. Draw a shape that has three angles.

   c. It is like a piece of pizza.

   d. Draw a shape that has three sides and three angles.

   e. A triangle is a shape that has three equal sides

   (If this definition is offered, draw a shape similar to the above shape on the board and announce that, based on this definition, this shape is not a triangle because its sides are not equal.)

3. Review the properties of a triangle that the students discovered during this assessment.

Notes

■ This is a fun way to introduce the concept of triangles. Students learn that their prior knowledge of triangles allows them to identify triangles, but for most students, it is insufficient to create an accurate definition of a triangle.

■ Performance indicators are not provided for this activity. Log what is commonly understood, as well as misconceptions, about triangles and then use this information to plan instruction.

■ This activity is appropriate for other geometric shapes and can be used to assess as well as to introduce attributes of those shapes.

Content Areas

Geometry and Spatial Sense

Activity Type

Manipulative

➤ Representational

Abstract

Strategies

Interviews

Observations

Portfolios

Student Self-Assessment

➤ Performance Tasks

Student Writing

Understanding
a Bar Graph

Outcome

■ To read, construct, and interpret bar graphs.

Materials

■ Pencil and paper
■ Crayons
■ Graph paper

Assessment Activity

1. Explain to students that they will construct a bar graph and on it record the hair color of the people in the class.

2. Indicate which people to use for the graph (e.g. whether to include the teacher or students who are out of the room at the time of the activity).

3. Explain that they each must decide on hair color categories and on the color of each person's hair.

4. Ask students to write a paragraph describing how they completed this task.

Notes

■ Give each students 5 points for doing a graph. Points may be given as follows:

▲ 1 point for correctly setting up a bar graph
▲ 1 point for correct total number graphed
▲ 1 point for correctly scaling the graph
▲ 1 point for correctly labeling the categories
▲ 1 point for correctly graphing the data

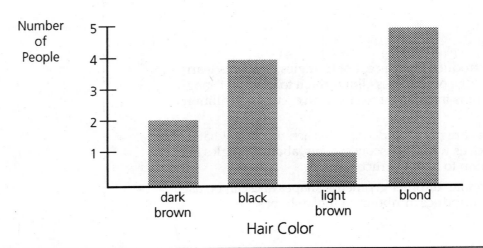

Content Areas

Statistics and Probability

Activity Type

Manipulative
➤ Representational
Abstract

Strategies

Interviews

Observations

Portfolios

Student Self-Assessment

➤ Performance Tasks

Student Writing

- The activity may be modified for other graphs.
- Students may select what type of graph they wish to do.
- Ask students to make two different graphs for the same data.
- Ask students to write interpretative statements.
- Suggest that students collect data from other classes, make appropriate graphs, and discuss comparisons.
- Students may collect data on another variable (e.g., eye color), or make graphs that would help them discuss whether the two attributes (e.g., hair and eye color) are related.
- This activity could be used as a self-assessment if the student was to evaluate himself or herself on the 5 points.

Outcome

■ To read, construct, and interpret bar graphs.

Sample Performance Indicators for Student Who Is

Not Understanding	Developing	Understanding/Applying
▲ Is unable to begin ▲ Does not know what a bar graph is ▲ Needs frequent prompts	▲ Draws bar graph but numbers or labels incorrectly ▲ Is unable to make bar length match up with correct number ▲ Records only some of the data ▲ Has only some of the categories	▲ Correctly sets up graph without assistance ▲ Includes all data ▲ Correctly numbers and labels the graph ▲ Correctly graphs data

Understanding Fractions

Outcome

- To understand fraction concepts.

Materials

- Fraction Quiz Worksheet
- Pencils

Assessment Activity

1. Ask the student to pretend to be a teacher and to grade the three anonymous answers by giving each a score from 0 to 10.
2. Ask the student to explain in writing why the grades he or she gave were reasonable.

Notes

- As a variation for the second part of this assessment, ask the student to write notes explaining to the students who answered the problem incorrectly why their answers were incorrect and how to correct them.
- The three samples provided are actual responses of students.
- The activity assumes that students:
  - ▲ have been discussing and sharing various problem-solving approaches to a given problem.
  - ▲ have experience analyzing alternative approaches.
  - ▲ have experience with writing in mathematics classes.

Content Areas

Fractions, Decimals, Ratio, and Percent

Activity Type

Manipulative

➤ Representational

➤ Abstract

Strategies

Interviews

Observations

Portfolios

Student Self-Assessment

Performance Tasks

➤ Student Writing

Outcome

■ To understand fraction concepts.

Sample Performance Indicators for Student Who Is

Not Understanding	Developing	Understanding/Applying
▲ Is unable to identify and explain errors ▲ Has difficulty expressing reasons in writing ▲ Is incorrect in analysis of others' work ▲ Provides incorrect answers ▲ Does not provide explanations	▲ Can determine correct and incorrect response ▲ May have difficulty explaining reasons	▲ Is able to identify correct responses ▲ Is able to identify incorrect responses and to explain why it is wrong ▲ Is able to figure out someone else's strategy ▲ Is able to articulate reasons in writing

Fraction Quiz

Name _____ Date _____

Last month, Tamara went to buy a new airplane model. At the store, she found out that the $14.00 she had in her pocket only covered $\frac{7}{9}$ of the cost of the model. On the following day, she brought the correct amount of money to the store and bought the model. How much money did she bring to the store the second day?

Here are three student answers to the problem:

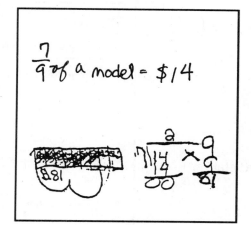

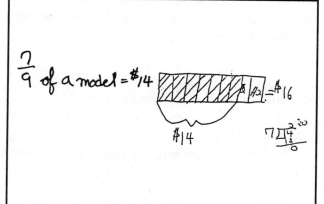

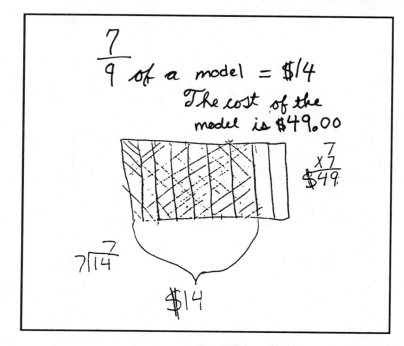

Understanding Multiplication Facts

Outcome

■ To know multiplication facts though 20.

Materials

■ Pencil and paper
■ Unifix® cubes (optional)

Assessment Activity

1. Distribute paper to students, and direct them to show in writing or in drawings how to solve the problem 6×3.
2. Tell them to pretend that they are explaining this to someone who does not know how to multiply.

Notes

■ This assessment could be used as a pretest or posttest.
■ Students also could use Unifix® cubes to show how to make 6×3. This could be done in an interview.
■ For the student who has difficulty writing, record the student's dictation.

Content Areas

Multiplication and Division

Activity Type

Manipulative
➤ Representational
➤ Abstract

Strategies

➤ Interviews
Observations
Portfolios
Student Self-Assessment
Performance Tasks
➤ Student Writing

Outcome

■ To know multiplication facts though 20.

Sample Performance Indicators for Student Who Is

Not Understanding	Developing	Understanding/Applying
▲ Is unable to begin writing or drawing ▲ Suggests finger counting to attain the answer but does not tell what numbers to count	▲ Draws picture of problem but does not match the problem (for instance drew 4×6, but wrote the problem 3×6) ▲ Draws the problem correctly but is unable to explain ▲ Sees multiplication as repeated addition (e.g., suggests adding $6 + 6 = 12$ and adding 6 more) ▲ Needs prompts to get started	▲ Suggests counting by 3s up to 6 of them ▲ Suggests drawing three groups of six and then counting them all ▲ Sees multiplication not only as repeated addition but as groups or arrays (area model)

Sample Student Work

Not Understanding

If you wanted to know how to QO 3 X 6= you could count with your fingers to git the anserw. If you git the wrong anwser And if you have a ruler with the X problems and aosers use that insted of pour fingers. But the Anser is 18.

Developing

3 X 6=
Six Pluse Six = 12 and anohter Six = 18 So you no how to Put Six Pluse Six and add anohter Six and counte it on and you got the answer and the answer is 18

Understanding/Applying

Take 6 x 3 for an example draw three groups of six now count all of them together. whats your anser?

Understanding Patterns

Suggested Grades

K–2

Outcomes

- To create a pattern using concrete objects.
- To recognize and interpret patterns (e.g., ABAB or colors).
- To extend a given pattern.
- To insert missing elements into a pattern.

Materials

- Unifix® cubes or other attribute materials (e.g., buttons, pattern blocks, shells)

Assessment Activity

1. Tell the student to use the Unifix® cubes to create a pattern. The student should choose the pattern (e.g., ABABAB, AABBAABB).
2. Ask the student to read (interpret) the pattern that was built.
3. Begin a pattern, and ask the student to extend the pattern.
4. Show a pattern that has a missing element (e.g., ABBABBA_B), and ask the student to name the missing element.

Note

- This activity may be done with individual students or small groups.

Content Areas

Problem Solving
and Logic

Algebraic Ideas

Activity Type

➤ Manipulative

Representational

Abstract

Strategies

Interviews

➤ Observations

Portfolios

Student
Self-Assessment

➤ Performance
Tasks

Student Writing

Outcomes

- To create a pattern using concrete objects.
- To recognize and interpret patterns.
- To extend a given pattern.
- To insert missing elements into a pattern.

Sample Performance Indicators for Student Who Is

Not Understanding	Developing	Understanding/Applying
▲ Plays with objects ▲ May ask, "What do you mean?" ▲ Quickly builds anything with no comprehension of building a pattern, even with prompts ▲ Can copy but cannot extend the pattern	▲ Starts to create a correct pattern but does not complete it ▲ Can build or extend the pattern but cannot verbalize it ▲ Needs reaffirmation from teacher ▲ Can copy and extend simple patterns easily but may have difficulty with more complex patterns ▲ Cannot insert missing elements into a pattern	▲ Builds pattern correctly ▲ Develops and extends patterns correctly ▲ Can generate and explain different patterns ▲ Uses a harder pattern than ABAB when asked to create ▲ Identifies missing elements in a pattern easily

Understanding Time

Outcome

■ To tell time to the nearest five minutes.

Materials

■ Paper and pencil

Assessment Activity

1. Instruct students to write a letter to someone else, explaining how to tell time.
2. Ask them to include an illustration of a clock to help make the explanation clearer.

Notes

■ This is a good activity to note any misconceptions that students may have about time. Be specific about the expectations; otherwise the concepts written may be too general.

■ Other ideas for writing about time include the following:

▲ What new ideas did you learn about time that you did not know before?

▲ Explain what the hands and the numbers on the clock mean.

▲ What hint can you give someone who is having trouble telling time?

Content Areas

Measurement

Activity Type

Manipulative

➤ Representational

➤ Abstract

Strategies

Interviews

Observations

Portfolios

Student Self-Assessment

Performance Tasks

➤ Student Writing

Outcome

■ To tell time to the nearest five minutes.

Sample Performance Indicators for Student Who Is

Not Understanding	Developing	Understanding/Applying
▲ Is unclear ▲ Rambles without making sense ▲ Provides no details	▲ Includes partial information ▲ Leaves unanswered questions	▲ Explains idea that numbers stand for five-minute intervals ▲ Includes difference between minute and hour hands ▲ Explains a particular time

Sample Student Work

Not Understanding	Developing	Understanding/Applying

Not Understanding

Dear Orca This is the way
to tell time.
the little arm is the hour and
the big arm is the minute arm
12, 3, 4, 5, 6, 7, 8, 9, 10, 11, 12,
is all are minutes and hours.
See how goes.

Developing

Dear Orca This is the
way you tell time when the
short hand is pointing to the 12
it is called o clock. like in 1 oclock.
when the small
hand is pointing to
6 it is called 30.
Like in 10:30.

Understanding/Applying

Dear Orca
This is how you tell time.
The long hand tells you the hour.
The short hand tells you the minute.
1) ... You first look at the hour hand.
If it is a little before the 12 then the
hour is it but if it is a little after 12
then it is 12.

The minute hand tells you the minutes.
You count by 5 each...
There are 4 little lines
In between each number.
The 4 lines tell you
the time in between the 5's.

Using Calculators Correctly

Outcomes

- To demonstrate how to use a calculator.
- To demonstrate how to check classwork with a calculator.

Materials

- Calculators

Assessment Activity

1. Place five to ten calculators on a table to create a calculator learning center.
2. While the class is doing math seatwork, call small groups of students to the center. Let students correct their seatwork with the calculators.
3. Observe students to determine whether they are using the calculator correctly.
4. If necessary, ask questions about the following items to determine students' proficiency with the calculator.
   a. Recognizing and using specific keys and features
   b. Using on/off, number, clear, and operation keys
   c. Using the constant function
   d. Using M+, M−, MRC, MC
   e. Understanding calculator codes
   f. Recognizing common limitations
   g. Checking reasonableness of answers

Note

- Have other calculator activities available at the center that allow students to learn how to use the calculator and to demonstrate their proficiency.

Content Areas

Calculators

Activity Type

➤ Manipulative

Representational

➤ Abstract

Strategies

Interviews

➤ Observations

Portfolios

Student Self-Assessment

➤ Performance Tasks

Student Writing

Outcomes

- To demonstrate how to use a calculator.
- To demonstrate how to check classwork with a calculator.

Sample Performance Indicators for Student Who Is

Not Understanding	Developing	Understanding/Applying
▲ Wastes time playing with calculator ▲ Does not know how to use keys and features correctly ▲ Watches to see how others do it	▲ Is not sure whether answers are correct ▲ Needs help with some keys or features ▲ Tries to figure out how to do some things or asks ▲ Can answer some questions	▲ Corrects work correctly using calculator independently ▲ Can answer questions about how to use calculator ▲ Can help others having difficulty with calculator

What's in a Shape?

Outcome

■ To use estimation strategies.

Materials

■ What's in a Shape? Worksheet
■ Calculator

Assessment Activity

1. Sketch this problem on the board.

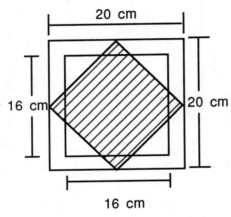

2. Have students pair up and discuss possible strategies for estimating the shaded area in the drawing. Discuss strategies different people used. If necessary, generate additional examples.
3. Distribute handouts. Students estimate the shaded area and explain in writing the strategy that was used.

Notes

■ You may want to remind students that estimating does not require an exact answer.
■ This lesson can be done as an individual or group activity.
■ An extension of this activity would be to have students describe several ways to estimate area for each sketch.
■ Students may wish to generate examples.
■ You may want to have students present their strategies to each other.

Content Areas

Estimation and Mental Computation

Activity Type

Manipulative

➤ Representational

➤ Abstract

Strategies

Interviews

➤ Observations

Portfolios

Student Self-Assessment

➤ Performance Tasks

➤ Student Writing

Outcome

■ To use estimation strategies.

Sample Performance Indicators for Student Who Is

Not Understanding	Developing	Understanding/Applying
▲ May not recognize an unreasonable estimate	▲ May or may not justify estimate as reasonable	▲ Can justify, and may refine, estimate
▲ Needs review on area	▲ May need review on area	▲ Knows how to find area
▲ Needs direction about what strategy to use and how to use it	▲ Can implement a strategy if it is modeled first	▲ Can select and demonstrate at least one strategy, including partitioning
▲ May need step-by-step instructions	▲ Can demonstrate how to use a specific strategy	▲ May demonstrate several strategies
▲ Struggles to understand other strategies	▲ May need occasional prompts or assistance	▲ Can understand someone else's strategy
	▲ Can understand someone else's strategy	

What's in a Shape?

Name _____ Date _____

Estimate the area of the shaded region. Then, explain the strategy you used to
get your estimate.

Drawing   **Estimate**   **Explanation of Strategy**

1.

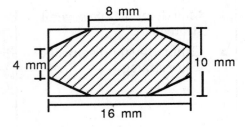

2.

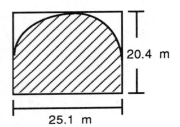

3.

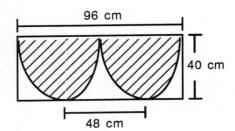

Drawing	**Estimate**	**Explanation of Strategy**

4.

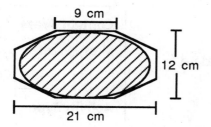

5.

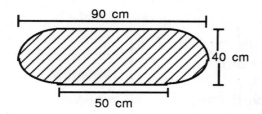

6.

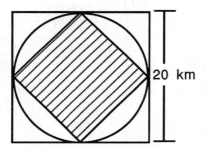

Describe other strategies to use on any of the drawings.

How do the estimates compare?

Working with Kragels

Outcome

■ To measure the perimeter and area of a rectangle by using a nonstandard unit of measure.

Materials

■ Working with Kragels Worksheet and a pencil
■ Scissors

Assessment Activity

1. Hand the student the Working with Kragels Worksheet and a pencil. Direct the student to cut out the Kragel Square carefully.

2. Explain that the student must use the Kragel Square to measure the area and perimeter of the rectangle. Then the student is to tell you the area and perimeter and why he or she thinks the answers are correct.

3. Record what attempts the student makes, what strategies are used, the student's attitude and level of confidence, and the student's explanation.

Notes

■ To save time and supplies, laminate a copy of the Working with Kragels Worksheet. Use a sharp, single-edge razor blade to cut out the Kragel Square. All students can use this same Kragel Square as a measuring tool and also an erasable marker to make measurements that can later be wiped off the laminated rectangle. Otherwise you will need to erase the marks each student makes or copy one worksheet for each student.

■ This is a good activity to use to reinforce the concept of placing a measuring tool end to end when measuring. It might be helpful to do this before asking students to do it with a ruler.

■ Using the same tool to measure perimeter and area will help students see the relationship between one- and two-dimensional shapes and what units should be used to measure them.

Content Areas

Measurement

Activity Type

➤ Manipulative
➤ Representational
  Abstract

Strategies

➤ Interviews
➤ Observations
  Portfolios
  Student
  Self-Assessment
➤ Performance
  Tasks
  Student Writing

Outcome

■ To measure accurately the perimeter and area of a rectangle by using a nonstandard unit of measure.

Sample Performance Indicators for Student Who Is

Not Understanding	Developing	Understanding/Applying
▲ Randomly places Kragel-Square on figure ▲ Does not correctly find area and perimeter ▲ Asks for help before trying ▲ Says does not know what perimeter and area are ▲ Measures area in terms of Kragels ▲ Measures perimeter in terms of Square Kragels	▲ Estimates end of measuring tool but does not mark it before moving it to new location ▲ Measures all four sides to find perimeter and repeatedly places Square Kragel over the rectangle to get the area ▲ Knows the answer is correct but cannot mathematically communicate why ▲ Needs a few prompts to accurately use the measuring tool, to make the measurement, or to explain the answer	▲ Uses Kragel by putting it down, marking the end point, and putting it down again directly next to the mark ▲ Measures only two sides using Kragels to find perimeter and two sides using Square Kragels to find area ▲ Can explain why his or her answer is correct ▲ Uses correct unit for each measurement

Working with Kragels

Name _____ Date _____

```
┌──── Kragel ────┐
↑                ↑
│    Square      │
Kragel  Kragel   Kragel
│                │
↓                ↓
└──── Kragel ────┘
```

Working with Patterns

Outcome

■ To recognize, extend, reproduce, and create a pattern.

Materials

■ 2 colors of Unifix® cubes or other attribute materials (e.g., shells, buttons)

Assessment Activity

1. Arrange the materials in an AAB pattern.
2. Ask, "What do you think I am beginning to make?" (recognize)
3. Ask, "What do we call this?" (recognize)
4. Ask, "Can you keep my pattern going?" (extend)
5. Ask, "Can you make one just like mine?" (reproduce)
6. Say, "Make a pattern of your own. " (create)

Note

■ Use increasingly complex patterns.

Content Areas

Problem Solving
and Logic

Algebraic Ideas

Activity Type

➤ Manipulative

Representational

Abstract

Strategies

➤ Interviews

➤ Observations

Portfolios

Student
Self-Assessment

➤ Performance
Tasks

Student Writing

Outcome

- To recognize, extend, reproduce, and create a pattern.

Sample Performance Indicators for Student Who Is

Not Understanding	Developing	Understanding/Applying
Recognize ▲ Has difficulty identifying it is a pattern	**Recognize** ▲ Can observe it is a pattern ▲ Can recognize, with prompting, a pattern	**Recognize** ▲ Reads the pattern orally ▲ Can identify patterns in everyday surroundings ▲ Figures out and explains someone else's pattern ▲ Can verbalize or physically mimic a pattern
Extend ▲ Randomly adds on	**Extend** ▲ Selects items with same attributes but fails to order correctly	**Extend** ▲ Continues pattern three or more times
Reproduce ▲ Is unable to look at a given pattern and copy it	**Reproduce** ▲ Tries to impose previous pattern on new pattern	**Reproduce** ▲ Can reproduce a pattern with same or different materials
Create ▲ Randomly orders cubes	**Create** ▲ Makes an attempt to create a pattern	**Create** ▲ Creates own pattern

Writing About Fractions

Suggested Grades

4–6

Outcome

■ To demonstrate the meaning of fractions.

Materials

■ Paper and pencil

Assessment Activity

1. In this activity students will explain the meaning of a fraction by using the following three-part definition:

   a. define the whole

   b. divide the whole into as many equal parts as are stated by the denominator

   c. emphasize the number of parts as stated by the numerator

2. Instruct students to write a letter to an alien. The alien understands English but knows nothing about fractions. Ask students to define or explain the concept of a fraction to the alien.

Note

■ This activity may be used as a review after fraction concepts are taught or as a preassessment to help plan instruction. It will assess the students' knowledge and understanding about fractions.

Content Areas

Fractions, Decimals, Ratio, and Percent

Activity Type

Manipulative

➤ Representational

➤ Abstract

Strategies

Interviews

Observations

Portfolios

Student Self-Assessment

Performance Tasks

➤ Student Writing

Outcome

■ To demonstrate the meaning of fractions.

Sample Performance Indicators for Student Who Is

Not Understanding	Developing	Understanding/Applying
▲ May not have all of the steps ▲ May not list steps in correct order ▲ Cannot elaborate ▲ May provide incorrect example (e.g.,) ▲ May avoid using mathematical terms	▲ Is able to name steps ▲ Has difficulty elaborating and providing clarification on each step ▲ May list parts but writing does not indicate total understanding ▲ Uses correct terminology but may or may not demonstrate understanding of it ▲ Can provide example	▲ Is able to name steps ▲ Elaborates or clarifies each step ▲ Can provide example ▲ Uses correct terminology

Sample Student Work

Not Understanding

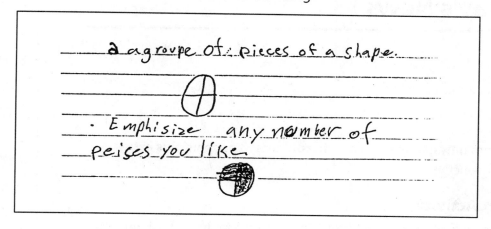

a a groupe of pieces of a shape.

· Emphisize any number of peices you like.

Developing

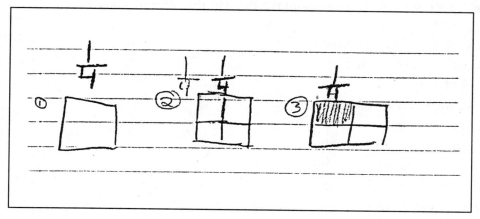

Understanding/Applying

1. First find the whole - □
2. Divide the whole into equal pieces - ⊞
4. The bottom number of the fraction is called a denominator. It tells how many equal pieces the fraction is divided into. ¼
3. Indicate how many pieces are shown. ⊞
5. The top number is the numerator it tells how many pieces are indicated - ¼
6. Put the denominator & numerator together you have a fraction. ¼ = ⊞

Yesterday's News

Outcome

■ To interpret a variety of graphs.

Materials

■ Graphs from newspapers or magazines, at least 3 per pair plus extras
■ Paper and pencil

Assessment Activity

1. Group the class into pairs. Set out the graphs on a table, and ask one student from each pair to select three graphs.
2. Tell each pair of students to choose one of the three graphs and to answer the following questions:
   a. What is the source of the information?
   b. How were the data collected?
   c. What type of graph is it?
   d. What does each unit represent?
   e. What is the purpose?
   f. Can you see and describe a pattern?
   g. Is this graph easy to interpret? Why or why not?
   h. Why use a graph instead of words?
   i. Can this information be shown in a different way?
   j. Can you write questions using the information shown?
   k. How can this information help you understand the subject of the graph?
   l. Can you summarize the data shown?
   m. What other information would have helped you write your summary?
3. After students have finished answering the questions, tell them that they have ten minutes to prepare a brief presentation about their graph.
4. Have students share their information with the class.
5. Write the words *descriptive* and *interpretative* on the board. Ask each pair of students to give one fact from their graph. Ask the class to determine whether the fact is a descriptive or an interpretative statement.
6. Direct each student to select one of the remaining graphs. Ask students to answer individually the thirteen questions (from step 2 above).
7. After the questions have been answered, have students write as many descriptive and interpretative sentences as they can (at least three).

Notes

■ This lesson will take two days. Doing steps 6 and 7 on the second day works well.
■ Use a record-keeping device to record students' actions during steps 1 to 5.

Content Areas

Statistics and Probability

Activity Type

Manipulative

➤ Representational

➤ Abstract

Strategies

Interviews

➤ Observations

➤ Portfolios

Student Self-Assessment

➤ Performance Tasks

➤ Student Writing

Outcome

- To interpret a variety of graphs.

Sample Performance Indicators for Student Who Is

Not Understanding	Developing	Understanding/Applying
▲ Is not able to read graph ▲ Is not able to understand information presented ▲ Is not able to describe data ▲ Is not able to generate descriptive or interpretative statements	▲ Is able to read the graph with assistance ▲ Is able to do some processes (read, understand, describe, apply data), but not all ▲ Needs prompts to complete tasks ▲ Generates descriptive and interpretative statements but mislabels them	▲ Independently analyzes graph ▲ Uses correct mathematical terms ▲ Writes several descriptive and interpretative statements

0 to 100%:
How Well Did You Score?

Outcome

■ To use a graph and calculator to help assess performance on a series of tests.

Materials

■ Series of student's test or quiz scores (e.g., 9 weeks of scores on 10-word spelling tests)
■ Calculator
■ Pencil and plain paper

Assessment Activity

1. Give student copies of their test scores in one subject.

2. Ask each student to construct a graph showing his or her scores. Students may choose to use any type of graph as long as they can accurately present the test scores.

3. Ask students to interpret the graph by answering the following questions:

   a. What is your average (mean) test grade?
   b. What test grade did you get most frequently (mode)?
   c. Why did you choose to use the type of graph that you did?
   d. What patterns or trends do you see?
   e. How can you explain these patterns?
   f. Are these patterns what you expected to see? Why or why not?

4. Ask students to predict future trends by answering the following questions:

   a. Can you indicate on your graph or on a new one what you think your next four weeks of scores will be?
   b. Why did you make the predictions that you did?
   c. What factors will affect your scores?
   d. What new strategies will you use to achieve your desired scores?

5. In four weeks, return students' graphs and answers to them. Have them graph their actual test scores and compare them to their predictions. The original questions can be asked again. Students can repeat this activity throughout the year to help them learn to assess their performance and to learn to improve it. Ask students to construct a different type of graph each time this activity is done.

Content Areas

Statistics and Probability

Calculators

Activity Type

Manipulative

➤ Representational

➤ Abstract

Strategies

Interviews

Observations

➤ Portfolios

➤ Student Self-Assessment

➤ Performance Tasks

➤ Student Writing

Notes

■ Ask students to use calculators whenever they need them.

■ Some students may choose graphs that make it difficult to find trends (see pictograph 1 and circle graph). These students will need extra guidance.

■ Some students may set extremely low expectations for themselves. Other students may set unrealistically high expectations. Discuss the predictions with students before accepting their work to avoid these problems.

■ Ask students to answer a question related to one of the concepts discussed in math that week. The results will show who understands what was taught (and so should have enrichment opportunities and who needs extra support and activities related to that concept. Students could graph these scores, or test scores in any other content area.

■ This activity gives students an opportunity to see how skills they are learning in math can help them in their daily lives.

Samples

Week Number	1	2	3	4	5	6	7	8
Quiz Score	4	5	4	2	3	4	5	5

Circle Graph

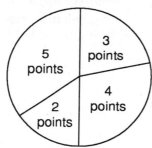

Bar Graph

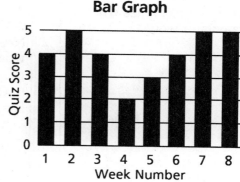

Pictograph 1

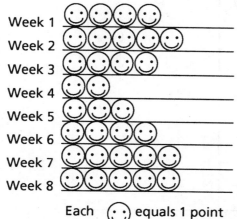

Pictograph II

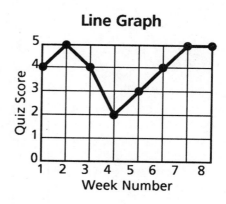

Line Graph

Outcome

■ To use a graph and calculator to help assess performance on a series of tests.

Sample Performance Indicators for Student Who Is

Not Understanding	Developing	Understanding/Applying
▲ Does not know how to construct any type of graph	▲ Can construct graph with prompts	▲ Is able to construct a graph independently
▲ Creates graph that does not accurately show test scores	▲ Creates same type of graph each time activity is done	▲ Is able to construct a variety of graphs to communicate information
▲ Cannot interpret graph	▲ Constructs graph but then cannot interpret it	▲ Can interpret graph
▲ Does not accurately assess own work	▲ Can understand information on graph but cannot extrapolate	▲ Recognizes and understands patterns in graphs
▲ Does not suggest realistic strategies to improve future grades	▲ May need help understanding how some factors relate to performance	▲ Can assess own work
▲ Does not recognize when a calculator would be helpful	▲ Needs suggestions about what strategies to try	▲ Seeks new strategies to improve test scores
	▲ Does not recognize all of the times a calculator can help him or her	▲ Uses calculator as time-saving device

Resources

Baratta-Lorton, Mary. *Mathematics Their Way.* Menlo Park, CA: Addison-Wesley Publishing Company, 1976.

Briars, Diane J. "Assessing Students' Learning to Inform Teaching: The Message in NCTM's Evaluation Standards." *Arithmetic Teacher* (December 1989), pp. 22–26.

Burton, Grace M. "Writing as a Way of Knowing in a Mathematics Education Class." *Arithmetic Teacher* (December 1985), pp. 40–45.

Burns, Marilyn. *About Teaching Mathematics: A K–8 Resource.* Sausalito, CA: Marilyn Burns Education Associates, 1992.

California Mathematics Council. *Assessment Alternatives in Mathematics: An Overview of Assessment Techniques That Promote Learning.* Berkeley, CA: EQUALS, 1989.

Charles, R., F. Lester, and P. O'Daffer. *How to Evaluate Progress in Problem Solving.* Reston, VA: National Council of Teachers of Mathematics, 1987.

Curriculum and Evaluation Standards. Reston, VA: National Council of Teachers of Mathematics, 1989.

Exploring Mathematics: Calculator Sourcebook. Glenview, IL: Scott, Foresman and Company, 1991.

Ford, Margaret. "The Writing Process: A Strategy for Problem Solvers." *Arithmetic Teacher* (November 1990), pp. 35–38.

Fullerton, Olive. *Mathtime 2.* Toronto: Copp Clark Pitman, Ltd., 1987.

Garland, Cynthia, ed. *Mathematics Their Way Summary Newsletter.* Saratoga, CA: Center for Innovation and Education.

Greens, C., et al. *TOPS Problem Solving Card Decks.* Menlo Park, CA: Dale Seymour Publications, 1980.

Katterns, Bob and Ken Carr. "Talking with Young Children About Multiplication." *Arithmetic Teacher* (April 1986), pp. 18–21.

Labinowicz, E. *Learning from Children: New Beginnings for Teaching Numerical Thinking.* Menlo Park, CA: Addison-Wesley, 1988.

Liedtke, Werner. "Diagnosis in Mathematics: The Advantages of an Interview." *Arithmetic Teacher* (November 1988), pp. 26–29.

Lindquist, M. "Assessment: The Key to Change in the K–4 Curriculum." Salt Lake City, UT: National Council of Teachers of Mathematics Annual Conference, 1990.

Long, Madeleine J. and Meir BenHur. "Informing Learning Through the Clinical Interview." *Arithmetic Teacher* (February 1991), pp. 44–46.

McKillip, William D. and George M. A. Stanic. "Putting the Value Back into Evaluation." *Arithmetic Teacher* (February 1988), pp. 37–38, 52.

Mumme, Judith and Nancy Shepherd. "Communication in Mathematics." *Arithmetic Teacher* (September 1990), pp. 18–22.

Pandy, Tej. *A Sampler of Mathematics Assessment.* Sacramento, CA: California Department of Education, 1991.

Peck, Donald, Stanley M. Jencks, and Michael L. Connel. "Improving Instruction Through Brief Interviews." *Arithmetic Teacher* (November 1989), pp. 15–17.

Reys, Robert E. "Testing Computational Estimation—Some Things to Consider." *Arithmetic Teacher* (March 1988), pp. 28–30.

Richardson, Kathy. "Assessing Understanding." *Arithmetic Teacher* (February 1988), pp. 39–41.

Robinson, G. Edith. "The Purpose of Testing." *Arithmetic Teacher* (September 1987), p. 33.

Russell, Susan Jo, and Rebecca B. Corwin. *Used Numbers: Statistics: The Shape of the Data.* Menlo Park, CA: Dale Seymour Publications, 1989.

Schoen, H. and M. Zweng, ed. *Estimation and Mental Computation: 1986 Yearbook.* Reston, VA: National Council of Teachers of Mathematics, 1986.

Stevens, S. "Opening the Door to Alternatives: A Different Look at Assessment." Salt Lake City, UT: National Council of Supervisors of Mathematics Annual Conference, 1990.

Szetela, Walter. "The Problem of Evaluation in Problem Solving: Can We Find Solutions?" *Arithmetic Teacher* (November 1987), pp. 36–41.

Trafton, Paul. "Tests—A Tool for Improving Instruction." *Arithmetic Teacher* (December 1987), pp. 17–18.

Trafton, P. and A. Shulte, ed. *New Directions for Elementary School Mathematics: 1989 Yearbook.* Reston, VA: National Council of Teachers of Mathematics, 1989.

Valencia, Sheila, "A Portfolio Approach to Classroom Reading Assessment: The Whys, Whats, and Hows." *Reading Teacher* (January 1990), pp. 338–340.

"Vermont State Assessment: Criteria for Evaluating Mathematics Portfolios and/or Best Pieces." Evanston, IL: National Council of Teachers of Mathematics, 1990.

Wilde, Sandra. "Learning to Write About Mathematics." *Arithmetic Teacher* (February 1991), pp. 38–43.